1994

Managing the Mosaic™

W9-DFF-762

Addressing Workforce Diversity and Managing Institutional Change in Health Care

*Trisha A. Svehla
and Glen C. Crosier*

Foreword by R. Roosevelt Thomas, Jr.

AHA

AHA books are published by
American Hospital Publishing, Inc.,
an American Hospital Association company

This publication is designed to provide accurate and authoritative information in regard to the subject matter covered. It is sold with the understanding that neither the authors nor the publisher is engaged in rendering legal, accounting, or other professional service. If legal advice or other expert assistance is required, the services of a competent professional person should be sought.

The views expressed in this publication are strictly those of the authors and do not necessarily represent official positions of the American Hospital Association.

Library of Congress Cataloging-in-Publication Data

Svehla, Trisha A.
    Managing the mosaic: addressing workforce diversity
and managing institutional change in health care / Trisha A.
Svehla and Glen C. Crosier.
        p.   cm.
    Includes bibliographical references.
    ISBN 1-55648-115-2 (pbk.)
    1. Health facilities—United States—Personnel
management.   2. Minorities—Employment—United States.   I.
Crosier, Glen C.   II. Title.
RA971.35.S95 1994
362.1'1'0683—dc20   94-5214
                                                                     CIP

Catalog no. 088170

©1994 by American Hospital Publishing, Inc.,
an American Hospital Association company

Printed in the USA

AHA is a service mark of the American Hospital Association used under license by American Hospital Publishing, Inc.

Text set in Goudy
3M—5/94—0369

Richard Hill, Acquisitions/Development Editor
Lee Benaka, Production Editor
Cheryl Kusek, Cover Designer
Peggy DuMais, Production Coordinator
Marcia Bottoms, Books Division Assistant Director
Brian Schenk, Books Division Director

Contents

List of Figures and Tables

About the Authors

Trisha A. Svehla is the president of Svehla Consultants, Inc., of Downers Grove, Illinois, a firm that specializes in human resources consulting. Ms. Svehla has worked for more than twenty years as a hands-on practitioner in all aspects of the human resources function. Before forming her consulting practice, she was employed for more than thirteen years by the American Hospital Association (AHA), where her responsibilities included both human resources and operations management. While at the AHA, Ms. Svehla was the prime initiator and facilitator for the association's internal organizational change efforts and contributed immeasurably to the achievement of the association's human resources and other corporate objectives.

In addition to working in the health care field, Ms. Svehla has held human resources positions in the manufacturing and service sectors. She is an active member of numerous professional organizations, including the Human Resource Management Association of Chicago and the Midwest Society of Professional Consultants. She also serves as an adviser to Project Reach, a joint venture of the American Hospital Association, the American College of Healthcare Executives, and the National Association of Health Services Executives which seeks to address the problem of insufficient opportunities for minorities in health services management.

Ms. Svehla is a frequent keynote speaker and trainer at national and regional business and association conferences on various critical human resource issues, including workforce diversity, organizational change, and organizational leadership. She holds a master's degree in management from Northwestern University, Evanston, Illinois, and she serves as an adjunct professor in the area of workforce diversity management at Illinois Benedictine College in Lisle, Illinois.

Glen C. Crosier has more than twenty years experience in business and consulting in the United States and overseas. He currently serves as associate executive director for the Council for Jewish Elderly, Chicago, Illinois, an organization that operates a skilled nursing home and Alzheimer's center and provides group and assisted living programs, home counseling, adult day care, and other health services to the elderly.

As a consultant and president of Advanced Change Management, Inc., New Lenox, Illinois, Mr. Crosier has worked with many organizations in helping them optimize and reposition their businesses. His clients have included service, manufacturing, retail, real estate, and health care organizations in both corporate and divisional locations.

Mr. Crosier holds a master's degree in psychology and sociology from St. Francis College, Fort Wayne, Indiana, and is a noted speaker, lecturer, and adviser to top-level management.

Foreword

I am delighted to see this book by Trisha A. Svehla and Glen C. Crosier. It meets a definite need.

Although most of my research and educational experiences have been conducted within the business community, I have from time to time worked with health care organizations. In these cases, I was struck by the diversity of the workforces and also the diversity of the professions. I came away believing that diversity issues existed in many forms throughout these organizations.

A barrier in most of these situations has been the lack of health care-specific materials. Stated differently, I have found that health care professionals can have difficulty relating to "business" concepts. Svehla and Crosier have penned a book that is keenly sensitive to the realities of the health care sector. It provides a comprehensive, health care-specific framework for addressing diversity. The book is ambitious and timely and should be valuable to the health care professional in the foreseeable future. I make this statement for several reasons.

First, this book is a helpful blend of conceptual applications and practical how-tos for the practitioner. The authors take embryonic diversity concepts developed primarily in the business setting and apply them to health care. Presenting these concepts in a health care-specific context is important. It negates the "not-invented-here" syndrome on the part of those health care professionals who are turned off by "business" concepts. So, in this regard the work is original. It offers a vehicle by which health care practitioners can learn about diversity theory in a friendly context.

But more than conceptual awareness is involved here. The book also offers how-to suggestions for launching diversity processes. So, readers can gain conceptual understanding and also prepare realistically for moving forward. This is a unique combination in the diversity field. Most books in this area have tended to be heavy on concepts or implementation. Svehla and Crosier have struck a good balance.

A second reason this book is an important contribution is that it is more than a prescription for moving forward with diversity management in health care. It is a blueprint for fostering fundamental transformation in health care organizations. The health care change agent who follows the book's suggestions

will find his or her ability greatly enhanced, not only with respect to workforce diversity, but also with regard to implementing any major change.

Another factor contributing to the book's significance is that it explicitly
and implicitly says that *managing* in the health care field is legitimate and important. In many organizations centered around professionals, such as universities, professional firms, and hospitals, *administering* is valued more than managing.
Administrators carry out the will of the professionals and often serve on a rotating basis. Although more valued than management, the administrative function itself is viewed more as a necessary evil to be shared.

The authors presume that managing as empowerment is legitimate in the
health care organization. Empowerment managers accept responsibility for ensuring that the enterprise's culture, systems, climate, and norms encourage the
behavior needed to achieve the organization's objectives. Without this role in
place, or at least emerging, following the book's suggestions will be most difficult.

Svehla and Crosier rightly ascribe central importance to the managerial role
as empowerment; however, our research here at The American Institute for Managing Diversity indicates that this is the case in relatively few circumstances. Indeed,
we have found the lack of empowerment management to be the biggest barrier
to progress with diversity issues. So by squarely emphasizing its importance, the
authors are getting at what I consider to be the core of the matter.

Finally, the book is timely and important because of the current debate
about the delivery of health care. As in many other sectors, health care professionals have tended to see their organizations as institutions. Institutions give
off a feel of being permanent and all-knowing. Often, they are housed in impressive buildings that convey permanence and security. This notion, as has been
the case in other sectors, has changed.

Now, all aspects of the health care field are up for examination. The focus
is not just on *efficiency* (using assets economically), but also on *effectiveness*
(achieving objectives). Even physicians and their roles are not beyond scrutiny.
Further, the external constituencies of customers, communities, and government agencies are modifying their expectations of health care organizations.
Similarly, employees are changing in terms of demographics and expectations.
All of this makes the health care sector very fluid.

Svehla and Crosier provide a much-needed health care framework for thinking and acting around diversity issues and, indeed, change in general. This
book should set the stage for productive discussion and meaningful launch-
ings of diversity efforts.

R. Roosevelt Thomas, Jr.
President
The American Institute for Managing Diversity
Morehouse College
Atlanta, Georgia
March 1994

Acknowledgments

To set out on a journey to write a book is in itself a frightening task. In accomplishing this task, Ms. Svehla would like to acknowledge the following friends and business associates who were important but "unseen" partners in making this book possible:

- Dr. Vicky Gordon Martin, whose advice on those "writer's block" days to "just set a goal of writing ten pages a day" kept Ms. Svehla burning the midnight oil;
- Dona Young, not only for her encouragement but the loan of numerous books to assist Ms. Svehla in unleashing energy for her creative writing;
- Carole Rebello and Dorothy Ware, for their unshakable friendship and their daily phone calls demanding progress reports;
- Ken Svehla, Ms. Svehla's husband of twenty years, for his encouragement, support, research, and assistance on a seemingly endless task;
- Richard Hill and Anita Samen, the book's primary editors at American Hospital Publishing, Inc., for their encouragement, assistance in resolving numerous obstacles, and patience and perseverance in keeping the book on course.

It is with great appreciation that Mr. Crosier would like to recognize David A. Milberg, partner, Advanced Change Management, Inc., for his assistance and patience during the writing of this book. Mr. Crosier drew upon Mr. Milberg's knowledge and experience to provide the reader with a broader perspective on the management of workforce diversity. As a friend and partner, Mr. Milberg has contributed unselfishly to this multiyear effort and has in many respects made this book possible.

Workforce 2000: A Preview of Your Future Workers

Workforce 2000 captured the attention of the American business community when it was published by the Hudson Institute in 1987.[1] The dire picture painted by the U.S. Department of Labor and the Hudson Institute was clear: the pool of qualified applicants from which organizations could select employees was shrinking and changing dramatically. The report predicts that by the year 2000, for the first time in the history of American business, human capital will be as vital an asset as physical facilities, real estate, and financial assets. Health care institutions, which are projected to remain at the pinnacle of job growth, will be strongly affected by the change in workforce demographics. These institutions will need to look beyond the traditional pool of workers to recruit and retain employees of unparalleled diversity, including dramatically increased numbers of women, minorities, aliens, older workers, and the differently abled.

Overview of American Health Care Workforce Demographics

According to projections in a recent study conducted by the Bureau of Labor Statistics (BLS), over 50 percent of the top 15 job-growth areas in the 1990s will be in health care.[2] (See table 1-1.) For most of the health care job categories listed in the BLS study, there is already a shortage of workers qualified to fill available jobs. The projected continued growth in these job categories will exacerbate these shortages. Note that many of the jobs listed in table 1-1 are in nontraditional health care settings—that is, outside the four walls of a primary care facility—indicating that health care institutions should reexamine the paradigms they use to define health care settings to keep pace with national health care trends.

This reexamination has already begun. The dramatic changes that have been occurring in the hospital field during the 1980s and 1990s—such as significant financial and organizational restructuring and movement from independent community hospitals to interdependent health care systems—have caused

Table 1-1. Fastest-Growing Jobs of the 1990s

Industry	Number of Workers in 1988	in 2000	Percent Change
Health Care			
Medical assistants	149	253	70.0
Home health aides	236	397	67.9
Radiologic technologists and technicians	132	218	66.0
Medical records technicians	47	75	59.9
Medical secretaries	207	327	58.0
Physical therapists	68	107	57.0
Surgical technologists	35	55	56.4
Physical and corrective therapy assistants	39	60	52.5
Other			
Paralegals	83	145	75.0
Data processing equipment repairers	71	115	61.2
Operations research analysts	55	85	55.4
Securities and financial services sales workers	200	309	54.8
Travel agents	142	219	54.1
Computer systems analysts	403	617	53.3
Social welfare service aides	91	138	51.5

Source: U.S. Bureau of Labor Statistics, 1990.

some to refer to health care organizations of the future as "hospitals without walls." This expansion of the concept of "health care setting" carries with it an expansion of responsibilities, skills, and sheer numbers of health care workers.

An excellent analysis of the change affecting today's hospitals can be found in *Strategic Choices for America's Hospitals*, by Stephen Shortell, Ellen Morrison, and Bernard Friedman. The authors outline the growth of the hospital field, including the introduction and rise of private health insurance coverage in the 1930s; the passage of the Hill-Burton Act in the 1940s, which brought about hospital expansion; and the October 1983 prospective payment system (PPS) legislation that mandated fundamental changes in how health care organizations were reimbursed for patient care. After 1983, the availability of unlimited government funds to cover patient care became a thing of the past. According to the authors, this third change required three major paradigm shifts by hospital executives and their organizations:

1. Moving from a *product orientation* (hospitals provide services to patients brought in by the medical staff) to a *market orientation* (hospitals define market needs and preferences and actively develop programs to meet these needs)
2. Moving from a *caretaking mentality* (the hospital executive's job is to be a steward of the hospital's assets) to a *risk-taking mentality* (the hospital executive's job is to increase the hospital's assets)

3. Moving from *operational management* (hospital executives run a good shop) to *strategic management* (hospital executives must position the organization to seize future opportunities)[3]

Although the discussions of health care reform in the mid-1990s have encouraged a reexamination of these paradigms, it is crucial to keep in mind that such changes in orientation, attitude, and management style are critical as we examine the issue of workforce diversity. Hospitals are human capital intensive; their success depends on recruiting, training, and retaining sufficient numbers of employees with the right mix of skills to meet organizational objectives. The following sections examine five demographic facts presented in *Workforce 2000* that emphasize the increased diversity of the health care workforce of the future.

Slowing Population Growth

By the year 2000, the population and workforce will be growing more slowly than at any time since the 1930s. Population growth, which was climbing by approximately 1.9 percent per year in the 1950s, will slow to only 0.7 percent per year by the year 2000. The labor force, which exploded by 2.9 percent per year in the 1970s, will expand by only 1 percent annually during the 1990s.[4]

The slow growth rates of the 1990s will decrease the pool of available workers, forcing employers to look at alternative, previously untapped sources of labor. This shift will enhance the importance of a new category of employee—the so-called gold-collar worker over the age of 55.

Rising Average Age of Workers

In the 1990s and beyond, the average age of the U.S. population and workforce will rise, and the pool of young workers entering the labor market will shrink. As a result, gold-collar workers will be sought by U.S. employers as never before. American industry is already attempting to woo retired workers back into the workforce and to entice currently employed gold-collar workers to remain in the workforce.

Advantages and Stereotypes of Employing Older Workers

Workers over the age of 55 are becoming desirable to employers not only because of the shortage of qualified younger workers but also because studies have shown that, in comparison to younger workers, they are more dependable, are more experienced, take the job more seriously, have fewer absences, have fewer accidents, and have no child care responsibilities that can conflict with work.[5]

Some employers, however, still maintain unfortunate and invalid stereotypes of older workers—for example, that they are less productive than younger workers or that they are unable to adapt to new technologies. Such misconceptions have discouraged some employers from actively recruiting from this pool of workers. It is crucial that employers realize that older workers are a diverse group with a mosaic of backgrounds, experience, skills, and interests. Many older workers are eager to advance, develop new skills, and earn more money. With increasing life expectancies in the United States, older workers have decades of productive work years ahead of them. They are an excellent source of labor to fill projected staff shortages in the coming decades.

Increased Demand for Younger Workers

Younger workers will also benefit from the aging of the workforce. As increasing numbers of workers over the age of 55 remain in the workforce, baby boomers age, and dwindling numbers of workers between the ages of 18 and 26 enter the workforce, the average age of the workforce will increase from 36 in 1990 to 39 by the year 2000. The number of young workers between the ages of 16 and 24 will drop by approximately 8 percent.[6]

The financial implications of this dearth of younger workers cannot be overlooked. Because younger workers tend to be paid less than older workers, organizations have traditionally grown by adding large numbers of younger, lower-paid workers. These workers, who will already be in short supply by the year 2000, will also be in demand, which will have the paradoxical effect of increasing the salary scale.

Increasing Feminization of the Workforce

During the 1990s and beyond, women will continue to enter the labor market in increasing numbers. Approximately two-thirds of new entrants into the workforce between now and the year 2000 will be women. Sixty-one percent of all working-age women are expected to have jobs by the year 2000.[7]

The feminization of the workforce has focused attention on the needs of women workers, such as day care, elder care, maternity and paternity benefits, flexible working hours, and flexible working stations. The Family and Medical Leave Act of 1993, which mandated that companies that employ more than 50 people provide unpaid leave for workers to care for newborn or newly adopted children or ill family members, was a milestone in recognizing the family responsibilities of working women.

Despite the progress of the past two decades, there is still much progress to be made by women in the workplace. For example, although there are increased numbers of women in the executive suite and in policy-making positions, managerial ranks continue to be dominated by men. And many male managers continue to have reservations about women in the workplace. As Felice Schwartz, president of Catalyst (a nonprofit organization that consults with top U.S. corporations on women's issues), argued:

Until babies, babies, babies have a place on the business agenda, we will all continue to fail. I think [that] . . . as soon as [men] think "women" they think "babies" and as soon as they think babies, they think of lack of commitment. All women are suspect: the single woman, the woman who doesn't have children but who is married, the woman who has children but puts her career first, the woman who has children but puts her children first or is committed to both.[8]

As *Workforce 2000* illustrates, however, women will continue to be increasingly important participants in the labor market. As of 1991, 75 percent of all men were participants in the labor force, compared with 57 percent of all women. This means that, although the number of males entering the workforce between now and the year 2000 will be minimal (because most men are already employed), the number of women who are working or are willing to work will continue to rise.[9] Organizations will be forced to deal more effectively with issues specifically related to women in the workplace.

Increasing Importance of Minority Workers

In the years to come, members of minority groups will constitute a growing segment of the workforce. According to *Workforce 2000*, minorities will account for 29 percent of net additions to the workforce between 1985 and 2000 and will make up more than 15 percent of the overall workforce by the year 2000.[10]

This prediction reverses the trend that characterized the 1970s and 1980s, in which the proportion of male minority workers in the labor force actually decreased. Between 1970 and 1984, the percentage of African-American men in the labor force dropped from 79 percent to 74 percent. *Workforce 2000* points out that as recently as 1987 African-American women outnumbered African-American men in the workforce.[11] Table 1-2 provides the data supporting this trend of decreasing minority participation in the workforce during the year 1983.

The decreased participation of minorities in the workforce of the 1970s and 1980s can be attributed in part to the fact that African-Americans and Hispanics of both genders tended to be employed in occupations that declined

Table 1-2. Minority Participation in the American Labor Market, 1983

	White	African-American	Hispanic
Labor force participation	64.3	61.5	63.8
Unemployment rate	8.4	19.5	13.7
Median family income, weekly	$487	$348	$366
Percentage below poverty	12.1	35.7	28.4
Median years of schooling	12.8	12.5	12.1

Source: U.S. Bureau of Labor Statistics, U.S. Bureau of the Census, 1983.

during this period. A study conducted by the Equal Employment Opportunity Commission concluded that both minority groups were 35 percent more likely than whites to be employed in occupations projected by the BLS to lose the most employees between 1978 and 1990.[12] Although the BLS projects that minorities and women will remain underrepresented in most professions, the diminishing pool of workers in the 1990s will increase employers' dependency on minority employees and women to fill positions at all levels.

Unfortunately, minority workers are less likely to have had the necessary postsecondary education and on-the-job training to be prepared for the majority of new jobs created between 1987 and the year 2000, according to the research reported in *Workforce 2000*. In addition, these workers may have language, value, and cultural differences that may prevent them from taking advantage of the jobs that exist today or will be created in the near future. Health care employers therefore need to address their workforce needs and to determine the roles they will play in providing workers with more knowledge of the job opportunities existing within health care. Employers also need to examine whether and how they will create outreach programs to establish a pool of qualified workers in an increasingly tight labor market. Chapter 6 discusses proactive efforts that can be taken by health care institutions to address these issues.

Increasing Importance of Alien Workers

Related to the projected increase of minority workers in the workforce is the increase in the number of alien workers. During the 1990s and beyond, aliens are projected to show the greatest increase in overall population and workforce participation since the end of World War I. Immigration officials estimate that approximately 600,000 aliens—both legal and illegal—will enter the United States annually during the 1990s. Two-thirds or more of those aliens who are of working age are expected to enter the labor force.[13]

Implications of Predictions in *Workforce 2000*

In summary, according to the predictions of *Workforce 2000*, minorities, women, older workers, and aliens will make up over five-sixths of the net new additions to the workforce between 1987 and the year 2000.[14] In addition, both younger workers and older workers will benefit from changing workforce demographics. Table 1-3 summarizes the findings of *Workforce 2000*. Even today, the shortage of workers has created a "seller's market" for health care employees and has increased opportunities for nontraditional workers. Although there is no comparable "buyer's market" for consumers of health care services, rising costs and increased information have helped consumers to become more cautious and critical when considering health care options.

Table 1-3. Entrants into the Workforce, 1985–2000

	1985 Labor Force	Net New Workers 1985–2000
Total number	115,461,000	25,000,000
Native white men	47%	15%
Native white women	35%	42%
Native nonwhite men	5%	7%
Native nonwhite women	5%	13%
Alien men	4%	13%
Alien women	3%	9%

Source: Reprinted with permission from W. B. Johnston and A. Packer. *Workforce 2000.* Indianapolis, IN: The Hudson Institute, 1987.

Significant Changes Affecting the Health Care Labor Environment

Health care consumers and health care workers have adopted a more demanding and less complacent attitude toward health care organizations. To continue to attract customers and workers in the future, health care organizations will need to respond to these changes. The following subsections examine changes in consumer attitudes, levels of union activity, worker expectations, and patterns of communication and how these changes will affect the current and future labor environment in health care institutions.

Changing Consumer Attitudes

The heated debate over health care reform that has characterized the early 1990s has highlighted growing consumer concerns about the perceived crisis in the quality, affordability, and availability of health care. Most Americans consider ready access to high-quality health care, regardless of ability to pay, to be a basic human right. As the cost of health care has risen, Americans have become more knowledgeable and discerning consumers. They are demanding "more bang for the buck" than ever before from health care institutions and providers.

Current projections indicate that by the year 2000, 15 percent of the gross national product will be spent on health care.[15] As health care costs continue to rise, government mandates and interventions are also likely to increase, creating additional demands upon hospital personnel.

Consumers are concerned about rising costs, but they are also concerned about what they perceive to be decreasing service. They expect every health care employee they encounter to provide high-quality, *efficient* care. Not only must health care institutions and providers supply good medical care, they must also supply good customer service. As a health care consumer interviewed for this book put it:

I drive 30 minutes across town in horrendous traffic [although] there is a hospital within walking distance of my home because [the nearby] hospital never meets its appointment times, loses the medical chart of myself and my family members, and has discourteous front office staff. I drive to another hospital . . . because of the quality and efficiency of their staff.

The increasing demands on already-overburdened health care workers, the climate of job insecurity that began in the late 1980s, and the realization that there is a shortage of qualified workers are among the many factors that have increased health care workers' interest in labor unions.

Increased Union Activity

In April of 1991, the U.S. Supreme Court ruled that the National Labor Relations Board (NLRB) acted within its legal bounds in adopting the rule that presumptively established eight bargaining units in acute care hospitals.[16] These units are physicians, nurses, other professionals, technical employees, business office clerical employees, skilled maintenance employees, guards, and all other nonprofessionals.

Not surprisingly, the Supreme Court's decision was expected to increase union organizing within health care organizations, though it may still be too early to tell what the effect of the decision will be on union activity. There is a wide range of unions interested in organizing hospital employees, including, to name just a few:

- Service Employees International Union
- American Federation of State, County and Municipal Employees
- International Union of Operating Engineers
- American Federation of Teachers/Federation of Nurses and Healthcare Professionals
- National Union of Hospital and Healthcare Employees
- International Brotherhood of Teamsters
- American Nurses Association

In March 1992, the American Society for Healthcare Human Resources Administration (ASHHRA) and The Omni Group, Inc., conducted a survey of ASHHRA members to determine the scope of union organizing activity in the health care field. Of the 494 hospitals that responded, 111 (or 22.5 percent) reported union activity of various kinds, especially in Pennsylvania and New York. The major findings of the survey were as follows:

- Unions were targeting hospitals with more than 5,000 employees about 43 percent of the time.
- Registered nurses, nonprofessional employees, and skilled maintenance employees were the primary targets.

- Unions had learned to capitalize on their successes by using grassroots approaches, such as selective employee contact, direct mail, handbills, and home meetings.
- The top two employee issues targeted by union organizers were "pay" and "relations with top management/administration."[17]

A report prepared by the American Hospital Association's Labor Relations Advisory Committee offers in-depth information about, and strategies for dealing with, increased union activity in health care organizations.[18] Additional information on unions is available in *Future Work*, a report by Joseph Coates, Jennifer Jarratt, and John Mahaffies, which points out that because the majority of jobs in the future will be service jobs, union recruiting activity will focus increasingly on service workers, who traditionally have not been union members.[19] Further increasing the likelihood of rising union popularity is the fact that unions advocate higher wages, improved benefits, and greater job security. Health care workers who survive massive layoffs and witness the poor treatment of departing employees often become demoralized, which makes them strong candidates for labor-union membership. Increased labor activity, along with anxiety about job security and the increasingly diverse workforce, are also creating altered worker expectations.

Changing Worker Expectations

The employment relationship between employees and employers has changed in the 1990s. Workers are less willing to assimilate because, after all, workers have observed that no matter how hard one tries to fit into an organization, one may become the victim of corporate downsizing. The new workplace has changed from a melting pot to a colorful salad or stew in which each ingredient retains its individual flavor.

Examples of this increased differentiation—or *diversity*—can be seen throughout American industry. During the 1970s, when women joined the workforce in great numbers, dressing for success meant downplaying femininity and wearing adaptations of men's business attire—tailored suits, starched shirts, and even ties. In today's workforce, however, women's attire is more varied and includes dresses, suits, and pants in bright colors and pastels, demonstrating that women are more confident of their rightful place in the workforce. Although the so-called glass ceiling that prevents women from ascending to the top of the corporate ladder still exists, women are represented in increasing numbers in the professions and in the executive suite. This progress has made it easier for them and for the women they supervise to feel comfortable in the workplace and under less pressure to blend in.

Minority workers also are less willing than in the past to assimilate into the corporate melting pot and risk losing their ethnic identities. This change may be partly due to the fact that minorities have few role models in upper management to demonstrate the benefits of melting in. Unfortunately, many minority workers experience the effects of the glass ceiling at fairly low levels in the organization.[20]

Members of the younger generation of workers (workers born between the years 1967 and 1975) are perhaps the least willing to assimilate. They challenge the status quo on everything from work rules to the use of ecologically unsound styrofoam cups in the cafeteria. This new generation of workers does not see company loyalty as a worthwhile attribute. Many have seen family members or friends laid off after years of loyal service and have witnessed the destruction of the dream of worry-free retirement after decades of hard work. Younger workers join a company thinking, "I will give you 100 percent while I work for you, but I will stay on the lookout for a better opportunity." They reject the workaholic mentality of the 1980s and the need to work 10 hours or more a day. After all, their parents (who often missed out on school plays, Little League games, and other family activities) were laid off despite their long work hours. Merciless downsizing in today's corporations has helped to bury the old Protestant work ethic.

Worker expectations also have been changed by the large number of highly educated workers with advanced degrees in the workforce. These workers expect to participate actively in decision making and will not accept being managed in the traditional hierarchical style. They expect their expertise and educational achievements to be appreciated and utilized to the fullest by their employers.

The expected future job growth in the health care field will require increased reliance on the groups of workers discussed in the preceding sections. Health care organizations will need to be especially careful to identify and respond to the new expectations and needs of an increasingly diverse workforce.

Changing Patterns of Communication

The present and future workforce, which includes ethnically diverse and differently abled workers, will alter patterns of communication at work. Workplaces will need to adapt to the use of languages other than English and adapt facilities to accommodate employees with impaired vision or hearing. Such changes, although seemingly difficult to achieve, will not only maximize worker productivity but will also enhance relations with customers who have a variety of cultural backgrounds and physical abilities.

Adapting to Nonnative Speakers of English
With aliens and minorities making up an ever-increasing percentage of the new labor pool and the overall population, communicating effectively with customers and workers who speak little or no English has become a major organizational concern. Many companies, including health care organizations, have developed programs to teach English to employees at the work site. These programs have been shown to improve not only language skills but also self-confidence, morale,

and productivity. However, the increase in alien and minority workers has also resulted in a form of backlash. A number of employers have mandated that only English can be used in their workplaces. However, courts have recently ruled that "English-only" mandates are illegal. For example, in *Gutierrez v. Municipal Court of Huntington Park,* the state of California established that the use of foreign languages in the workplace may be restricted only when there is a compelling business-related need to do so.[21] According to Equal Employment Opportunity Commission (EEOC) guidelines,

> The primary language of an individual is often an essential national origin characteristic. Prohibiting employees, at all times in the work place, from speaking their primary language, or the language they speak most comfortably, disadvantages an individual's employment opportunities on the basis of national origin. It may also create an atmosphere of inferiority, isolation and intimidation based on national origin, which could result in a discriminatory working environment. Therefore, the commission will presume that such a rule violates Title VII and will closely scrutinize it.[22]

Most English-only rules are instituted by employers because of employee complaints about coworkers, subordinates, or supervisors who do not speak English or who do not speak it well. Instituting training programs to help employees respect and value cultural differences can reduce conflicts among workers with different cultural backgrounds. Such programs should aim at eliminating misconceptions about non-English-speaking employees, such as, "They want to live in this country, but they don't want to learn the language." Most non-English-speaking employees are highly motivated to learn English; they realize that their lack of language skills inhibits their chances for career advancement.

Many companies have come to realize that multilingual employees can enhance business. For example, U.S. West, a Denver-based telecommunications company, found that many of its customers spoke mostly Spanish, or even only Spanish, and these customers found it difficult to communicate with service representatives who spoke only English. When U.S. West began to utilize Spanish-speaking representatives for such customers, their level of customer satisfaction — and their business — improved.[23]

In health care, many consumers of health care services, as well as service providers, are not native speakers of English. Enhancing the English-language skills of employees while encouraging them to use their native languages when appropriate not only is necessary but also makes good business sense.

Adapting to Workers with Hearing or Vision Impairments

Today's health care institutions must also accommodate the communication needs of workers with impaired hearing and vision. The passage of the Americans with Disabilities Act requires health care organizations to accommodate

the needs of differently abled workers—and customers. The shortage of qualified job applicants has made it especially important for health care institutions
to be ready to employ workers with hearing and vision impairments. Equipping work stations with telecommunications devices for the deaf (TDDs) and
providing signs, forms, and training materials in large type or in Braille can
allow health care organizations to tap a whole new source of qualified workers.

The Ongoing Shortage of Health Care Workers

The historical shortage of qualified health care workers shows no sign of letting
up. The nursing shortage crisis of the 1980s has abated only slightly during
the early 1990s. As table 1-1 demonstrated, more than half of the fastest-growing
job categories in the 1990s will be in health care. This is not good news to
health care organizations, which already are coping with understaffing problems.
Tables 1-4 and 1-5 show supply-and-demand figures for 19 health care worker
categories in the years 1990 and 2000 and list estimated shortages based on
current vacancy levels and rates of attrition.[24] Many of the areas of projected
job growth are outside of the typical acute care setting. Also, many of the jobs
(such as respiratory therapists, physical therapists, and occupational therapists)
reflect the projected needs of an aging population.

According to *Health Care 2000*, three primary factors will increase the need
for qualified health care workers in the decades to come:[25]

1. *The creation and utilization of new technologies:* Sophisticated equipment, new
   technologies, and a growing need for labor-intensive acute care, multiple
   doctors' visits, and laboratory tests will increase the demand for workers with
   relevant specialized training and skills.
2. *The aging of the population:* Persons over the age of 75 use significantly more
   health care services and have longer and more frequent hospital stays than
   the overall population. The population between the ages of 75 and 84 is
   expected to grow from 9.5 million in 1988 to 12.0 million by the year 2000.
   The number of people age 85 and older, who use twice as many hospital
   days per capita as persons 10 years younger, will increase from 3 million in
   1988 to 4.6 million by the end of the 1990s. Both of these groups are growing much faster than the population as a whole. Nursing homes, home health
   care providers, and hospice facilities can expect increased demands for their
   services as the population ages.
3. *The AIDS epidemic:* It is estimated that by the year 2000 there will be 10
   times as many diagnosed AIDS patients who require medical care as there
   were in 1989.

The current trend toward increased utilization of outpatient facilities, nursing homes, home health care services, and AIDS treatment centers will continue to boost the demand for health care workers at all levels who have relevant

skills and experience. The implications of this emphasis on relevant skills will be discussed in the following section.

Maintenance of a Supply of Skilled Workers

Americans were up in arms in 1992 when a Japanese official called American workers uneducated and lazy. In fact, America's service-oriented economy has created "smarter" jobs: More than half of all the jobs that will be created through the year 2000 will require postsecondary education, and almost a third of those jobs will be filled by college graduates.[26]

Table 1-4.   Year 1990 Employment Figures

Professions	Demand[a]	Supply[b]	Vacancies	
Nursing				
Registered nurse	1,780,000	1,630,000	150,000	(8%)
Licensed practical nurse	710,339	664,167	46,172	(7%)
Allied Health				
Respiratory therapist	59,288	56,000	3,288	(6%)
Occupational therapist	39,759	33,000	6,759	(17%)
Physical therapist	81,900	68,000	13,900	(17%)
Radiation therapy technician	9,378	8,159	1,219	(13%)
Sonographer (ultrasound technician)	22,346	20,000	2,346	(10%)
Radiographer	224,766	204,537	20,228	(9%)
Nuclear medicine technician	13,293	12,230	1,063	(8%)
Cardiac perfusionist	2,001	1,781	220	(11%)[c]
Medical technologist	238,995	219,660	20,335	(9%)
Histology technologist	1,042	917	125	(12%)
Cytogenetic technologist	1,725	1,307	418	(24%)
Cytology technologist	7,470	5,543	2,017	(27%)
Medical assistant	160,215	149,000	11,215	(7%)
Miscellaneous				
Social worker	1,182,795	1,100,000	82,795	(7%)[c]
Pharmacist	172,000	123,862	48,138	(28%)
Accredited records technician	41,463	28,195	13,268	(32%)
Registered record administrator	16,748	12,687	4,061	(32%)

Source: Reprinted with permission from *Health Care 2000: A World of Human Resource Differences,* copyright 1992 by the American Hospital Association, p. 4.

Note: Figures are derived from all health care settings except as noted.

[a]The demand figures represent the number of professionals who are, or will be, required to fill all available openings.

[b]The supply figures represent the number of professionals who are, or will be, available to serve their respective professions.

[c]The percent vacancy number is drawn from a survey limited to hospitals.

Table 1-5. Year 2000 Employment Figures

Professions	Demand	Adjusted Supply	Vacancies	
Nursing				
Registered nurse	2,190,000	1,930,000	260,000	(12%)
Licensed practical nurse	855,000	717,000	138,000	(16%)
Allied Health				
Respiratory therapist	79,000	64,229	14,771	(19%)
Occupational therapist	48,000	37,461	10,539	(22%)
Physical therapist	129,000	110,140	18,860	(15%)
Radiation therapy technician	11,253	11,623	0	(0%)
Sonographer (ultrasound technician)	26,815	23,197	3,618	(13%)
Radiographer	260,537	245,120	15,417	(6%)
Nuclear medicine technician	15,230	14,680	550	(4%)
Cardiac perfusionist	3,098	5,196	0	(0%)
Medical technologist	296,000	160,874	135,125	(46%)
Histology technologist	2,052	1,765	287	(14%)
Cytogenetic technologist	2,222	1,603	619	(28%)
Cytology technologist	9,337	5,827	3,510	(37%)
Medical assistant	253,000	161,039	91,961	(36%)
Miscellaneous				
Social worker	1,644,518	1,414,286	230,232	(14%)
Pharmacist	206,000	131,657	74,343	(36%)
Accredited records technician	45,112	27,284	17,828	(40%)
Registered record administrator	29,309	13,534	15,775	(54%)

Source: Reprinted with permission from *Health Care 2000: A World of Human Resource Differences*, copyright 1992 by the American Hospital Association, p. 6.

In health care, educational requirements and skill levels for even entry-level jobs are rising, placing increasing demands on health care institutions to attract better-educated workers and provide better training for new workers. In addition, increasingly rigorous requirements for the continuing education of current employees are leading employers to offer increased opportunities for in-service training and skill development and enhancement.

According to a professor at Columbia University's Teachers College, as of 1990, every fifth person hired by American industry was both illiterate and innumerate, despite increasing worker educational requirements and skill levels.[27] The August 1989 cover of *Personnel Administrator* shocked many. In boldface type was the caption, "27 Million Americans Cannot Read This." The U.S. Department of Labor has estimated that the majority of the growth in the labor pool will come from minority students, of whom nearly 40 percent are considered functionally illiterate.[28]

Clearly, Americans are faced with a disparity between the skills required by the jobs of the present—and the future—and the abilities of the candidates available to fill them. Corporate America can no longer sit back and point the finger at the educational system. Corporate America must now take action by creating innovative training and in-service programs to ensure that there will be a supply of literate, work-ready applicants to meet future needs.

Preparation for the Coming Challenges in Health Care Staffing

This chapter provided a brief overview of the changes in workforce demographics facing American employers in general and the health care industry in particular. The effective management of an increasingly diverse workforce will be the major challenge employers face in the coming decades. The homogeneous workforce of the past, in which all workers could be assumed to have similar expectations and could be managed with traditional management techniques, is gone forever—if, in fact, it ever really existed. This book describes approaches that have been effective in meeting the challenges of workforce diversity. However, the reader must keep in mind that each workplace is unique and that an effective approach to managing workforce diversity must be tailored to the specific needs and concerns of each individual organization. There is no formulaic set of solutions that will work for everyone. Understanding the issues that are of concern to health care workers is the first step toward effective management of the diverse health care workforce of the future.

References

1. Johnston, W. B., and Packer, A. *Workforce 2000*. Indianapolis: The Hudson Institute, 1987.

2. U.S. Department of Labor, Bureau of Labor Statistics, 1990.

3. Shortell, S. M., Morrison, E. M., and Friedman, B. *Strategic Choices for America's Hospitals*. San Francisco: Jossey-Bass, 1990, p. 9.

4. Johnston and Packer, p. xix.

5. First there was blue-collar and white-collar . . . now prepare for the gold-collar workforce. *The Personnel News*, Sept. 1990, p. 20.

6. Johnston and Packer, p. xx.

7. Johnston and Packer, p. xx.

8. Interview with Felice Schwartz. *Chicago Tribune*, May 3, 1992, section 6, p. 3.

9. U.S. Department of Labor, Bureau of Labor Statistics. *Employment and Earnings*, Table A4, May 1991.

10. Johnston and Packer, p. xx.

11. Johnston and Packer, p. 89.

12. Racial stereotyping: an old, virulent virus. *Chicago Tribune*, May 13, 1992, p. A1.

13. Johnston and Packer, p. xx.

14. Johnston and Packer, p. xx.

15. Shortell and others, p. 3.

16. American Hospital Association v. National Labor Relations Board et. al. No. 90–97, argued Feb. 25, 1991, decided Apr. 23, 1991.

17. American Society for Healthcare Human Resources Administration and The Omni Group, Inc. *ASHHRA/OMNI Semi-Annual Labor Activity Report*. First report, March 1, 1992. Chicago: ASHHRA, 1992.

18. Labor Relations Advisory Committee. *Collective Bargaining Units in the Health Care Industry*. Chicago: American Hospital Association, 1991.

19. Coates, J., Jarratt, J., and Mahaffie, J. *Future Work*. San Francisco: Jossey-Bass, 1990, pp. 399–406.

20. U.S. Department of Labor. *A Report on the Glass Ceiling Initiative*. Washington, DC: U.S. Department of Labor, 1991.

21. Gutierrez v. Municipal Court of Huntington Park, S.E. Judicial Dist., Los Angeles County, 838 F.2d 1031 (9th Cir. 1988).

22. Equal Employment Opportunity Commission Guideline, Title VII.

23. Geber, B. Managing diversity. *Training*, July 1990, p. 28.

24. American Society for Healthcare Human Resources Administration. *Health Care 2000*. Chicago: ASHHRA, 1992.

25. ASHHRA, p. 2.

26. Johnston and Packer, p. 98.

27. Wanting workers. *The Wall Street Journal Reports*, Feb. 9, 1990, p. R11.

28. *Personnel Administrator*, Aug. 1989.

Chapter Two

Managing Workforce Diversity: The Cutting-Edge Concept

Chapter 1 described the changing demographics that have created a diverse 1990s workforce. This chapter provides a brief overview of the legislative changes that have mandated and will continue to encourage workforce diversity. The chapter then discusses some of the difficulties in attracting a viable workforce for today and for the future. The chapter closes by discussing some common obstacles that prevent us from valuing diversity. Understanding and applying the information presented in this chapter can help health care organizations arrive—and remain—at the cutting edge of diversity management.

The Impact of Federal Legislation

The first step in managing a diverse workforce is to become familiar with key federal legislation that, since the mid-nineteenth century, has made the workplace more open to all. Federal laws have helped ensure equal employment opportunities for all applicants and employees in all aspects of employment: recruitment, working conditions, compensation, relocation, employee development, performance assessment, advancement, discipline, and termination. Perhaps the best known of these laws are the various civil rights acts, which through the years have caused sweeping and long-standing changes in American society as well as in employment practices.

The Civil Rights Acts

The passage of the Civil Rights Act of 1866 ensured that all persons have the right to make and enforce contracts, including employment contracts, and provided for civil action to enforce those rights. In 1870 the act was amended to ensure the right of all citizens to inherit, purchase, lease, sell, hold, and convey real and personal property. In 1871 the act was further amended to provide for enforcement of the 14th Amendment, which prevents state laws from infringing upon citizens' rights, privileges, and immunities.

After a period of almost 100 years during which no new federal civil rights legislation was passed, the Civil Rights Act of 1964 became law. Title VI of the act specifically prohibits employment discrimination on the basis of race, color, and national origin in programs and activities that receive federal financial assistance. Title VII outlaws employment discrimination based on race, color, religion, sex, or national origin by all employers with 15 or more employees.[1]

The Civil Rights Act of 1991 made employers liable for compensatory and punitive damages when they are proved guilty of intentional discrimination on the basis of sex, religion, disability, and other categories. In addition, the act allows the awarding of substantial damages to victims of sexual, ethnic, and religious harassment even when a job loss or adverse employment action did not occur.

In so-called disparate impact claims (charges that an employment practice affected female or minority-group members more adversely than white males), employers must prove that the employment practice is job related and is justified by business necessity specific to the job in question. Prior to 1991, employers were required to demonstrate only business *justification,* not necessity.[2]

The Pregnancy Discrimination Act

The Pregnancy Discrimination Act of 1978 amended Title VII of the Civil Rights Act of 1964, expanding the definition of discrimination "because of sex" to include discrimination against pregnant women. The Pregnancy Discrimination Act requires companies with 15 or more employees to treat pregnancy as they would any other medical disability. That means that an employer must hold a job for a woman on maternity leave if the job would routinely be held for an employee of either gender who was recovering from a temporarily disabling condition such as a heart attack, a bout with cancer, or a broken leg. The act also prohibits companies from firing, refusing to hire, or denying promotions to women solely because they are pregnant.

As of early 1994, 19 states go beyond the requirements of the federal law and mandate job-protected leaves to women recovering from childbirth or caring for newborns. Nonetheless, according to *Working Woman* magazine, "from 1985 to 1990, new mothers were 10 times more likely to lose their jobs than other employees on leave."[3] The article found that discrimination against pregnant women has become much more subtle than the blatant denial of equal opportunity that was routine prior to 1978. "Employers are much more sophisticated about the law . . . and very conscious about not putting themselves in a litigious position," says Ellen Galinsky, co-president of the Families and Work Institutes.[4]

The most common discriminatory ploys used by employers include departmental restructuring that just happens to eliminate the pregnant woman's position or a sudden discovery of performance problems that were not documented before the employee's pregnancy that result in termination or demotion. Given that women of childbearing age make up a large proportion of the current and future workforce, companies should be looking for ways to retain women, not exclude them. This observation is particularly applicable to health care organizations, which as discussed in chapter 1, can expect unprecedented job growth in the 1990s and beyond.

Affirmative Action

Out of the civil rights acts came the principle of affirmative action, which attempts to actively address and rectify past discrimination. A series of executive orders issued over the past 30 years established the principle of affirmative action to ensure fair employment practices by businesses engaged in transactions with the U.S. government. Writing in the *Harvard Business Review,* R. Roosevelt Thomas, Jr., identified five premises about the workforce that support the need for affirmative action:[5]

1. Adult white males make up something called the "U.S. business mainstream."
2. The U.S. economic edifice is a solid, unchanging institution that nevertheless has more than enough space for everyone.
3. Women, aliens, African-Americans, and other minorities should be allowed in to the business mainstream as a matter of public policy and common decency.
4. Widespread racial, ethnic, and sexual prejudice keeps such groups out of the mainstream.
5. Legal and social coercion are necessary to bring about the changes needed to ensure equity.

The specific executive orders that implemented affirmative action prohibit federal contractors from discriminating against employees on the basis of age (Executive Order 11141); require federal contractors to take affirmative action to ensure that applicants are considered for employment regardless of race, color, religion, or national origin (Executive Order 11246) or sex (Executive Order 11375); and prohibit federal employers from discriminating on the basis of race, color, religion, sex, national origin, handicap, or age (Executive Order 11478). Because of its focus on age discrimination, Executive Order 11478 received additional federal attention when the Age Discrimination in Employment Act was passed in 1967.

The Age Discrimination in Employment Act

The Age Discrimination in Employment Act (ADEA) of 1967 prohibits discrimination against employees or job applicants on the basis of age. The ADEA, enacted to prevent discrimination against workers over age 40, applies to all employers with 20 or more workers employed for at least 20 weeks per year. Even without the help of the ADEA, changing workforce demographics will make recruitment and retention of workers over 40 a top priority. Not only will such workers become greater in number, but their skills, maturity, and experience will make them ideally suited to the kinds of jobs that will proliferate in the 1990s and beyond. Corporate America, however, is not yet targeting this segment of the population to fill its employment needs. Small business seems to be more enlightened. According to a survey conducted for the Small Business Administration, businesses with fewer than 25 employees account for more than two-thirds of new hiring of workers age 65 and over.[6]

Even if corporate America continued to ignore the value of older workers and even if changing demographics were not making older workers a crucial segment of the workforce, the ADEA makes it unlawful for certain employers to discriminate against older workers.

The Americans with Disabilities Act

In 1991 President George Bush signed into law the Americans with Disabilities Act (ADA), the world's first comprehensive civil rights law for protecting the rights of individuals with disabilities. Passage of the ADA represented a milestone in America's commitment to full and equal opportunity for all of its citizens. The president's emphatic directive on that day, "Let the shameful walls of exclusion finally come tumbling down," neatly encapsulated the simple yet long-overdue message of the ADA: that differently abled Americans are full-fledged citizens who are entitled to equal opportunity and access to mainstream American life.[7] The ADA defines a person with a disability as: (1) an individual who has a physical or mental impairment that substantially limits one or more of his/her major life activities; (2) an individual who has a record of such an impairment; or (3) an individual who is regarded as having such an impairment.

Even before passage of the ADA, however, society's attitudes toward the differently abled were beginning to shift. Before 1975 it was not uncommon to find what were known as "ugly laws" in city statutes and ordinances throughout the country. One such "ugly law" from a large midwestern city read as follows: "No person who is diseased, maimed, mutilated or in any way deformed so as to be an unsightly or disgusting object or improper person is to be allowed in or on the public ways in this city, or shall expose himself to public view, under penalty of not less than $1 nor more than $50 for each offence."

Thankfully, attitudes changed, helped along by legislation such as the Rehabilitation Act of 1973. For example, a 1975 amendment to the 1969 Education of the Handicapped Act established the right of all children to a "free appropriate public education in the least restrictive environment," meaning that differently abled children could mix with the general public in public schools.[8] Prior to this 1975 amendment, only 15 states provided any public education for the differently abled.

The enactment of the ADA moved the United States toward full acceptance of the differently abled as vital and important members of the workforce and society as a whole. Differently abled employees who have been discriminated against are entitled under the ADA to the same relief, including compensatory and punitive damages, as prescribed by the Civil Rights Act of 1991.

To allow qualified differently abled persons to perform essential job functions, the ADA requires all employers to make "reasonable accommodations" to the known physical or mental limitations of a qualified applicant or employee with a disability unless it can show that the accommodation would cause an undue hardship on the operation of its business. *Undue hardship* is defined by the ADA as "an action that is excessively costly, extensive, substantial, or disruptive, or that would fundamentally alter the nature or operation of the business." In determining undue hardship, factors to be considered include the nature and cost of the accommodation in relation to the size, financial resources, nature, and structure of the employer's operation, as well as the impact of the accommodation on the specific facility providing the accommodation.[9]

The ADA has been viewed by many organizations as a legal and economic burden imposed by the government. However, in view of the present and future shortage of qualified workers, the ADA should be viewed as an opportunity to tap a large source of qualified workers. According to statistics supporting the ADA, there are 43 million Americans who are differently abled, and a large portion of them are not active participants in the labor market.[10]

Having to make "reasonable accommodations" is not the biggest barrier to hiring the differently abled—prejudice is. Common misconceptions about the differently abled include the following:

- *Certain jobs are more suited to the differently abled:* This statement is the same as saying that only certain jobs are suitable for women and minorities. This attitude limits the opportunities for the differently abled to excel in the workplace.
- *Differently abled workers are better workers:* This seemingly flattering stereotype exists because the few differently abled workers in the workplace tend to be overqualified for the jobs they hold. However, this misconception creates expectations that make it extremely difficult for the differently abled employee of average abilities to function in an organization.
- *Managers need special training to supervise differently abled employees:* In general, the only special managerial training necessary is sensitivity training to help managers interact effectively with differently abled employees.
- *Reasonable accommodation is expensive:* According to a survey by the Job Accommodation Network, a database that tracks disability accommodations, over 70 percent of such accommodations cost under $500. Moving a computer to a lower desk for an employee in a wheelchair costs nothing. A stepladder that will enable an employee with dwarfism to reach high file drawers costs under $50. A telecommunication device for a hearing-impaired employee costs about $200. Adapting a bathroom stall to accommodate a wheelchair costs under $500.[11]

Many large organizations, especially in the service industry, are slowly beginning to tap the differently abled to fill gaps in their workforces. For example, the McDonald's Corporation, a pioneer in the hiring of large numbers of older workers, is now actively recruiting differently abled workers. Health care organizations, too, should look to differently abled workers to meet growing employment needs. In addition to bringing much-needed skills to the workplace, differently abled workers can help health care organizations become more sensitive and responsive to the needs of differently abled customers.

The Immigration Reform and Control Act

In addition to the differently abled, another group of nontraditional employees—aliens—will become an increasingly important source of workers in the coming years. Recent legislation has made it increasingly likely that U.S. employers in general and health care organizations in particular will find a steady stream of qualified aliens to fill the highly skilled jobs that will experience the most growth in the 1990s and beyond.

The Immigration Reform and Control Act of 1986 amended the Immigration and Nationality Act, which was enacted to administer programs for the admission of aliens and temporary foreign workers for employment opportunities in the United States. The 1986 act prohibits discrimination based on citizenship status and national origin. A further revision of the act in 1990 mandates major increases in the number of visas for aliens who are highly skilled professionals, such as researchers, engineers, and scientists; "priority workers" with "extraordinary abilities" in the arts, science, education, business, or athletics; and workers with advanced degrees, "exceptional ability," or highly developed work skills. The law also calls for an increased number of visas over a three-year period for aliens from 35 countries with low immigration rates during recent decades. All the aliens must have the equivalent of a high school education or two years of specific work experience.[12]

This 1990 immigration law puts a new slant on the proverbial "huddled masses" of immigrants at Ellis Island. The U.S. government's move to encourage the immigration of highly skilled and educated workers was prompted in part by current and projected shortages of such workers in the present workforce. Many health care organizations have already begun to use foreign-born physicians and nurses to fill staff shortages and thus have had to develop strategies to accommodate increasing workforce diversity.

The Family and Medical Leave Act

All employers, including those in health care, are making additional major adjustments to accommodate the requirements of a sweeping and long-awaited piece of legislation—the Family and Medical Leave Act of 1993. Signed into law by President Bill Clinton on February 5, 1993, the Family and Medical Leave Act was the first piece of legislation signed under the new administration.

The act requires that any employer with 50 or more employees offer unpaid leaves of absence totaling 12 weeks over a 12-month period for the following reasons:

- *The need to care for a child in the first 12 months after birth, adoption, or foster placement:* It is important to note that the employer can require that the leave be taken all at one time.
- *The need to care for a spouse, child, or parent who has a serious health condition:* Such leave may be taken intermittently, or the employee may reduce his or her hours at work (for example, by working half-days or less than five days per week), but only when a reduced schedule is needed because of the sick person's specific medical condition. The care of parents-in-law, siblings, and children-in-law is not covered by the act. A *serious health condition* is defined as a health condition that either requires inpatient care in a hospital, hospice, or residential medical care facility or requires continuing treatment by a health care provider.
- *The employee's own serious health condition that prevents the employee from performing his or her job:* As with a family member's illness, leave can be taken intermittently or, if medically necessary, by reducing work hours.[13]

The passage of the Family and Medical Leave Act of 1993 is proof that the government recognizes that women in the workforce are a fact of life, that the majority of women with children work outside the home, and that an aging population has made it increasingly likely that workers will have to attend to the needs of aging or disabled spouses or parents. A survey conducted by the Travelers Corporation found that approximately one out of every five of its own employees over the age of 30 provided some care to an elderly parent and that most of the employees providing such care were women, even when the elderly parent was the spouse's.[14] The Family and Medical Leave Act of 1993 recognizes that workers of both genders need to be able to attend to family needs or health crises without fear of job loss.

With or without legal sanctions, however, employers can ill afford to ignore the needs of a large proportion of the workforce, given the predicted shortages of skilled and qualified workers in the years to come. Women, workers with families, older workers, differently abled workers, minority workers, and aliens will all be vital components of the workforce of the future. The laws described in the preceding sections have made it difficult for employers who might want to ignore demographic evidence and exclude such workers. Whether one attributes it to demographics or legal necessity, employers will have to become more responsive to issues of diversity in order to attract and retain a viable workforce.

The Growing Difficulty in Attracting a Viable Workforce

Even if the fact that the number of entrants into the labor pool will decrease by about 500,000 each year between the early and mid-1990s does not impress health care organizations, the changing workforce skills mix and growing work-force skills gap should draw everyone's attention.[15] Increased demand for a dwindling supply of skilled workers, increased specialization and educational requirements for jobs, and a growing literacy crisis are issues of grave concern to health care organizations.

Increased Demand, Dwindling Supply

Health care already experienced a major labor shortage during the nursing shortage crisis of the 1980s. Hospitals quickly developed creative recruitment and retention practices, including offering monetary bonuses to new employees and parental leave, child care, and elder care to all employees. Health care organizations have offered seminars on work and family issues and have instituted flexible spending accounts that allow employees to lower their personal taxes by using pretax dollars to pay for eligible expenses. (Flexible spending accounts also benefit employers in that the accounts save on payroll taxes.) The Bureau of Labor Statistics projects that, although the overall civilian labor force will increase by 16 percent by the year 2000, employment in health services will grow by 41.9 percent, or by almost 3 million workers.[16] Therefore, employers in general—and health care organizations in particular—will have to continue to listen to and respond to workers' needs with new and creative programs if these organizations are to attract and retain qualified workers.

Mismatch between Applicants' Education and Job Requirements

In addition to a dwindling supply of workers available to fill an increasing number of jobs, other factors will contribute to projected labor shortages in health care. For example, disagreements about licensing, certification, competency testing, and the degree of formal education needed by health care professionals are likely to limit the number of viable applicants. Most health occupations require at least some postsecondary training. According to the Bureau of Labor Statistics, the major shortfall that may materialize is the lack of individuals with the education needed to qualify for the necessary postsecondary education or training.[17]

Although minorities are an increasingly important segment of the new workforce, they are more likely than nonminorities to have left high school before graduation. However, the projected educational mismatch is a double-edged sword. Paradoxically, an increasing number of high school graduates, both minority and nonminority, are going on to college, which may make them over-qualified for or unwilling to accept the technical jobs that comprise the majority of health care positions.[18]

The Literacy Crisis

An issue related to education is the growing literacy crisis in America. As was discussed in chapter 1, it is estimated that every fifth person now hired by

American industry is both illiterate and innumerate. According to a survey conducted in 1990 by the American Society of Training and Development, 70 percent of Fortune 500 companies plan to increase the amount of money they spend on employee education and training, as well as to emphasize remedial education.[19] Because of this literacy crisis, businesses must institute educational programs to help a growing number of their employees master the basics of reading, writing, and mathematics. Chapter 6 will explore in detail how health care institutions are dealing with the education and skills mismatch and the literacy crisis.

The variations in the educational and literacy skills of U.S. workers add another dimension of diversity to the workforce of the future. The sections that follow explore the various aspects of diversity.

The Many Faces of the Diverse Workforce

The new diverse workforce has many aspects and faces. Workforce diversity encompasses a mosaic of races, ethnic and religious backgrounds, sexual orientations, family situations, ages, and physical abilities. Workforce diversity can also refer to diverse functions within an organization. The workplace clearly is no longer a man's world and it is increasingly less a white man's world, but it was for white men that most corporate structures, policies, benefits, and norms were established.

To fully appreciate the complexity of diversity, it is helpful to break down diversity into two categories: *primary diversity*, which consists of elements of diversity over which one has no control, and *secondary diversity*, which consists of elements of diversity that are subject to choice, that is, that one can control.[20] The following are examples of elements of primary and secondary diversity:

- Primary
  - Age
  - Ethnicity
  - Gender
  - Physical abilities and qualities
  - Race
  - Sexual orientation
- Secondary
  - Educational background
  - Geographic location
  - Income
  - Marital status
  - Military experience
  - Parental status
  - Religious beliefs
  - Work experience

Each of us has a culture and value system that develops throughout our lives and that we bring with us to the workplace. We then blend our unique personal cultures with the culture of the particular institution for which we work. *Workforce diversity* thus can refer to a wide spectrum of differences and recognizes that every person is unique and different from other people in some way. However, it is difficult for some people to accept workforce diversity, and sometimes playful approaches can help break down barriers.

Examining Diversity through Games

An interesting way for groups to explore and understand workforce diversity is to use learning exercises such as the Diversity Mix Game or Diversity Bingo.[21] Brief overviews of the games show how such games can be useful in helping staff to accept the many faces of diversity. (See appendix A for information on ordering Diversity Bingo.)

The Diversity Mix Game

The Diversity Mix Game is intended as a nonthreatening "icebreaker" activity in a diversity training workshop. The game can be run by internal or external consultants conducting the diversity training. To play the Diversity Mix Game, workshop participants form small groups of equal size. (For example, a group of 20 participants would break into four groups of five members.) Each group then considers ways in which its members differ from one another. Points are assigned on the basis of categories of differences. The group with the highest score "wins" as the most diverse team.

Examples of Diversity Mix Game categories and point values include the following:

- *Gender:* 1 point
- *Race:* 1 point
- *Ethnicity:* 1 point per ethnic heritage (for example, Irish/German = 2 points)
- *Age:* 1 point for each decade represented (that is, under 20, 20 to 29, 30 to 39, 40 to 49, 50 to 59, and over 60 years of age)
- *Organizational role:* 1 point for each different job description
- *Employment history:* 1 point for each different job held ("job-hoppers" can rack up the points here)
- *Origins:* 1 point for each state a person has lived in
- *Experience:* 1 point for each year on the job
- *Familiarity:* 1 point for each person in the group whom other members of the group had never met before

Playing the Diversity Mix Game helps participants see the diversity of the group exclusive of race and gender. They gain a better understanding of the many aspects of employee diversity.

Diversity Bingo

Diversity Bingo is played much the same way as traditional bingo, though the game should ideally be conducted by a trained diversity facilitator. In this game, the two categories of diversity, primary and secondary, are further broken down into 25 descriptors of diversity, each of which occupies a square on a traditional bingo card. As group members play the game and the descriptors are called out, players try to guess which members of the group fit into each called category. Throughout the game, attitudes, stereotypes, and preconceptions about each descriptor of diversity are explored and discussed. The game is effective because it enables participants to examine stereotypes without "owning" them.

The 25 bingo categories are these:

- A person over 60 years of age
- A person born and raised on a farm (it is interesting to note whether some group members believe that this category does not include people of color or aliens)
- A person with a southern accent
- A person who speaks more than one language (this category explores stereotypes about foreign accents and people who speak English as a second language and whether some accents are more acceptable than others)
- A differently abled person
- A Muslim (do group members assume that a Muslim must be from a foreign country?—over 2.5 million of the almost 1 billion Muslims in the world are American)
- A naturalized citizen
- A person of Hispanic-Latin American heritage
- A woman
- A left-handed person (although this may be a minor diversity issue, left-handed people live in a right-handed world and must adapt for a lifetime)
- A military veteran (do group members assume that veterans are all men?)
- A person with red hair
- An inhabitant of planet Earth (this square ends up being the free space on the bingo card)
- A person who has received welfare
- A person of African ancestry
- A man
- A person of Native American heritage
- A high-school graduate (investigate whether group members have stereotypes and prejudices about various levels of education or public versus private education)
- A single parent
- A person who is over six feet tall
- A grandparent

- A vegetarian (does the group assume that this practice must be for cultural or religious reasons? what barriers does this create in the work environment?)
- A person of Asian heritage
- A person who is Jewish
- A person who is gay or lesbian

The last category makes most groups uncomfortable, and it is not uncommon to hear participants make "jokes" or sarcastic remarks. It is important to examine these biases and prejudices to ensure that the work environment allows each person to reach his or her full potential in the organization. Is the organizational culture biased against diversity in sexual orientation?

In the authors' experience, discussions of stereotypes throughout this game tend to be very frank, and heated arguments are possible. Trained facilitators know how to diffuse such arguments. In the event that a trained facilitator is not present, the following are some helpful tips:

- Know the game (or any exercise for that matter) so well that issues can be confronted and addressed with confidence.
- Manage time effectively to keep the game moving. If a participant is overly resistant on a particular issue, offer to meet with that participant privately after the workshop is completed.
- Explain your role as a facilitator and establish rapport and trust with the participants. Explain that the game is intended to help participants better understand themselves and each other.
- Encourage and foster participation from everyone. Provide positive reinforcement by thanking participants for their responses, answers, and opinions.
- Learn to be comfortable with silence. Sometimes people need time to think about how to respond to questions. In addition, avoid making any participant feel uncomfortable or "on the spot." If someone cannot or chooses not to respond, move on to another participant.
- Pay attention to group dynamics at all times. Watch for difficulties and step in to assist participants in moving on when such difficulties arise. It is important that every participant feel respected and valued regardless of his or her opinions, attitudes, or responses.

Both the Diversity Mix Game and Diversity Bingo demonstrate the many types of diversity that exist in society and in the workplace. The games provide a vehicle for addressing diversity elements in a nonthreatening atmosphere. In general, games and learning exercises are useful in bringing to light attitudes and stereotypes that may hinder the understanding and valuing of differences.

Stereotypes and prejudices may be the most obvious obstacles to embracing diversity in the workforce. But they are not the only ones.

Identifying Obstacles to Understanding and Valuing Diversity

In order to effectively manage the diverse workforce of the future, organizations and their managers must learn how to recognize and overcome the major obstacles to understanding and valuing diversity. Stereotypes and prejudices held by managers, coworkers, and clients are obvious barriers to valuing diversity, but some not-so-obvious barriers include the time-honored beliefs that America is a "melting pot" and that following "the Golden Rule" leads to goodwill and harmony. Preconceptions about communication styles and personality types can also be stumbling blocks to valuing workforce diversity.

Stereotypes and Prejudices

The authors of *Workforce America* define *stereotype* as "a fixed and distorted generalization made about all members of a particular group."[22] *Webster's Ninth Collegiate Dictionary* defines *prejudice* as "an injury or damage resulting from some judgment or action of another in disregard of one's rights." It is human nature to either ignore differences or view them as bad. Likewise, the beliefs, behaviors, and characteristics of the majority, or the dominant group, are often thought of as good. For example, many people label the following opposite personality traits as good and bad:

- Good
  - Assertive
  - Aggressive
  - Independent
  - Powerful
  - Intelligent
- Bad
  - Submissive
  - Passive
  - Dependent
  - Powerless
  - Stupid

If one substitutes the words *male* for *good* and *female* for *bad* or substitutes *white* for *good* and *black* for *bad,* one can understand how easy it is for dominant groups to justify their intolerance of people who are "different." Understanding that this *cultural myopia*—the belief that one's particular culture and value system is appropriate in all situations and relevant to all others—exists is an important step in managing organizational diversity.[23]

Prejudices and stereotypes are often self-fulfilling prophecies because many people tend to seek out examples that validate their faulty reasoning. Diversity workshops conducted by the authors of this book have revealed a number of prejudices and stereotypes prevalent in the workforce and in society in general. These stereotypes and prejudices include the following:

- Ethnic and racial
  - African-Americans: good at dancing and sports; absentee fathers; lazy; want something for nothing; militant

- —Asians: excel at math and science; sneaky; team players; industrious
- —Hispanics: illegal aliens; macho; good lovers; abusive husbands
- Gender
  - —Male bosses: insensitive; control freaks; in charge of everything; cannot be trusted
  - —Women bosses: bitchy; suffer from premenstrual syndrome; emotional; always try to prove themselves; sleep their way to the top
- Physical abilities
  - —Differently abled: can do only certain jobs; do not pull their own weight; better workers than most; thankful to have a job
- Age
  - —Younger workers: no loyalty or dedication; want to change everything; less qualified; inexperienced
  - —Older workers: dead wood; resist change; old dogs who cannot learn new tricks; useless in today's world
- Sexual
  - —Lesbians and gays: likely to have AIDS; emotional; insecure; artistic

In workshops conducted by the authors, participants have been able to list numerous examples to "justify" their prejudices and stereotypes. To value and manage diversity, organizations must help employees to identify prejudices and stereotypes that interfere with positive work relationships. Understanding and recognizing the cultural baggage that each individual brings to the workplace is necessary to understanding, recognizing, and valuing the differences of others. Differences are neither good nor bad; they are simply different.

Although prejudices and stereotypes definitely affect workers' abilities to understand and value diversity, there are two other obstacles that are harder to overcome because they are based on long-standing beliefs held by most Americans: (1) America is a melting pot of different people and cultures, and (2) Americans should practice the Golden Rule, that is, "Do unto others as you would have them do unto you." It may seem surprising that these basic tenets of life in America are being branded as obstacles to embracing diversity, but the discussion that follows reveals some of the problems they create for effective diversity management.

America as a Melting Pot

The problem with the notion that America is a melting pot is evident in the metaphor itself. In a melting pot, differences get melted away, and those who exhibit differences are the ones who get melted. When white male workers dominated the workforce, the melting pot philosophy might have been effective and its results might have been desirable, but it is no longer practical or desirable to strive to homogenize the many elements of the workforce and melt away differences. The diversity of the American workforce reflects the diversity of the American society, and it is no longer possible or desirable to ignore or eliminate all differences.

The Golden Rule and Nichols's Model of Cultural Difference

In a diverse workforce—and society—the Golden Rule, "Do unto others as you would have them do unto you," may need to be restated as "Do unto others as they would have you do unto them." Edwin J. Nichols, a cultural anthropologist, has spent decades studying the philosophical aspects of cultural differences. He contends that to understand cultural differences, one must understand the following concepts:[24]

- *Axiology*: What different cultures value
- *Epistemology*: How different cultures learn
- *Logic*: How various cultures reason
- *Process*: How learning takes place in different cultures

In his studies, Nichols divides the world's population into three major ethnic/cultural groups, each with several subgroups: (1) Europeans and Euro-Americans, (2) Africans, Afro-Americans, Hispanics, Arabs, and some Native Americans, and (3) Asians, Asian-Americans, Polynesians, and other Native Americans. Table 2-1 details Nichols's model for the philosophical aspects

Table 2-1. Nichols's Model: The Philosophical Aspects of Cultural Difference

Ethnic Groups	Axiology	Epistemology	Logic	Process
European Euro-American	Person–Object: The highest value lies in the object or in the acquisition of the object	Cognitive: One knows through counting and measuring	Dichotomous: Either/or	Technology: All sets are repeatable and reproducible
African Afro-American Native American Hispanic Arab	Person–Person: The highest value lies in the interpersonal relationship between people	Affective: One knows through symbolic imagery and rhythm	Diunital: The union of opposites	Ntuology: All sets are interrelated through human and spiritual networks
Asian Asian-American Native American Polynesian	Person–Group: The highest value lies in the cohesiveness of the group	Conative: One knows through striving toward the transcendence	Nyaya: The objective world is conceived independent of thought and mind	Cosmology: All sets are independently interrelated in the harmony of the universe

of cultural difference. If one of Nichols's cultural concepts—for example, axiology—is examined across the different cultures, one can gain an understanding of Nichols's model. By helping his readers to understand the broad differentiations in value systems across the three groups, Nichols demonstrates the danger in thinking ethnocentrically about values and beliefs, that is, in assuming that the values of a dominant culture are right and that everyone else's values must be measured against the dominant values.

According to Nichols's model, African-Americans value relationships more than objects and therefore may put the requirements of a relationship ahead of those of a job. For example, if a relative is ill and needs assistance, an African-American employee may reason, "I can get another job, but I cannot get another family member to replace the one who is ill." A Euro-American, according to Nichols's model, is unlikely to think that way because objects or the acquisition of objects (the job, money, status, and other things that can be counted and measured) is paramount.

Nichols's theory of value differentiation can be used to understand the following scenario. A Euro-American supervisor has an African-American secretary. If the supervisor does not understand the difference in values, she can inadvertently violate the secretary's value system by dropping a report on the secretary's desk first thing Monday morning and, without any explanation, stating that she needs it typed up by 10:00 a.m. At first glance, this may not seem to be an unreasonable request. After all, it is the secretary's job to do the supervisor's typing by whatever deadline the supervisor specifies. However, the supervisor creates easily avoided stress by not first acknowledging the relationship that exists between her and her secretary before moving to an object-driven agenda (the report). According to Nichols's model, the African-American secretary's highest value is interpersonal relationships. The supervisor can create a more positive and less stressful work environment by simply acknowledging the interpersonal relationship between herself and her secretary, for example, by asking, "How are you? Did you have a good weekend? Did you do anything special?" This quick and simple acknowledgment of the relationship enables the supervisor and the secretary to satisfy their value systems and achieve work goals harmoniously.

In another scenario, a Euro-American manager likes to conduct staff meetings in which *brainstorming*—the process of coming up with solutions to problems by throwing out ideas in an informal fashion—is a regular and important feature. The manager notices that his Asian employees are reluctant to participate in the informal brainstorming sessions. According to Nichols's model, Asian cultures place the highest value on the cohesiveness of the group, making it difficult for Asian employees to brainstorm ideas that might create disharmony or disunity in the group. If these employees are hesitant to participate in future sessions, the manager can ask them for their ideas before the sessions begin.

These are just two examples of the kinds of conflict that can arise when people do not understand different cultures and value systems. It is crucial to remember that not everyone in a particular cultural or ethnic group will behave in the same way or share the same values. However, the general value differences discovered by social scientists such as Nichols have proved to be accurate and predictive of various cultural groups' values and beliefs.

This new understanding of the Golden Rule requires us to challenge the assumptions we hold about those who are different from us and *not* to assume that everyone shares our value system and wants to be treated as we do. Equal treatment is not necessarily fair treatment. The concept of equal treatment tends to put differences in a bad light, leading people to ignore differences in the workplace, which then creates discomfort for the different person. For example, if a person remains standing when talking to a person in a wheelchair, both parties can become uncomfortable because one person is standing over the other and eye contact is difficult. Taking the time to sit down not only literally puts one on the same level as the person in the wheelchair, but also makes it possible for both parties to converse more directly. When interacting with a severely disfigured person, avoiding direct eye contact so that one does not appear to be staring is a common practice, but this practice also can cause discomfort for both parties. To truly embrace diversity is to accept, acknowledge, and value differences, not to ignore them or try to eradicate them.

Communication Styles

To attract and retain an effective workforce in the years to come, health care organizations must become aware of, and responsive to, the different communication styles characteristic of different cultures and genders. Job applicants from diverse backgrounds and cultures may not have communication styles that readily convey the qualities that many managers are looking for. Men and women, too, have different communication styles that can lead to applicant–manager barriers. If asked to name the characteristics and behaviors that an ideal applicant would exhibit in an interview, most managers would include the following:

- Speaks clearly
- Volunteers information
- Asks questions of the interviewer
- Is assertive and animated
- Maintains good eye contact
- Presents a personable yet professional image
- Verbalizes his or her achievements
- Seems knowledgeable about the company
- Shows examples of his or her work

Applicants from some cultures, although they might make suitable and desirable employees, may not exhibit the preceding characteristics in an interview. For example, in some Asian cultures, children are taught that "the nail that sticks up gets hammered down" or "the quacking duck gets shot." In some East Indian cultures, children are taught that it is disrespectful to make direct eye contact. How would job applicants from these cultural backgrounds fare in a typical interview situation?

Edward T. Hall, a cultural anthropologist, studied cultures around the world and developed a "context continuum" that helps to explain different communication styles across cultures. (See figure 2-1.) The context continuum classifies cultures according to how important they consider nonverbal communication to be. So-called high-context cultures place a high value on nonverbal communication. Hall maintains that no culture is exclusively at either end of the context scale, but that some cultures (such as Asian, Hispanic, and African-American) are high context, whereas others (such as Northern European) are low context. The significance of this model is that most of the new entrants to the U.S. workforce are from high-context cultures, but most managers are from medium-to-low-context cultures. In high-context cultures, communication is for interaction, not just for information exchange; communication is a way to establish and maintain a relationship. This observation is consistent with Nichols's model of the philosophical aspects of cultural differences. In high-context cultures, a verbal exchange consists of not only words but also the social setting, the participants' phrasing, the participants' gestures and tone of voice, and the participants' history, status, and posture. In low-context cultures, however, words alone tend to carry the meaning of the verbal exchange.

The concept of high- and low-context cultures is also useful in differentiating between the communication styles of most men and women in our country. The communication styles of Anglo-American women tend to have more in common with members of high-context cultures than with Anglo-American men. That is, Anglo-American women tend to use communication interactions to establish or maintain relationships, whereas Anglo-American men tend to be low-context communicators who often use interactions to exchange only information. According to Deborah Tannen, author of *You Just Don't Understand:*

> White American males engage the world as an individual in a hierarchical social order in which he's either one up or one down. In a white American man's world, conversations are negotiations in which people try to achieve and maintain the upper hand if they can and to protect themselves from others' attempts to put them down and push them around. Life then is a contest, a struggle to preserve independence and avoid failure. Women and culturally diverse people approach the world as a network of connections. In this world, conversations are negotiations for closeness in which people try to seek and give confirmation and support and to reach consensus.[25]

Understanding these seemingly dichotomous communication styles is a major step toward understanding communication difficulties that may arise in the workplace.

Figure 2-1. Diversity in Context

Low	Medium–Low	Medium	High
Northern European	Anglo-American male	Southern European	Asian
Swiss	Anglo-American female	Middle Eastern	Hispanic
			American Indian
			African-American

Note: Cultures may be placed on a continuum of low to high context, based on the relative importance of nonverbal communication. High-context cultures place more value on body language and other cues than do low-context cultures.

Just as a misunderstanding of different communication styles can lead to conflict and misunderstandings in the workplace, ignorance of different personality types can also have a negative effect on an organization's ability to attract and retain a qualified workforce.

Personality Types

People are different in fundamental ways. They want different things. That is, they have different motives, purposes, aims, values, needs, and drives. They also think, conceptualize, perceive, understand, and comprehend differently. They even believe differently.

Many times, differences in work style can create conflicts in the work environment. For example, why are some people's offices meticulously in order while others' are in complete disarray, yet both types of workers are valuable contributors to the work team? In a similar vein, why are some people naturally talkative while others are more quiet and introspective? Furthermore, why do some employees see the forest and others see only the trees?

These differences were studied by Swiss psychologist and physician Carl G. Jung in the 1920s in his study of psychological typology. An admirer of Jung's work, Katherine Briggs, began in the same decade to look for a way to make Jung's theory of psychological types available to the public. Briggs and her daughter, Isabel Myers, designed an instrument, known today as the Myers-Briggs Type Indicator (MBTI), and began to develop a database to measure attitudes, feelings, perceptions, and behaviors for the various psychological types. Data were gathered on thousands of participants throughout the 1950s and 1960s. In 1962, Myers approached the Education Testing Service with the data, after which ETS continued collecting, validating, and testing the data until 1975. Today the MBTI is one of the most widely used psychological testing instruments for understanding individual differences in work styles, work values, and work attitudes.

For the purpose of diversity management, the MBTI is a particularly useful and practical tool to help managers gain an understanding of the different personality types that exist across cultural and gender classifications.[26] The MBTI is an easy-to-use questionnaire that identifies various human preferences, strengths, and temperaments. Utilizing 126 short questions and word-pair combinations, the MBTI delineates differences in perception, judgment, energy direction, and life-style that characterize different personality types. The MBTI does not attempt to rate degrees of psychopathology, nor does it measure intelligence. The questionnaire responses are tabulated by a certified specialist and the end results are compiled in individual report forms that pinpoint how individuals gather information, make decisions, derive and direct energy, and deal with their environments.

The application and uses of the MBTI are numerous. By improving the organization's understanding of the needs and behavioral preferences of staff, managers can harness the rich differences of the people within the organization for the improvement of everyone's work life. Otto Kroeger and Janet Thueson, in *Type Talk at Work*, explain that the MBTI can be utilized to:

- Conduct meetings more effectively by allowing various points of view to be heard and differing needs to be met
- Match an individual's potential with job requirements by understanding individual strengths and weaknesses
- Address career enhancement needs or career changes by understanding and accepting those strengths and weaknesses
- Resolve conflicts quickly and effectively
- Break work-flow bottlenecks by allowing each person to work according to his or her own style
- Set more realistic and widely accepted organizational goals by including a broader range of different perspectives, needs, and ideas
- Reduce stress levels by understanding what motivates and energizes different people
- Meet deadlines by realizing that different types of people deal with time in different ways[27]

The information provided by the MBTI will help health care managers and employees to gain a better understanding of themselves and how they interact with others. This understanding will in turn help to prevent conflicts among the many personality types that will make up the diverse workforce of the 1990s and beyond.

Setting the Stage for Action

This chapter has examined the difficulties that health care organizations will face in attracting a viable and diverse workforce in the years to come, as well as the legislation that has made such a diverse workforce possible. This chapter has also explored the many faces of diversity and the most prevalent obstacles to understanding diversity. The information in this chapter will help health care organizations make the critical decision to achieve the cutting edge of diversity management. As the past chairman of Xerox, David Kearns, once said, the company that gets out in front managing diversity will have a competitive edge.

The next chapter will explore how a health care organization can conduct an environmental assessment to determine its current "diversity climate." Once this climate is assessed, the organization can truly begin to effectively manage its workforce diversity and, in the process, better meet the expectations of an increasingly diverse customer base.

References

1. *Guide to Federal Labor Laws.* Washington, DC: Bureau of National Affairs, 1991.

2. U.S. Department of Labor. *The 1991 Civil Rights Act.* Washington, DC: U.S. Department of Labor, 1991.

3. Harris, D. You're pregnant? You're out. *Working Woman,* Aug. 1992, p. 48.

4. Harris, p. 50.

5. Thomas, R. R., Jr. From affirmative action to affirming diversity. *Harvard Business Review,* Mar.–Apr., 1990, p. 107.

6. Marketplace. *Wall Street Journal,* July 17, 1992.

7. U.S. Equal Employment Opportunity Commission. *Americans with Disabilities Act Handbook.* Washington, DC: U.S. Equal Employment Opportunity Commission, 1991.

8. Education of the Handicapped Act of 1969 (91-230, Title VI).

9. U.S. Equal Employment Opportunity Commission.

10. Thompson, R. Equal Access. *Successful Meetings,* May 1991, p. 44.

11. *Sensitivity to People with Disabilities.* Washington, DC: Bureau of National Affairs, 1991.

12. Politics and policy. *Wall Street Journal,* Nov. 15, 1990.

13. Hewitt Associates. Family and medical leave legislation. Report to clients, Hewitt Associates, Lincolnshire, IL, 1993.

14. Friedman, D. Eldercare: the employee benefit of the 1990's. *Across the Board,* June 1986.

15. Herren, L. H. The new game of HR: playing to win. *Personnel,* June 1989.

16. Dunlop Group of Six. *Health Workforce: Trend and Projected Demand.* Chicago: American Hospital Association, 1991.

17. Future jobs. *American Demographics,* Mar. 1990.

18. Future jobs. *American Demographics,* Mar. 1990.

19. American Society of Training and Development, 1990 survey.

20. Loden, M., and Rosener, J. *Workforce America*. Homewood, IL: Business One-Irwin, 1991.

21. Advancement Strategies. *Diversity Bingo*. San Diego: Pfeiffer & Company, 1992.

22. Loden and Rosener, p. 58.

23. Loden and Rosener, chapter 3.

24. Nichols, E.J., presented at a seminar sponsored by the American Hospital Association, Chicago, 1989.

25. Kennedy, J., and Everest, A. Put diversity in context. *Personnel Journal*, Sept. 1991, p. 53.

26. Further information on the use of the Myers-Briggs Type Indicator (MBTI) can be obtained from the Consulting Psychologists Press, Inc., 3803 E. Bayshore Road, Palo Alto, CA 94303.

27. Kroeger, O., and Thueson, J. *Type Talk at Work*. Washington, DC: Tilden Press, 1992, p. 11.

Chapter Three

Assessing the Environment:
A Step toward Effective
Diversity Management

Chapter 2 argued for the need to effectively manage the diverse health care workforce of the 1990s and beyond and presented the many challenges of managing such a diverse group. Before health care organizations begin to devise effective diversity management strategies, they must first determine their diversity climate, both internally (within the organization) and externally (in the surrounding community that comprises the organization's customer base). *Diversity climate* refers both to the degree of diversity in the health care organization and the surrounding community and to the way in which various groups interact within the organization and throughout the community. In order for health care organizations to determine their diversity management goals and how best to achieve them, organizations must first understand their diversity climate.

Successfully utilizing the talents of people from many cultures, socioeconomic backgrounds, and ethnicities, as well as managing a mosaic of workers with different genders, sexual orientations, ages, and physical abilities, is a difficult undertaking. Managers who cannot effectively manage workforce diversity affect organizational morale, productivity, efficiency, and ultimately viability. These managers do not see the big picture, and when problems arise they often treat the symptoms rather than the real cause. Determining their organizational diversity climate and then undertaking a gap analysis will enable health care organizations to effectively and successfully manage the increasingly diverse workforce of the decades to come.

The most effective method for health care organizations to determine their diversity climate is to conduct internal and external *environmental assessments*. The environmental assessment process consists of three stages: (1) an internal culture and value analysis; (2) studies of current and projected workforce demographics, including recruitment, training, turnover, and retirement trends; and (3) an external culture and value analysis. The environmental assessments use standard survey and research techniques, including written surveys, telephone surveys, and focus groups, to gather and analyze data from employees at all levels of the organization, as well as from patients and members of the community. These data will point out problem areas and guide health care organizations in developing effective diversity management strategies.

Survey and focus group questions prepared for the internal institutional workforce survey should be different than the questions for the external survey of patients and community members. All questions should be carefully chosen to cross-check answers and perceptions, and survey and focus group participants should be assured that their responses will be kept strictly confidential. Some participants, whether they are employees, patients, or community members, may have special language or literacy needs or physical conditions that hinder their participation in written, oral, or English-language surveys. Facilitators with the requisite skills and knowledge should be available to assist participants when required. If these responsibilities are too burdensome, organizations may opt to utilize an outside consultant or testing firm to prepare and administer surveys, lead focus groups, and tabulate results. Appendix A contains a list of consulting firms that specialize in environmental assessment surveys. The following sections describe the purposes and procedures of internal and external environmental assessments.

Assessing the Internal Environment

Performing an internal environmental assessment, or a comprehensive self-study, enables a health care organization to gauge the diversity, characteristics, and attitudes of its workforce; chart its comparative strengths and weaknesses; and then use these data to plan for future organizational needs.

The following four-step plan for conducting an internal culture and value analysis is a methodical approach to a complex process. The four steps also help management and staff achieve a sense of ownership of the process, which in turn helps to ensure an atmosphere of workplace trust and openness that will lead to valid and useful results. The entire internal analysis process should be conducted within 60 days given that longer time frames can disrupt organizational operations and dilute the impact of the assessment results.

Step 1: Gathering Preliminary Management Input

The health care organization's top-level management should select a group of key managers, ranging from first-line supervisors to division managers, from each of the organization's departments. The size and representation of this managerial group depend on the size of the institution and its scope of services, but its membership should be kept to a reasonable number. An organization that operates one primary institution, such as a hospital, should select a manager from each major area of institutional operation. Alternatively, an organization that operates institutions in a number of locations and/or in multiple areas of health care service should select key managers from each location or area of service to ensure that all aspects of the organization's operations are represented.

The duties of this group should be to gather general information about the current organizational workforce diversity, the problems within and among diverse groups, and possible strategies for solving these problems. The duties of the managerial group are preliminary; that is, managers highlight the major issues identified by each organizational operation as a starting point for more detailed work at a later time. This group's activities also provide an opportunity for management ownership of the internal environmental assessment and enable the group to determine the next steps in the process. Group discussions must be structured to focus on set objectives and an organized process for identifying problems and solutions.

The managerial group should meet twice over a 10-day period. The first meeting should identify problems and frame them in a way that facilitates the identification of solutions. The second meeting should outline possible solutions and identify appropriate strategies for implementing those solutions.

A skilled facilitator can help the managerial group understand diversity issues and how to characterize them. This facilitator should introduce the subject of workforce diversity in the first meeting and present a process for identifying diversity issues and approaches to addressing those issues. If no such facilitator exists within the organization, the group may want to invite an outside consultant who specializes in helping organizations to assess their cultural environment and improve their diversity management. A consultant can be particularly valuable in guiding the group to make an initial list of likely solutions to workforce diversity problems.

The information gathered from the two managerial group meetings should be summarized for top-level management and used to create a knowledge base for taking the next three steps. At this point, top-level management should appoint five managers to serve as a steering committee for the remainder of the internal culture and value analysis process. The steering committee should immediately meet to obtain staff input on diversity issues and then conduct the internal culture and value analysis described later in this chapter.

Step 2: Gathering Preliminary Staff Input

After analyzing the management group's input (resulting from its two meetings), the steering committee should prepare an outline for a second set of meetings, this time with a representative group of staff members from throughout the health care organization. (More than one staff group may be required, depending on the size of the organization.) The staff group should represent a cross section of rank-and-file employees from all major areas of the organization. The group should also include staff members from as many different cultural and ethnic backgrounds as possible. A diverse and representative staff group is crucial to the steering committee's ability to zero in on diversity issues facing the organization.

The staff group should also meet twice over a 10-day period. The first meeting should gather information on staff perceptions of key workplace diversity issues. The second meeting should discuss potential solutions and compare staff-generated solutions to those solutions generated earlier by the management group. Solutions may emerge when staff group members discuss diversity problems they have encountered in the workplace.

To introduce the first meeting, a facilitator should provide staff representatives with an overview of the management group's findings. The facilitator should also explain the steering committee's mission, provide a structure for the staff group's meetings, and list the objectives to be achieved by the staff group—the identification of critical diversity issues and potential solutions to diversity problems. The facilitator should emphasize that the problems and solutions identified by the staff representative group need not agree with the findings of the management group. For the second meeting, an outside consultant may again be helpful in facilitating an open, productive discussion and ensuring high-quality information. The results of the staff group's discussions should be summarized in a written report to the steering committee. The steering committee should then evaluate the information from both the management and staff group sessions before beginning step 3.

Step 3: Conducting an Internal Culture and Value Analysis

The steering committee should next develop a five- or six-page written questionnaire, based on the results of the management and staff group meetings, to be given to all employees of the health care organization. (See appendix B for a model internal culture and value analysis survey.) Depending on the ethnic makeup of the organization, it may be desirable to have the questionnaire prepared in non-English languages. If this is not practical, ensuring that translators are provided to those who require assistance will also improve the questionnaire response rate. If time and resources allow, the convening of focus groups can greatly complement the individual employee surveys. (Appendix C provides a model format for conducting employee focus groups as part of a health care organization's internal culture and value analysis.)

This questionnaire, the internal culture and value analysis survey, is the keystone of the internal environmental assessment. Honest and complete answers to several fundamental questions will help health care organizations develop an effective diversity management program that will help them achieve the long-term goal of managing an increasingly diverse workforce. These fundamental questions include the following:

- Does the organization have a clear concept of workforce diversity that can be easily communicated to decision makers, supervisors, and rank-and-file employees?
- Can the organization's culture accommodate diversity, or is there an underlying assumption that workers from diverse backgrounds or with different abilities should adapt to fit the organization's culture?

- Do the organization's recruitment, training, and management systems work for or against the valuing of diversity? What are the real criteria used in determining job offers, promotions, performance appraisals, job requirements and responsibilities, and financial rewards?
- Do human resources strategies exist to help the organization cope with a workforce consisting increasingly of women, minorities, older persons, the differently abled, and aliens?
- Does the organization exhibit ideological or cultural barriers to effective diversity management?

The results of the internal culture and value analysis survey should provide answers to these questions. Although the surveys may point to the need for changes that seem overwhelming and difficult, health care organizations that accept the challenge and develop effective diversity programs will be on the cutting edge of diversity management and will maximize their chances for future growth and success. Organizations that fail to meet diversity challenges will be ill-equipped to cope with future labor shortages and may find that their very survival is in jeopardy.

In addition to addressing fundamental questions about an organization's diversity management, an internal culture and value analysis survey should target specific employee concerns. Every organization is composed of a unique group of employees who create their own workplace culture. Recognizing and understanding this unique corporate culture is critical in discerning employees' views concerning issues relating to the organization's corporate culture, including, for example:

- How effective (from the employees' point of view) is the organization's management of workforce diversity?
- How is the current working relationship among peers?
- How do employees feel about the health care institution for which they work?
- How do workers feel about the health care industry in general and about other local health care organizations in particular?
- How do employees feel about the patients and clients they serve, as well as local community members?
- Do employees feel that members of certain ethnic and cultural groups are best suited to certain health care jobs, whether the jobs are high ranking and prestigious or require minimal skills?
- Do employees feel that the organization is experiencing any effects (positive or negative) of increasing gender diversity in health care? Examples of gender diversity include the growing number of female physicians (a field previously dominated by males) and male nurses (a field previously dominated by females).
- Do employees feel that the organization is experiencing any effects (positive or negative) of increasing openness about sexual orientation?

- How do employees feel about coworkers and patients who are HIV positive?
- How do employees feel about women and minorities in executive and supervisory roles?
- How do employees feel about working with older persons and the differently abled?
- How do employees from different ethnic, racial, and cultural backgrounds interact?
- How do members of specific cultural, racial, and ethnic groups interact with homosexuals?
- What different value systems exist among the cultural, racial, and ethnic groups employed by the organization? (Chapter 2 provided an overview of value systems as they relate to workforce diversity.)

The model culture and value analysis survey form in appendix B and the model focus group format and questions in appendix C will help the steering committee collect crucial diversity data relating to the preceding questions. It cannot be emphasized enough that to obtain the most frank, complete, and useful responses in surveys or focus groups, those administering the surveys or moderating the focus groups should reassure employees that their responses will be kept completely confidential and will not have any effect—positive or negative—on their jobs.

Employees should be given time during their regular working hours to complete the questionnaire or participate in focus groups. Questionnaires can be distributed in a variety of ways depending on the subtlety of organizational diversity issues and the complexity of the questionnaire. (Complex diversity issues require complex questionnaires.) The easiest way to distribute questionnaires is to ask department heads to hand them to their staff; however, a confidentiality mechanism must be in place so that all questionnaires can be returned directly to the steering committee. Signatures of respondents must remain optional, but questionnaires must be coded so that at least the employee's department can be identified. Although it is not necessary for staff to complete the questionnaire under controlled conditions, the steering committee may obtain a better response rate if groups of employees are gathered in a meeting room, for example, to complete their questionnaires.

Questionnaire and focus group results should then be summarized by an experienced analyst. This analyst can be a staff member (usually a trained human resources person), but preferably the analyst should be a skilled outside consultant working in tandem with a staff member. When summarizing results, the analyst should examine the following key areas:

- Diversity issues related to hiring, promotion, and operational efficiency
- Relationships among departments
- Current organizational policies and procedures related to diversity
- Management attitudes and perceptions related to diversity

The analyst should prepare a written report for the steering committee. The committee in turn compares the report with data gathered from earlier managerial and staff group meetings (steps 1 and 2). This comparison should provide the steering committee with a direction for seeking solutions to diversity-related problems, as well as prepare the committee for step 4 of the analysis process.

Step 4: Presenting the Analysis Results

After the human resources analyst and/or independent consultant has examined and summarized the questionnaire and (if applicable) focus group results, the analyst's report should be presented by the steering committee to a joint meeting of the managerial and staff groups formed during steps 1 and 2. These groups should be encouraged to discuss the report's findings in an atmosphere of openness.

This joint meeting should result in identification of diversity-management barriers that may hamper a health care organization's productivity and efficiency, as well as its reputation. Consequently, diversity-management barriers negatively affect the organization's ability to recruit and retain employees and, even more important, to attract and serve patients. In other words, an organization's success and revenue are affected by its internal environment. Diversity-management barriers to success identified by the internal culture and value analysis may include:

- Inability to keep the organization sufficiently staffed to maintain an acceptable level of service
- Lack of understanding on the part of management concerning the needs, expectations, and aspirations of diverse groups within the organization's workforce
- Mistrust among the diverse workforce population
- Unclear definitions of authority and responsibilities at all levels of the organization
- Misunderstanding among employees concerning what is expected of them due to culture-specific job interpretations
- Lack of understanding that different cultures and ethnic groups may have different work ethics (for example, observing holidays that are not observed by most employees)

The preceding barriers are simply examples. Some organizations may identify other barriers as a result of their internal culture and value analysis. Once barriers have been identified, the organization can not only take appropriate steps to overcome them, but can also use what it has learned about the barriers to enhance cooperation between management and staff.

Analyzing an Organization's Workforce Demographics

As stated earlier in this chapter, the internal culture and value analysis is the first stage of the internal environmental assessment; the second stage is analysis of workforce demographics. Many factors must be examined when analyzing an organization's workforce demographics. Each of these factors must be analyzed independently as well as in relationship to the other factors. These key factors include:

- *The institution's organizational structure:* A detailed set of organizational charts should be developed or updated by the human resources department and/or an independent consultant to show all positions, how many full-time equivalents exist for each, and, if possible, which groups—African-Americans, Asians, women, Native Americans, Hispanics, older workers, the differently abled, and so forth—are currently represented in the workforce and in what proportions. It is essential for the steering committee to know the organizational structure in order to understand how the organization operates.
- *The skill levels of workers in each position:* Job skill levels throughout the organization should be assessed and jobs with similar skill levels should be identified. To accomplish this, all jobs should be listed, along with the departments they are in, the skill levels required to perform those jobs, and any additional skills that workers performing the jobs may have. This job skill assessment will identify whether staff members have the minimum required skill levels to do their jobs, or whether they have skills that could be used to perform additional activities.
- *The interrelationships among departments and employees:* Major job activities and processes performed by the organization should be charted. Then the departments, areas, and key employees involved in those activities and processes should be identified. Finally, the length of time required to perform these activities and processes should be measured to determine the extent of the department and employee interrelationships.
- *The level of employee education:* Educational requirements should be assessed by job title and by department, and efforts should be made to identify instances where additional training and education might be needed for employees lacking the education required by current job responsibilities.
- *The number of employees and the work flow for each function:* This analysis should be performed by department and should pinpoint imbalances in the number of employees that different departments require to perform similar tasks.
- *Management directions received:* The amount of management direction that major work activities receive should be quantified by department. This data should then be compared with how much management direction staff members feel could be eliminated (gathered during the joint meeting with the steering committee) and still get the job done, perhaps more efficiently.

All of these demographic data should be compiled in outline form so that they can be used by the steering committee as a backdrop for the internal environmental assessment. These data will help illuminate solutions to diversity barriers, which will in turn help the organization to become more efficient and productive in the future. However, more specific demographic information will be useful as the health care organization assesses its cultural barriers. Specific demographic areas to examine include current and projected recruitment needs, turnover trends, and utilization of older workers.

Current and Projected Recruitment Needs

The recruitment needs of health care organizations are at an all-time high and are likely to remain high in the decades to come. (Chapter 6 presents a detailed discussion of recruitment issues in health care organizations as they relate to workforce diversity.) To deal with present and future shortages of skilled labor, health care organizations must accurately assess their current and projected staffing needs. This assessment, as part of the overall internal environmental assessment, should include an analysis of work flow and identification of high- and low-priority tasks (some of the latter may be expendable). The results of the assessment, as performed by the human resources department, should be reported to the steering committee.

Current staffing needs should be assessed in terms of:

- What levels of the organization have the most job openings
- What types of jobs are open
- How long jobs have been open
- Which job shifts are open
- How effective current recruiting practices are
- How existing staffing in each area compares with the minimum level of staffing required to maintain high-quality service
- How alternative recruiting approaches compare to the current approach

The human resources department should also keep in mind the following factors:

- Changes in the institution that may occur as a result of future plans to eliminate certain service areas, add others, and so forth
- Increases in the cost of traditional recruiting practices, such as higher fees for classified ads and higher employment agency fees

This recruitment data should also be compiled in outline form so that the steering committee can quickly analyze changes in various departments and evaluate the effect of these changes on organizational recruitment demographics.

Turnover Trends

Because of present and future shortages of qualified health care workers, organizations should assiduously seek to avoid excessive turnover. (Chapter 6 provides a detailed discussion of how excessive turnover relates to workforce
diversity.) As part of the internal environmental assessment, the human resources
department should assess whether categories of workers covered by affirmative
action statutes have unusually high turnover rates. High turnover rates may
indicate that the organization needs to modify its recruitment, retention, or
training practices. Employee turnover analyses should examine each position
exhibiting high turnover rates and the departing employees. These data should
include:

- Level of position in the organization
- Tenure of the person leaving the position
- Promotions the departing employee received
- Training the departing employee received
- Salary when the departing employee was hired
- Salary when the employee resigned
- Ethnicity, nationality, and sex of the departing employee
- Reason the employee left

These data should reveal to the steering committee whether and why certain
groups or cultures are leaving the health care organization and why specific
jobs or job levels show high rates of turnover.

The results of the turnover analysis should be broken down into the
categories listed above and then should be further broken down according to
the following categories:

- The number of managers, supervisors, and professionals who have left the
  institution during a specific period of time
- Turnover as a percentage of each category (managers, supervisors, and professionals)
- Turnover percentages by department and job category (nursing, dietary, clerical, maintenance, and so on)
- Turnover percentages according to age, sex, salary level, and discipline of
  employees

The human resources department should keep all of these data current and
should run summary analyses monthly to identify trends as early as possible.

The authors of this book have determined, based on their experience, that
turnover rates *greater than* the following rates are excessive and indicate retention problems:

- Managerial—8 to 10 percent per year
- Professional—15 percent per year
- Secretarial and clerical—20 to 25 percent per year

Additional turnover statistics that can help confirm whether a health care organization's turnover is excessive are available from the Bureau of National Affairs, the U.S. Department of Labor, the Society of Human Resource Professionals, and local personnel associations such as the Human Resource Management Association of Chicago.

Utilization of Older Workers

As has been discussed in preceding chapters, older workers, including retirees who return to the workforce, are an excellent source of qualified employees for health care organizations' current and projected staffing needs. Retired persons are the largest group of trained workers in the United States, and they comprise the fastest growing group of employable people. With life spans becoming longer, many older workers can expect to be able to work beyond the age of 70. Health care organizations should adjust their work environment to retain older workers as long as possible and to recruit older workers, including retirees who are interested in beginning second careers. Retirement trends within the organization, as well as recruitment efforts, should be examined to assess how effectively the organization is retaining and recruiting older workers. Large numbers of early retirements and low rates of recruitment of older workers could indicate that the organizational work environment is unreceptive to this valuable source of labor.

After the steering committee has completed the internal culture and value analysis (in cooperation with the human resources department and/or a consultant) and after the workforce demographics have been analyzed in terms of current and projected workforce needs, trends, and resources, the health care organization should take a moment to assess overall organizational, management, and employee attitudes toward workforce diversity; how effectively current employees are being used; and how prepared the health care organization is for future labor shortages. The steps described so far—the internal culture and value analysis and the analysis of workforce demographics—should by now have helped the health care organization to understand the following crucial issues:

- The diversity makeup of the organization's workforce
- The organization's prevailing corporate culture
- How the quality of interactions among diverse groups in the organization affect the overall institution

After this reflection, the organization can proceed to the next step in assessing its environment: the external assessment.

Assessing the External Environment

Health care institutions do not exist in a vacuum; they affect and are affected by their external environment. It is estimated that for each patient, at least three to five additional people come into contact with the patient's health care organization and its staff. In addition, because health care institutions are currently receiving much public scrutiny, the general public is increasingly familiar with the policies and practices of health care organizations, and thus build certain expectations. A health care organization's external environmental assessment therefore involves obtaining information from three groups: patients, family and friends of patients, and members of the community surrounding the organization. There is often overlap among these groups, but for the purposes of this assessment it is helpful to consider them as three separate constituencies. The external environmental assessment, like the internal assessment, has as its main component a culture and value analysis. Also like the internal environmental assessment, it is best to gather assessment data by utilizing written surveys *and* focus groups. Appendix D provides a model external culture and value analysis survey, and appendix E provides a model format and questions for an external focus group.

All members of a health care organization's external environment—patients, family and friends of patients, and members of the community—should be considered to be the organization's actual or potential customer base. Therefore, it is useful to consider the external culture and value analysis as a method for determining customer expectations and satisfaction levels. If patients and other customers are reacting unfavorably to staff members from diverse backgrounds, it may signal that the organization itself is poorly managing its diverse workers.

Patient Expectations and Satisfaction Levels

Patient expectations and satisfaction levels can be difficult to accurately assess. People usually visit health care organizations because of a health problem and, as such, they may be anxious, wary, and unhappy to begin with and thus predisposed to consider the experience a negative one. Therefore, health care organizations must immediately make a positive impression on patients or else the patients will not even have a neutral perception of the organization when the provision of health care services begins.

What patient expectations are and how well the organization is meeting them can be assessed by collecting and analyzing input from previous patients on such issues as quality and timeliness of care, quality of food service, quality of housekeeping, helpfulness of volunteers, clarity of communication, fairness and accuracy of billing, and overall quality and courtesy of staff. A key ingredient in this assessment is a tool known as a *patient satisfaction and expectations survey*. For years this type of tool has proven useful, and interest in it has been gaining recently because of its potential for measuring patient and family satisfaction with regard to workforce diversity issues.

Workforce diversity issues can and should be addressed in any satisfaction survey that is conducted by a health care institution for two reasons:

- Diversity issues between hospital staff and patients and patient families are often the last to be expressed but can play a major part in a family's decision to return to the institution for treatment. Often families form their own opinions not only from gaining their own impressions but also from hearing the opinions of other patients who may or may not be as objective. Potentially negative impressions can influence an entire family when making future decisions on seeking inpatient, outpatient, or specialty care.
- Customer satisfaction surveys of patients and families are often underestimated as a tool for determining whether workforce diversity issues exist in the hospital. This is primarily due to the fact that diversity issues have been buried or unrecognized for such a long time. In the last few years, increases in lawsuits and family complaints have caused major concerns about customer satisfaction that the authors contend are often embedded in diversity issues.

Figure 3-1 lists examples of questions that could be used as part of a patient survey to address workforce diversity issues. It should be recognized that some of these questions are the same or similar to questions that would be asked in a typical customer satisfaction survey. The similarity further illustrates the close relationship that exists between workforce diversity and patient and family satisfaction. This relationship should not be underestimated.

In addition to asking questions such as are suggested in figure 3-1, a patient survey should also capture the patient's age, ethnicity, and cultural identification, as well as determine whether the patient is differently abled. This information will tell the steering committee whether some community groups perceive that they are receiving inferior service or that the quality of care they receive is negatively influenced by their race, culture, age, gender, or physical abilities. Depending on the ethnic makeup of an organization's patients, the organization may have to prepare the survey in more than one language. Additionally, some respondents may need help filling out the questionnaire if they do not understand some of the questions. Finally, these patient-specific surveys should be adapted so that they can be conducted over the telephone if necessary.

Given the demographics of many environments served by health care institutions as well as the mix of their workforces, it is probable that diversity issues have gone unnoticed even when a typical satisfaction survey has been analyzed. A recognition of these issues will give new meaning to patient surveys and help institutions to target this ongoing challenge.

Figure 3-1. Suggested Questions for Patient Surveys to Identify Workforce Diversity Issues

---

The following questions can be helpful in determining whether workforce diversity issues need to be addressed either among institutional staff members or between institutional staff members and patients and patients' families.

1. How well do the staff in the institution respond to your needs?

2. Were there any situations during your hospital stay which may have contributed to a delay in your receiving care from the staff? If so, please identify each situation.

3. What could have been done to minimize or eliminate the situations listed in question 2?

4. What standards would you use in determining proper responsiveness by staff to each situation listed in question 2?

5. On a scale of 1 to 10 (with 10 being the highest rating), please rate the ability of our institution to meet your needs for communicating with our staff.

6. Do you feel our institution has been effective in relating to your needs as a patient or to those of your family members?

7. What are your general impressions of how well the staff worked together? Please give some examples.

8. How did the staff appear to work together to meet your needs or the needs of your family?

9. What are some examples of how the staff worked poorly together?

10. As best as you can determine, how well do the staff get along with one another to get the job done? Please give some examples.

Community Expectations

The health care organization's surrounding community ultimately determines in large part whether the organization survives and prospers. Health care organizations must therefore get involved in and maintain good relations with the community. A key aspect of maintaining good community relations is to be a good neighbor to the community and provide the community with high-quality health care. A community-specific survey, similar in structure to the more general external culture and value analysis surveys in appendixes D and E, can be instrumental in assessing community expectations. The data obtained in the community surveys should be combined with data obtained from patient surveys.

Data concerning how patients and the community at large view the health care organization (the external environmental assessment) should be combined with data from the internal environmental assessment. This combination of data will reveal what the organization must do to bridge the gap between how it presently meets employee and customer expectations in terms of effective management of diversity and how the organization needs to meet those expectations to survive and prosper in the decades to come. The process of reviewing survey data and determining what organizational changes are necessary is known as performing a gap analysis.

Performing a Gap Analysis

Gap analysis is a standard term used in survey analysis to identify the difference between where an institution stands with regard to certain areas of operation as compared with where the institution needs to be. The gap analysis objectively identifies and lists areas of operation that need to be addressed for improvement. Gap analyses can focus on customer satisfaction, employee attitudes, services preferred or needed by the market, and workforce diversity issues.

Performing a gap analysis of diversity issues requires two steps: (1) reviewing how well the organization is currently managing diversity and (2) determining what the organization needs to do to manage diversity more effectively. The steering committee can determine how effectively the organization is currently managing the diversity of its staff, customers, and community by examining the results of the internal culture and value analysis, the survey of workforce demographics, and the assessment of the external environment. The committee can determine what the organization must do to improve diversity management by setting guidelines for determining the organization's priorities, gauging how much change the organization can reasonably implement, and deciding what kind of time frame will be required. Each health care organization must have reasonable latitude to set its guidelines according to its particular needs and circumstances.

Performing all of the steps involved in an environmental assessment and gap analysis and formulating a plan for improving diversity management are difficult and challenging undertakings. Furthermore, in order to be truly effective, these steps should be taken on a periodic, ongoing basis to ensure that the health care organization continues to meet the needs of an increasingly diverse workforce and general population. Because of the difficult and ongoing nature of performing these assessments, organizations may want to consider using a diversity consultant.

Using a Consultant

Some health care organizations may decide to hire a consultant who specializes in workforce diversity issues to administer some or all of the environmental assessment process. (Appendix A provides a list of such consultants.) Organizations that opt to use consultants should first clearly understand the nature of the consultant's services and should identify which responsibilities still remain with the organization.

The environmental assessment process is a journey of self-discovery. The role of the consultant is not to provide answers but to provide technical expertise. In preparing the questionnaires, developing and moderating focus groups, and analyzing data, the consultant's primary responsibility is to be *objective*. This objectivity means ensuring that all of the necessary questions are asked and all relevant issues are thoroughly considered. Then the consultant's role should be to help the organization target the specific changes that it needs to make to effectively manage diversity in its workforce and community. The health care organization's responsibility is to openly and honestly confront questions and issues that arise, and not to prejudge the assessment results or try to guide the consultant to recommend actions that support the status quo or justify current management practices.

It is imperative that the organization's top-level management be committed to effective diversity management and confident that environmental assessment will help the organization develop a workable game plan for increasing its effectiveness. The next chapter explores how managers can be trained to manage diversity more effectively.

Chapter Four

Formulating a Management Development Plan

A fter the health care organization has completed the internal and external
environmental assessments described in chapter 3 and analyzed the assessment results, it is crucial to ensure that managers at all levels of the organization become key players in the organization's diversity management efforts. This process is likely to involve training and education of even senior and highly experienced managers. Diversity management is a new enough concept that most managers will be inexperienced with its issues. It is not safe to assume that even the best managers have an intuitive knowledge of the problems and techniques of diversity management. Managers and the health care organization as a whole will benefit from an effective plan to develop managerial techniques for managing the increasingly diverse health care workforce of the 1990s and beyond.

Health care organizations are large and complex entities, and these qualities lead to diversity issues that go beyond the cultural diversity issues found in smaller institutions. For example, health care organizations are hierarchical; they have both an *actual hierarchy*—the different levels of employees diagrammed on the organizational chart—and a *perceived hierarchy*. The comparative status of departments and their managers, although unwritten and perhaps unspoken, is no less real. Certain departments or positions in the organization may be perceived as having a higher status than other departments or positions. The director of public relations, for instance, may be perceived as higher in status, and thus treated with more deference, than the director of custodial services, despite the fact that both are managers of divisions crucial to the organization. The director of finance or the director of nursing, in turn, may be perceived as being higher in status than the director of public relations. The perceived hierarchy adds to the formal stratification already imposed by the actual hierarchy and can lead to diversity management problems for health care organizations.

This stratification can be exacerbated by the personal stereotypes and prejudices people tend to develop over the course of a lifetime. Managers may have stereotypes about race, gender, ethnicity, sexual orientation, and physical ability that hinder their ability to manage a diverse workforce. By the same token, nonmanagerial employees may have prejudices that affect their ability to accept supervision from or work with people from diverse backgrounds.[1] To help managers overcome barriers caused by stereotypes and prejudice (their own and those of employees), health care organizations should formulate a management development plan tailored to managerial needs.

The Need for Managers to Address Workforce Diversity

Up until now, many health care managers have addressed the increasing diversity of the workforce only because of various affirmative action "quotas" they have felt obliged to fill. Practical or environmental considerations may have prevented these managers from considering workforce diversity as simply workers with distinct individual and group qualities that add to the strength of their organization.[2] As early as the 1960s, and up through the 1990s, health care managers have been expected to meet increasing levels of affirmative action recruitment and hiring. Health care organizations are affected especially strongly by affirmative action goals for two reasons. First, most health care organizations receive substantial public funds and thus are subject to affirmative action mandates. Second, health care organizations have many entry-level or low-skilled positions (for example, custodians, cafeteria workers) that present opportunities for inexperienced or nontraditional workers to enter the workforce.

It is one thing to require managers to recruit and hire specific numbers or percentages of women, the differently abled, older people, minorities, and aliens; it is another thing to prepare managers to utilize such workers effectively. This challenge is particularly true of managers who are resistant to change in general or who are antagonistic toward the affirmative action process.[3,4] Effective diversity management is complicated by the fact that many health care managers have had little formal management training. For example, a physician who is made chief of surgery probably did not take a management course in medical school. Likewise, a maintenance engineer who becomes director of custodial and building operations probably never studied management techniques. Many health care employees are promoted through the managerial ranks because of hard work, skill, ambition, determination, professional degrees, and sometimes just plain luck.

After becoming managers, these employees depend to a large extent on their own past experiences to develop and fine-tune their management style and technique (often through trial and error). New managers may make a conscious effort to either emulate or avoid the management styles of people who supervised or managed them as they moved up through the health care ranks. They may also use as role models the senior managers to whom they report or people whom they admire in the organization. However, this sort of emulation and modeling is no substitute for formal management training and development, let alone diversity management training.

In addition to limited exposure to management training, health care managers may have had only limited exposure to people from various cultures or ethnic groups, or to people with backgrounds, sexual orientations, or physical abilities different than their own. For example, a nursing supervisor who was raised and educated in a homogeneous rural area may never have met, let alone worked with or supervised, a Latina. With the influx of highly trained aliens into the United States, health care managers may also find that they are supervising people with advanced degrees or with training credentials that are not immediately transferrable. A medical technician supervisor, for example, may supervise a Russian immigrant who was a full-fledged medical doctor in Russia, but whose training and degrees are not recognized in the United States. Managers in such situations may feel awkward, uncomfortable, or insecure around people whom they perceive as different, and these feelings can make management difficult.[5]

However, trained health care managers are not exempt from diversity management troubles. The increasingly diverse health care workforce is proving to be a challenge even to managers well versed in management techniques. It is clear that health care organizations must take steps to ensure that *all* managers become well versed in effective diversity management.

The Process of Developing Effective Diversity Managers

The process of developing effective diversity managers involves considerable training and education and cannot be achieved overnight. Managers must first be convinced of the value and necessity of diversity training before they can be trained in effective techniques. As R. Roosevelt Thomas, Jr., points out in *Beyond Race and Gender*, diversity management is not just affirmative action or learning to appreciate diverse cultures and individuals; it is harnessing diversity in order to increase workforce productivity.[6] The process of preparing managers to be effective diversity managers consists of two steps: an assessment/ inventory of individual managers and an examination of the organization's structure and systems. Top-level management or the management steering committee should oversee this process.

Step 1: Individual Manager Assessment/Inventory

Before health care organizations can develop effective diversity management training programs, they must first determine what strengths and weaknesses their managers may have in relation to the management of workforce diversity. Although the internal culture and value analysis described in chapter 3 points out the organization's overall problems with workforce diversity, to properly train managers the organization must specifically assess each manager's diversity-related strengths and weaknesses.

An individual manager assessment/inventory should be uniform in format and should eventually become part of the health care organization's formal evaluation process for managers on an annual (or perhaps more frequent) basis. Integrating a diversity management assessment/inventory into the organizationwide management assessment/inventory emphasizes how integral diversity management is to the overall management process.

A diversity management assessment/inventory should be designed by the human resources department, preferably with the help of an industrial psychologist or a skilled outside consultant. The assessment should attempt to answer the following questions:

1. How does the manager perceive his or her staff: as effective, hardworking team players or as irresponsible, uncooperative employees in need of constant close supervision?
2. How do these employees perceive their manager: as an open-minded, strong, and fair leader and role model or as a closed-minded, prejudiced, unfair, capricious, and difficult leader and role model?
3. What does the manager feel are his or her strengths and weaknesses? Does the manager see himself or herself as patient or impatient? Open-minded or biased? Adaptable or inflexible? Does the manager see himself or herself as good at training others?
4. According to the manager's employees, what are the manager's strengths and weaknesses? (Consider those qualities mentioned in question 3.)
5. According to the manager's immediate supervisor, what are the manager's strengths and weaknesses? (Again, consider those qualities mentioned in question 3.)
6. What special circumstances, if any, have affected the manager's ability to effectively manage his or her staff? How many, and what kind of, staff problems has the manager had? How has the manager dealt with those problems? How quickly has the manager dealt with those problems? What patterns, if any, have emerged with regard to how the manager handles employee problems?
7. How does the manager relate to his or her peers and superiors? Is the manager candid in relationships with peers and superiors? Does the manager minimize barriers between his or her staff and the staff reporting to the manager's peers and superiors? How soon does the manager bring staff problems to the attention of his or her manager?
8. What areas of the manager's treatment of workforce diversity need improvement? Is he or she showing signs of bias, overlooking gaps in skills or training, or exhibiting insensitivity to cultural differences?
9. What areas of the manager's relationships with peers need improvement? Is he or she spending too much time socializing? Is he or she displaying contempt of peers in other departments? Is he or she exhibiting overly aggressive or passive behavior, or acting standoffish or unfriendly?

10. What areas of the manager's relationships with superiors need improvement? Is he or she insubordinate, disrespectful, hostile, or disgruntled toward superiors? Is he or she meek and unquestioning when relating to superiors?
    Is he or she overly sensitive to constructive criticism and supervision?
11. How can the manager's supervisor assist him or her in improving performance in the areas identified in questions 8, 9, and 10?

The individual manager assessment/inventory should be conducted by the supervisor. The supervisor must discuss each manager's assessment/inventory privately with the manager, and goals and objectives for improvement should be established in a manner consistent with the overall performance management system and with the goals and objectives of the team. Disagreements with the assessment should be noted by the supervisor and added to the personnel file. The human resources department should list each team's strengths and weaknesses as identified by the assessment/inventory and should use the profile of strengths and weakness among managers to tailor an organizationwide diversity management training program suited to the needs of the organization's management pool and the organization as a whole.

Step 2: Organizational Structure Examination

Effecting change in any health care organization requires that its structure, managerial hierarchy, and method for making and disseminating policy should be clearly understood. This structure, after all, provides the context in which managers perform their functions. Understanding organizational structure enables top-level management to change organizational or departmental structures if their current configurations hinder the addressing of diversity issues. Additionally, understanding managerial hierarchy helps to identify managers who might be having problems with diversity issues.

To perform a structural examination, top-level management or the management steering committee should ask the human resources department to devise two separate organizational charts (on the basis of the results of surveys described in chapter 3), each detailing reporting relationships, flow of the management system, and decision-making levels from the top to the bottom of the institution. The first chart should depict how senior management would *like* the organization to be. The second chart should illustrate how the institution is *actually* organized. Both charts should be compared by top-level management and the management steering committee along the following lines:

1. How are policy decisions made and communicated throughout the organization?
2. What criteria are (or could be) used to decide whether employees should be better managed, promoted, transferred, given specific training, left in the same position, or let go?

3. How quickly and efficiently does *change* (that is, adjusting to budgetary cut-backs, establishing new services, handling staff problems, and so forth) take place within the organization? What steps does (or could) the organization take to implement change and what kind of a time frame is used when implementing change? Do solutions to change-related problems tend to work? Is there an organizational structure that could better minimize problems resulting from change? How are solutions to change-related problems communicated to staff? How could such solutions be communicated more effectively?

4. What role do management and staff play in forcing, implementing, or at least supporting change, from the bottom of the organization to the top? Is there an organizational structure and team approach that encourages stronger support of change? If not, what kind of structure might help support change?

5. Which organizational structures have been affected by workforce diversity in terms of affirmative action measures? Which organizational structures have benefitted (or suffered) by valuing (or failing to value) diversity and using (or failing to use) diversity to increase departmental productivity?

6. Who in the organization establishes and communicates policies and programs related to implementing affirmative action, valuing diversity, and using diversity to increase departmental productivity?

7. What voluntary employee groups exist to deal with organizational diversity issues?

The answers to these questions will reveal the kind of institutional climate that exists for accepting and adapting to change. *Climate* refers to how staff members feel about the way their institution is structured and run and to whether management listens to staff and considers their opinions. An organization's climate can make a difference in how effectively a diversity management program can be implemented.

When the two organizational charts are compared, they may or may not reveal much disparity. More often than not, the comparison will illustrate how and in what areas the organization's structure should change to accommodate the changes necessary for effective diversity management. The comparison should persuade the chief executive officer (CEO) and top-level management to support any necessary structural changes. Without top-level management support, trying to implement a diversity program for managers would only create problems.

Because staff issues such as diversity have traditionally been overshadowed by financial issues in many health care institutions, it is essential for the CEO to persuade the senior management team that implementing a diversity program is necessary. Knowing how the organization actually functions and how that compares with how top-level management thinks it should function will guide top-level management in developing effective diversity management programs, as detailed in chapters 8 and 10 of this book.

Orientation, Training, and Empowerment of Managers and Teams for Diversity Management: Taking the First Steps

Once manager and organizational structure assessments have been examined and resulting strengths and weaknesses related to effective diversity management have been analyzed, the next task is to train managers and teams in effective diversity management. In order for managers to manage a diverse workforce, they must be committed to valuing diversity. Additionally, managers must be trained in diversity management techniques and empowered to make the necessary changes—in themselves and in their organization—before they can accomplish diversity management goals.

Because no two health care organizations are exactly alike in terms of workforce diversity, corporate culture, and the like, each organization must formulate its own plans and priorities for and expectations of its managers. Regulation and compliance, rapidly changing medical technology, increased costs of doing business, less profit, and shortages of qualified personnel have all complicated health care managers' jobs. Carefully targeted diversity management programs maximize the likelihood that managers will be successfully oriented, trained, and empowered.

However, before appropriate diversity training programs can be developed and implemented, health care organizations must enthusiastically embrace the concept of change. Health care organizations must give accommodating changes in workforce diversity the same high priority as accommodating changes in medical technology and regulatory and compliance issues. In other words, the diversity change process for management must be institutionalized.

Institutionalizing the Diversity Change Process for Management

Organizational change related to workforce diversity cannot occur without commensurate changes in management attitudes and behavior. However, managers cannot be expected to accomplish such sweeping changes if the concept of change is not institutionalized. The health care organization must communicate that change is a constant and positive element to be embraced rather than a temporary priority that will fade as management and staff lose interest and momentum and resort to old ways of doing things. The organization also must demonstrate its commitment to change by allocating the necessary time and resources to the change process.

Some health care managers may view workforce diversity as something forced upon them by affirmative action requirements rather than as a positive change that should be embraced.[7] This negative attitude toward diversity is often exacerbated by organizations'–and people's–natural tendency to resist change. For example, changing to a new telephone system or having to use voice mail can be difficult and stressful to employees accustomed to the former, albeit less efficient, system. Although most people accept that changing science and technology will alter their lifestyles, many find it harder to accept sweeping changes in business and organizational practices, such as embracing workforce diversity. In the workplace, old beliefs and habits die hard.[8]

The first step in the organizationwide process of accepting and embracing workforce diversity is for senior managers to demonstrate their commitment to the value of workforce diversity. This demonstration will help managers at all levels of the organization to understand and value the need to effectively manage diversity. Senior management's commitment must continue throughout the change process. After seminars and workshops have trained managers in the techniques and principles of diversity management, senior managers must follow up by supporting managers in their diversity management efforts. Without sufficient follow-up by senior management, managers may view diversity workshops and seminars as unwelcome interruptions in their tightly scheduled routines or as obstacles to meeting deadlines. Also, without sufficient follow-up, managers may not realize that effective diversity management, rather than the effective filling of quotas, is something on which they will be evaluated.

Thus, effective management development programs for workforce diversity should be identified as key parts of a major institutional initiative that will provide ongoing support for change. Most important, the commitment to institutional change must have the unqualified and dedicated support of the CEO and the board of directors.[9]

Preparing Managers for a More Diverse Workplace

Once a health care organization's senior management has made the commitment to institutionalizing the value of diversity management, the next step is to prepare managers to effectively manage the changes that will be necessary to implement diversity-management goals.[10] Preparing health care managers to manage workforce diversity more effectively must be integrated with other organizationwide initiatives. A good management development plan will help managers understand that successful business practices require good diversity management. Some managers will need more support than others in learning to manage change, and some health care organizations will have more change to manage than others. An example may be instructive to demonstrate how some health care managers and organizations are experiencing drastic changes in the diversity of their workforce and their client base.

Mount Sinai Hospital was founded by, and is still mostly funded by, Chicago's Jewish community. However, the hospital's neighborhood has changed and is no longer predominantly Jewish. The hospital's neighborhood, and its clientele, are now predominantly African-American. Today, the hospital serves a completely different clientele than the one it was created to serve in terms of race, religion, culture, and services needed. Previously, Mount Sinai was primarily a surgical, research, and general patient care center, but its client base now requires increased outpatient and trauma care services. The hospital's workforce in the past was predominantly white and Jewish, but now its workforce is more diverse, reflecting its urban setting. These changes, which affected every aspect of the hospital, required managers to learn to more effectively manage diversity within and outside the organization. Furthermore, Mount Sinai's diversity management has facilitated cooperation between the Jewish and African-American communities. The Jewish community continues to fund the hospital, and the African-American community now participates in fundraising and other outreach efforts, making it a vital resource for the hospital.

An effective management development plan requires more than just a mandate from an organization's CEO. The plan must be linked to the organization's performance management program in order to communicate the importance of diversity management to all members of the organization. Managers should be provided with sufficient training and information, including seminars, workshops, and presentations by experts in diversity management, to give them a full understanding of diversity management so that they can build mutual performance objectives with subordinates. The human resources department should simultaneously identify and prioritize the types of training most needed for all managers throughout the organization. Outside consultants who specialize in diversity-management training programs can be particularly valuable because of the expertise and objectivity they bring to the training process.

Although programs to help health care managers manage diversity should be customized to suit the unique attributes of each organization, basic steps, focusing on the actions of top-level management, should be included in all training programs. The subsections that follow provide an overview of these basic steps, which can be modified as necessary to design a customized diversity-management training program for managers.

Step 1: Top-Level Management Makes the Commitment to Change

Before making a commitment to change its management of workforce diversity issues, top-level management must first reevaluate and/or redefine its overall philosophy and mission and outline specific, achievable, and measurable goals. For example, a revised health care mission statement might be expressed like the following:

> Our organization is committed to providing high-quality care to our patients and the community. We strive to maintain a standard of excellent and trusted leadership that is unsurpassed in our field, which means that we must be (1) ethical and innovative in our methods, (2) respectful and appreciative of our employees' contributions and ideas, and (3) responsive to the changing needs of our patients, employees, and community, now and in the future.

The goal-setting process must result in qualitative and quantitative objectives based on the results of the organization's internal and external environmental assessments and employee skills inventory. (See chapter 3.) Goals and objectives must emphasize that the purpose of improving diversity management is to maximize the productivity and effectiveness of a diverse organization, not merely to satisfy affirmative action quotas. The goals and objectives should focus on measurable changes, such as improved customer satisfaction, increased team-building activities, and implementation of identified efficiencies. Initial goals of top-level management might be (1) to analyze the results of the manager assessments and structure examination within six months, (2) to ensure that the human resources department completes a personal skills inventory of all employees within six months, and (3) to prepare training materials and initiate diversity-management training programs for all managers within eight months.

Step 2: Top-Level Management Communicates Goals and Objectives and Obtains Feedback

Top-level management should clearly communicate the importance of diversity management and the diversity program's goals and objectives to the rest of the organization's managers and encourage their feedback. As they communicate the importance of diversity issues, top-level managers should prepare the groundwork for diversity management to become an integral part of the health care organization's overall commitment to change. To prepare this groundwork, top-level managers should do the following:

- Set unambiguous goals and expectations.
- Communicate the benefits of diversity management rather than simply making it a job requirement.
- Argue that increasing workforce diversity is an integral part of other fast-paced changes taking place in the organization, such as medical technology innovations, new regulatory and compliance issues, and so forth.
- Announce preliminary plans for training programs and other organization-wide activities to implement the changes.

Individual meetings should first be held with key middle- and lower-level managers, followed up with a memo reinforcing the organization's commitment to diversity management. Following these individual meetings, small meetings of no more than 10 managers each should be held to explain the organization's commitment to change and to obtain the managers' feedback, which should eventually be integrated into the organization's goals and objectives. Ample time should be allowed in these group meetings for discussion and give-and-take. After these meetings, a follow-up memo summarizing the meetings and any resulting modifications to the mission statement and goals should be distributed to all managers.

These meetings provide the opportunity to fine-tune and revise the organization's diversity-management plans based upon feedback from all levels of management. This manager feedback informs top-level management as to what types of management training tools are needed to accomplish its diversity-management goals and objectives, including any special assistance needed by managers who are resistant to change.

Additionally, two-way communication between top-level managers and all other managers will help ensure the success of the diversity-management program. This communication process will also teach managers how to present diversity-related goals and objectives to their staff members. Providing managers—and then staff members—an opportunity to contribute to the planning of the diversity program will help them all feel a sense of ownership of the process and will increase their desire to achieve a successful outcome.

Step 3: Top-Level Management Institutes Training and Education Programs

At this point in the manager-preparation process, top-level management should assign responsibility for implementing specific parts of the organization's diversity-management plans to managers throughout the organization. These assignments must be clearly defined and understood. Furthermore, managers should understand that their assignments and responsibilities will be instrumental in ensuring the management team's overall effectiveness. Top-level management must continuously monitor the success of these assignments and intervene as necessary to support the continuity of change. Adequate education of managers will help accelerate the diversity change process and ensure that its goals and aims are met.

There are two elements to the manager-education process. The first element is sharing the results of the internal and external environmental assessments with management as a team. This sharing should be done through oral presentations during meetings. Oral presentations represent an opportunity for managers to reflect upon their own management styles and consider how their styles have affected the organization's diversity climate. Group discussion at these meetings should allow an exchange of ideas about diversity-management problems and solutions and reinforce the true goals of diversity management—improved productivity, effectiveness, and efficiency for health care organizations.

The second element of the manager-education process is discussing stereotypes and prejudices about race, religion, ethnicity, sex, age, education, sexual orientation, different abilities, and so on. This discussion, which should be moderated by a trained diversity facilitator, should help managers to overcome their prejudices and stereotypes and value diversity.[11] Figure 4-1 provides an outline of a model one-day training program in diversity management for managers, which can be conducted by an outside consultant or by a skilled educator already employed by the health care organization.

Figure 4-1. Outline of Model One-Day Manager Training Program

7:30 a.m.–8:00 a.m.:	Continental breakfast
8:00 a.m.–8:30 a.m.:	Program introduction • Detail the day's schedule. • Emphasize the support and priority top-level management has given to the training program and its goals. • Outline the training program's specific goals.
8:30 a.m.–9:30 a.m.:	Presentation on the definition of diversity management *Learning objective:* Understand the meaning of diversity management and how it applies to the organization.
9:30 a.m.–10:00 a.m.	Presentation on workforce trends—nationally, in the health care field, and in the organization *Learning objective:* Understand the impact of national and health care trends on the organization.
10:00 a.m.–10:15 a.m.	Break
10:15 a.m.–11:00 a.m.	Presentation of the results of the organization's self-assessments *Learning objective:* Understand the current organizational culture, the organization's strengths and weaknesses, and how these strengths and weaknesses relate to the organization's goals.
11:00 a.m.–12:00 p.m.	Presentation on management's role in managing diversity and the impact of different management styles *Learning objective:* Fully understand managerial responsibilities, determine what type of manager each participant is, and how these categories relate to managing diversity.
12:00 p.m.–1:00 p.m.	Lunch [this time may be used to provide a motivational presentation on organizations benefitting from effective diversity management, perhaps using the case study in chapter 9 as an example]
1:00 p.m.–2:00 p.m.	Group role-playing exercises with managers and employees representing diverse groups *Learning objective:* Experience exposure to what current and new employees with diverse backgrounds might experience in the organization.
2:00 p.m.–2:15 p.m.	Break

Figure 4-1. (Continued)

2:15 p.m.–2:45 p.m.	Full group discussion of group role-playing results
	Learning objective: Learn ways that the organization can overcome inhibiting factors affecting diversity management and achieve greater value from its diverse workforce.
2:45 p.m.–3:30 p.m.	Presentation on the external community and how it affects the organization
	Learning objective: Understand the organization's role in the community and how the community affects the organization.
3:30 p.m.–4:30 p.m.	Group exercises on utilizing diversity management to maximize the organization's effectiveness, productivity, and degree of customer satisfaction and competitiveness
	Learning objective: Learn how to tie diversity management directly to the organization and departmental bottom lines.
4:30 p.m.–5:00 p.m.	Program summary and participant feedback • Include a written evaluation questionnaire. • Determine any new or unresolved diversity-management issues resulting from the day's program that require further action.
5:00 p.m.–5:30 p.m.	Refreshments

As training programs are implemented, top-level management must maintain its continued support for, and reinforce the importance of, these educational activities. Top-level management must ensure that all training programs are integrated and consistently emphasize organizational diversity-management goals. With the help of the health care organization's management steering committee or human resources department, top-level management should periodically follow up the manager training to assess the success of manager-education efforts and fine-tune future programs.

Step 4: Top-Level Management Monitors Results of Management Development

An effective training program must have measurable results. This step in the training process relates back to step 1, which involved setting goals. This monitoring process can be frustrating; once the management-development program has begun and has gained support and momentum, managers tend to expect quick results. Some diversity-management experts believe that realizing results from an effective diversity-management program can take as long as five years.[12] Although long-term organizational change, particularly with respect to diversity management, probably does take that long, it is essential that top-level management break overall goals down into meaningful, measurable objectives that can be achieved in a year or less. Without short-term, achievable goals, managers may become discouraged and lose interest and enthusiasm for the diversity-management process.

Top-level managers should set deadlines for specific training and team-building exercises to take place. They should schedule follow-up reports and map out a strategy for monitoring the results of those exercises. Firm deadlines should be set for achieving a quantifiable level of increased patient satisfaction.

Ultimately, top-level management should be able to gauge how effectively the organization is managing diversity as a result of management development programs. Top-level management should establish procedures for continuous monitoring, review, and revision of the organization's mission, systems, aims, and goals (and the means of achieving those goals) as they relate to managing diversity. Top-level management may need to intervene in the efforts of middle- or lower-level managers to maintain continuity and support the momentum of the change process. If it is determined that the structure of the organization needs to change to achieve the organization's aims and goals, plans should be made only with the full support of the CEO. Finally, due to managerial turnover or persistent diversity-management problems, top-level management will find it necessary to repeat the entire management development process periodically as well as the steps to preparing managers for a more diverse workplace.

Traditional versus Progressive Leadership Styles

When carrying out management development plans, most institutions find that management leadership styles can have a strong effect on the success or failure of diversity-management programs. This section discusses two prevalent health care leadership styles as they relate to the management of diversity and the formulation of a management development plan. Theories of management style tend to go in and out of vogue. However, the authors of this book have found that, for the purpose of managing diversity it is helpful to focus on traditional versus progressive management styles.

Traditional managers usually have not received formal management training and have learned how to manage on the job and by emulating the behavior of other managers. Traditional managers tend to feel most comfortable using management approaches and techniques that have worked for them in the past.[13] The longer these managers continue to see themselves as successful (as measured by promotions, raises, and longevity within the organization), the more likely they are to believe that theirs is the right and most effective management style. This belief may have been valid in earlier decades, when the health care field enjoyed technological and economic stability.[14] However, in the 1990s and beyond, the health care field will change rapidly and in many different ways at once. Traditional managers may find themselves unable to keep up with the health care field's rapid changes, especially in the area of workforce diversity management.

Employees tend to regard traditional managers unfavorably. Employees may claim that traditional managers play favorites and are wrapped up in organizational politics. Traditional managers inflexibly insist that employees do things their way and leave subordinates to fend for themselves, according to some employees. Additionally, employees may claim that traditional managers play subordinates against each other, protect the status quo, and fail to see the big picture.

Presently, traditional management is not highly regarded. This management style is often used in business management courses and texts as an undesirable ("before") example that is superseded by the currently preferable progressive style (the "after" example).

Progressive managers have often received formal training in the art of management, but they also sometimes emulate progressive role models. Progressive managers are more likely than traditional managers to keep abreast of current management trends by joining professional groups and routinely reading professional journals. Progressive managers are often described by their employees as facilitators of change, effective mentors, problem solvers, and team players. Additionally, these managers are often seen as willing to take risks to set examples and establish standards of excellence.

The progressive management style is preferable to the traditional style in the change process, especially when it involves managing workforce diversity. However, it is possible for traditional managers to change. Whether progressive or traditional, all health care managers must be developed and trained to be dynamic facilitators of change. In other words, health care managers must become what the authors of this book call "the 90s manager."

Profile of the 90s Manager

To meet the challenges of rapid change and unprecedented pressures in the health care field, the 90s manager must hone his or her ability to focus on the big picture, encourage independent decision making among subordinates, formulate and clearly communicate policies to staff members, and build strong teams. Many of these areas used to be the purview of the highest levels of management. Now, however, health care organizations sometimes require each manager, regardless of level, to utilize the management skills of a CEO. Or, as Napoleon stated nearly 200 years ago, "Every infantryman carries a field marshall's baton in his knapsack."

To meet the challenges of the decades ahead, the 90s manager must have considerable technical knowledge, a great deal of energy, and well-thought-out personal and professional ethics. The 90s manager will have to take the following actions:

- *Learn new, progressive management techniques.* These techniques include facilitating management goals, encouraging the group process, and equipping staff to respond to continuous change.
- *Operate at a new level of creativity.* Because the health care field faces constant pressure to create new solutions to complex problems, creative problem solving will be one of the most crucial attributes for health care managers in the 1990s and beyond.
- *Build organizational momentum.* Strong organizational momentum enables institutions to accomplish the seemingly impossible.
- *Become a participatory manager.* The 90s manager shares authority and decision making with staff and is receptive to their suggestions and ideas.
- *Win the commitment of employees.* Managers who demonstrate commitment and leadership and serve as good role models tend to foster commitment among their staff members. As Dwight D. Eisenhower once said, "Leadership is the art of getting someone else to do something that you want done because he wants to do it."
- *Turn employees loose, but be ready and available to help.* The 90s manager expects the best from staff members, gives them the freedom to do their jobs well, and supports and reinforces employees as needed. This management style is also known as the "Pygmalion effect"– molding worker performance to match supervisor expectations.[15]
- *Encourage employees to be good team members.* The 90s manager recognizes the value of a diverse workforce and encourages teamwork among workers with different backgrounds, cultures, genders, ages, and abilities. He or she has the skills to overcome conflicts, prejudices, and stereotypes that can destroy his or her team. Teamwork is the key ingredient to managing diversity effectively and productively.
- *Make a habit of risk taking.* If managers are afraid or reluctant to take prudent risks and make changes, then staff members will follow suit. The 90s manager must constantly evaluate new ways to perform tasks more successfully and efficiently, particularly if those tasks affect the organization's ability to manage diversity issues.
- *Generally understand how the organization operates while maintaining specific skills in two or three areas (finance, personnel, and so on).* The 90s manager must combine an understanding of the whole organizational organism with expertise in the workings of two or three of its organs, that is, the 90s manager must be a good generalist as well as a good specialist. Care should be taken to stay up-to-date in one's specialties.

Systems and departments in health care organizations, although more highly specialized than ever before, must work together more intensely and harmoniously than ever before. Improving synergy is the key to improving all of a health care organization's individual functions. A first step toward improving the all-important synergy among systems and departments is building a sense of teamwork among a health care organization's managers.

Management Team Building

Building effective management teams and making the best use of an organization's management resources are particularly important to the health care field, where changing technology and workforce dynamics must be managed to ensure the organization's productivity and effectiveness. *Management team building* can be defined as a process whereby managers are trained to work in informal groups when problems arise. These management teams are usually appointed by top-level management and are composed of those managers best qualified to address a particular problem. Management teams are often asked to define problems, suggest possible solutions, and outline a process for implementing the solutions. Upon completing its deliberations, the management team reports its findings to top-level management, which is ultimately responsible for initiating appropriate action.

To foster team building throughout the health care organization, managers must become an effective management team themselves. Not only does this team approach build synergy, it also helps each manager utilize his or her unique strengths and abilities. Leaders are important to the management team, but so are all the members whose contributions may not be as visible.

The team spirit advocated by successful athletic coaches is applicable to health care. For example, after basketball coach Chuck Daley completed his second straight world championship year with the Detroit Pistons, he was widely quoted as preferring to coach athletes who worked as a team rather than coaching a group of individual superstars. This should be the attitude of progressive health care managers of the 1990s.

As part of the team-building effort, top-level management must show that it appreciates the different styles, abilities, and specialties of each management team member. Top-level management must set the example so that other managers recognize and appreciate the diversity of their peers on the team. Top-level management should encourage all managers to work as a team to solve all problems, whether they are organizationwide or limited to one area or department. Team synergy will enable management to work through even the most difficult and complex problems.

Team-building exercises provide opportunities for managers to define and analyze individual and group roles in managing a diverse workforce. For example, a group of managers could address a serious problem that has been faced by the organization and collaborate as a team to create a hypothetical solution. During these exercises, managers should identify and define the problem, outline solutions and consider each alternative, and then define the steps of the most desirable solution. Other useful team-building exercises can be found in management literature concerning team building and problem solving, some of which is referenced throughout this book's chapters. The manager groups should meet periodically and proceed over time to more complex teamwork exercises.

References

1. Loden, M., and Rosener, J. *Workforce America.* Homewood, IL: Business One-Irwin, 1991, pp. 72–73.

2. Thomas, R. R., Jr. *Beyond Race and Gender.* New York City: AMACOM, 1991, pp. 17–22.

3. Loden and Rosener, pp. 29–31.

4. Thomas, pp. 23–24.

5. Loden and Rosener, p. 47.

6. Thomas, p. 10.

7. Thomas, pp. 41–42.

8. Waterman, R. H., Jr. *Adhocracy, the Power to Change.* Knoxville, TN: Whittle Direct, 1990, p. 10.

9. Waterman, pp. 15–16.

10. Pritchett, P., and Pound, R. *Business as Unusual.* Dallas: Pritchett Publishing, 1988, p. 10.

11. Thomas, p. 29.

12. Thomas, pp. 148–58.

13. Crosby, P. K. *Quality Is Free: The Art of Making Quality Certain.* New York City: McGraw-Hill, 1979, p. 142.

14. Crosby, pp. 142–43.

15. Ziglar, Z. *Top Performance.* New York City: Berkley, 1986, chapter 4.

Chapter Five

Integrating Strategies for Valuing Diversity and Managing Quality

D iversity management should be an integral part of effective quality management in health care organizations. In *Beyond Race and Gender*, R. Roosevelt Thomas, Jr., notes several similarities between quality management and diversity management:[1]

- Quality and diversity management efforts are strategies to ensure business success.
- Both efforts stress empowerment and involvement of employees. Total quality management (TQM) requires that all employees be fully involved with and committed to quality. Diversity management requires the empowerment of people from diverse ethnic, racial, and cultural backgrounds, as well as empowerment of older workers, the differently abled, women, and all the many groups that make up the diverse workforce of the 1990s and beyond.
- Quality and diversity management efforts are professional way-of-life changes; that is, they are management strategies that require fundamental changes in the way organizations operate.
- Both efforts require cultural changes for full implementation and should be preceded by organizational self-assessments. For quality management initiatives, organizations must analyze what they must do to make quality a norm that is endorsed and practiced by employees. For diversity management initiatives, organizations must determine what barriers prevent employees from participating fully in organizational activities. Additionally, for both efforts, organizational culture must accommodate the needs of employees and the business environment.

These similarities between TQM and diversity management reflect the changes occurring in health care organizations. The degree to which an organization can adapt to change and accommodate its many cultures will determine its ultimate success.

Historically, health care organizations have imposed structures on their workforces that, in most cases, have ignored their informal organizational structures. For example, traditional hierarchical management structures have been the norm in health care. Hierarchical structure engenders top-down (vertical) decision making, which can be inefficient. Top-down decision making sometimes produces the wrong solutions to problems because those who have first-hand knowledge of problematic issues are the last to be involved or are not involved at all.

Despite this hierarchical structure, informal health care work teams often operate outside the official management structure. Small groups of employees (such as nurses or radiology technicians) routinely meet in small groups to informally discuss issues and problems, and often these informal teams quickly arrive at effective solutions. However, administrators often fail to understand the validity of the group's solutions or even overrule the group out of fear of giving up power to lower-level staff members. In this way, corporate culture can prevent staff members from becoming full partners in TQM initiatives.

Cultural Barriers to Full Partnership in Quality Management

In order to overcome cultural barriers to full partnership in quality management, health care organizations must become aware of their own corporate cultures. Organizational success can only be achieved when the workforce is united and focuses on common goals that benefit both employees and the organization. To this end, corporate culture must encourage employees to strive for commonly accepted goals. It is a challenge to convince a diverse workforce to work together toward common goals without requiring the diverse groups to surrender their distinctiveness—to melt into the melting pot.

The organization's management must be committed to helping the organization and its employees define quality management goals, work together to achieve them, and share in the rewards. Support from management minimizes and breaks down cultural barriers, enhances goals and objectives, provides the incentive for employees to excel, and facilitates the quality improvement initiative.

The authors have witnessed several situations in which techniques to minimize cultural barriers have greatly improved quality management efforts. In one case, a large, diverse health care institution committed itself to addressing cultural barriers and achieved quick, dramatic benefits, including the following:

- Staff members became enthusiastic about change.
- Teams formed rapidly and spontaneously to address quality problems.
- Staff members developed greater commitment to their jobs and were eager to share their successes.
- Methods devised to improve the institution quickly became part of ongoing operations.
- Productivity increased significantly.
- Marked and steady cost savings were achieved.

Given that such positive results are possible, health care organizations should identify and strive to overcome the most prevalent cultural barriers to quality improvement. An excellent framework for considering such barriers is the work of W. Edwards Deming, who is famous for revitalizing Japanese industry.

Deming, a statistician, spent his career studying and developing quality as a system. When American businesses lost interest in these techniques after World War II, Deming took his techniques to Japan and refined his techniques during the 1950s and 1960s. In the 1980s and 1990s, when U.S. businesses began to note and admire Japanese productivity and management techniques, U.S. executives began to utilize Deming's methods and accept the validity of quality as a system.

This chapter discusses several of Deming's famous 14 points, known as the *Deming Management Method*, as they relate to workforce diversity and managing change.[2,3] For example, one of Deming's points mandates the removal of barriers that rob workers of their right to pride in workmanship. Deming believes that employees are eager to do a good job and become frustrated when poor supervisors, faulty equipment, inadequate methods of measuring performance, and similar barriers prevent them from doing so. The following sections discuss barriers that can limit an institution's performance: poorly implemented management systems, disrespectful and fearful work environments, interdepartmental antagonism, and weak leadership.

Poorly Implemented Organization Management Systems

When utilized properly, organization management systems are powerful tools for managing diversity and assuring quality in health care organizations. However, *organization management* must focus not only on developing optimal systems but also on reexamining every aspect of the individual worker's activities as well as how he or she fits into the organization.

Quality improvement programs often ignore or slight the importance of organization management systems in assuring quality and managing diversity. Deming suggests a reason for this phenomenon: 97 percent of any system within an organization is not measurable and therefore must be managed effectively to obtain optimal results. In terms of managing workforce diversity, the many changes being effected in an organization require a huge effort to bring about an overall change in attitudes, culture, beliefs, and feelings about one's fellow workers. Such attitudes, culture, beliefs, and feelings are all behavioral aspects of an organization and therefore cannot be measured fully, nor should they be. However, they must certainly be managed with the high level of effort that Deming suggests.

Organizations must move beyond a measurement mentality to recognize that lasting quality improvement comes from what you *can* manage. This enables organizations to focus on those changes that do make a lasting difference, not just short-term results.

Neither quality improvement nor effective diversity management can be achieved without a fully integrated and operational organization management system. Without an effective system of this type, complex health care organizations cannot monitor their operations, ensure quality- and diversity-management results, and identify the effects of change, diversity management, and quality improvement.

An organization management system should incorporate an understanding of an organization's mission and vision, which outlines corporate strategies and objectives. (See figures 5-1 and 5-2.) Carrying out an organization's mission, vision, strategies, and aims requires the delegation of divisional accountabilities and objectives, as well as careful job designs that clearly outline responsibilities. An effective system promotes trust of fellow workers as well as teamwork, shared vision, open communication, training and development (including the provision of needed tools to employees), and a focus on organizational aims and objectives—which in turn creates optimal organizational management. (This progression is charted in figure 5-1.) The more diverse, decentralized,

Figure 5-1.   Performance Management: An Integrated Approach

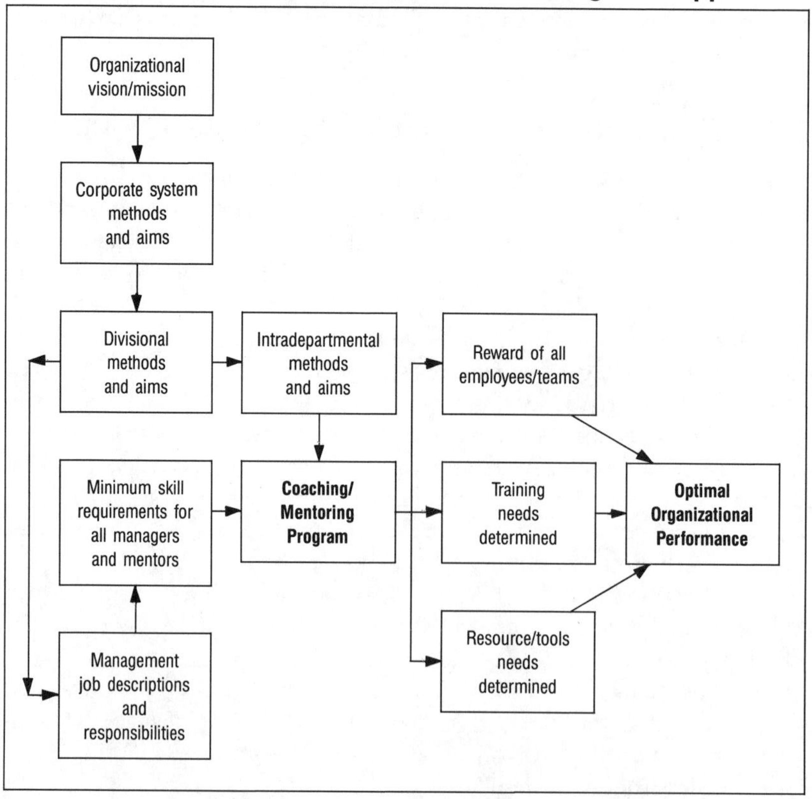

Figure 5-2. Performance Management Process: A Broad Overview

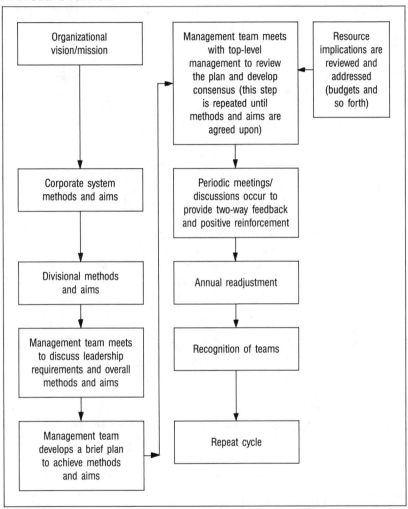

and complex the organization, the greater its need for an organized and systematic management system. Without such a system, health care organizations are likely to experience poor staff morale, high turnover rates, low customer satisfaction, and overall inefficiency.

In addition to being effectively designed, implemented, and managed, any overall system for organizational management must carefully address issues of methods and aims as well as of workforce diversity. In particular, the organization must encourage employee commitment to improving quality and valuing diversity. Organizations must be sensitive to the feelings and needs of all employees who are receiving constructive feedback. Management must reinforce the fact that the system applies to every employee and is intended to promote work-group teamwork and unity. In order to enhance employee commitment to improving quality and valuing diversity, organization management systems must:

- Praise groups of individuals. To effectively improve quality and teamwork, managers must de-emphasize individual recognition and focus instead on the group and its role in the overall system and aims of the organization. Too much emphasis on individual performance is counterproductive to encouraging teamwork and group decision making, where more knowledge can be applied to reach optimal solutions.
- Determine whether the method of group or organization recognition is difficult for employees from certain cultures. Public praise can make members of some cultural groups uncomfortable, and adjustments to the system should be made to avoid this discomfort.
- Develop a coaching system that is meaningful to members of various cultures in the organization. This system should focus on those areas that can help a person become more effective as a part of the team and the organization as a whole. A coaching system—not to be confused with a performance appraisal system—should address the following key questions:
  - How does an employee contribute to the team and to the overall aims of the organization?
  - How can the employee become a more effective part of the team and therefore enhance the team's contribution to the organization?
  - What tools are needed to enhance the employee's skills and contributions to the team?
  - What specific training is required for the employee to function more effectively as a contributor to the team?
  - What professional development would be beneficial toward making the employee more valuable to the team and to the organization?
  - What are the employee's ideas on how the organization and the team can work more effectively?
  - How can the employee's ideas be suggested to the team in the most constructive manner in order for the team to evaluate such ideas openly?

A coaching system can produce remarkable results in valuing diversity. The authors have observed several organizations that successfully implemented coaching systems to improve staff performance and attitudes and enhance work-group harmony.

However, a coaching system can only produce results if it is administered fairly and explained properly. It is critical that all of the diverse groups in the organization believe in the fairness and validity of the coaching system and that it is not a device to encourage individual competition. For example, nonnative speakers of English may have trouble understanding the system if their English comprehension is limited or if there are no comparable terms or concepts in their native language.

To ensure effective implementation of a coaching system, managers should do the following:

- Have in-depth, face-to-face discussions of the new system with all employees
- Allow ample opportunities for feedback and questions
- Explain procedures in detail, providing examples
- Outline the group decision-making process, providing examples

Some cultures are more responsive to the group decision-making process than the "ruggedly individualist" American culture. For example, cultures with tightly controlled family structures and strong community ties may comprehend the benefits of the group decision-making process and adapt to it more quickly than Americans. With proper explanation and support, however, health care organizations can readily accept a properly designed, group-oriented coaching system.

A well-implemented coaching system eliminates barriers and fosters continuous quality improvement (CQI). Applying the concept of CQI in health care should focus on the following improvements:

- Increasing patient satisfaction
- Eliminating unnecessary steps in delivering services
- Increasing staff morale and teamwork
- Enhancing cooperation and reducing stress levels for patients and staff
- Creating a better working environment with less turnover

Even the most up-to-date approaches to TQM and CQI can be negatively affected by outmoded performance appraisals, supervisory techniques, and management systems. Top-level management should encourage regular and accurate measuring and monitoring of new approaches to coaching to ensure the success and acceptance of these approaches and to prevent them from becoming barriers to quality improvement and effective diversity management.

Fearful and Disrespectful Workplace Environments

In addition to ineffective performance management systems, an organization's working atmosphere can be a barrier to successful performance. Deming wrote that fear should be driven from the workplace so that every employee can work to his or her best ability. Workers from the nontraditional groups as described in chapter 1 are especially likely to experience fear and disrespect in the workplace. Health care organizations that do not value diversity will lag behind in productivity and innovation in the increasingly diverse health care field. A fearful and disrespectful workplace will not bring out the best in employees. Conversely, a working atmosphere that fosters mutual respect and encourages employee sensitivity to the needs and cultures of diverse coworkers helps employees to respect and sensitively address the needs of patients and other health care customers. A workplace that is free of fear encourages employees to examine practices and procedures frankly and honestly, without fear of reprisals. Employees can then be free to creatively search for ways to improve the quality of care provided by their organization. Fear may be a strong emotion in departments with much cultural diversity; for example, alien employees may have grown up in countries with weak economies in which fear is a primary factor in job-related decisions.

To drive fear out of the workplace, management must demonstrate trust in its employees. Involving employees in designing practices and procedures—an empowering characteristic of CQI—is particularly effective in establishing a respectful, fear-free work environment that promotes employee confidence and innovation. By encouraging employees, especially frontline employees, to openly share their ideas, health care organizations can improve quality and help produce operational success. To ensure that all of their diverse employees feel respected and free of fear, health care organizations must continuously monitor their working atmospheres. Once this fear and disrespect is eliminated, an optimal work environment that supports teamwork can be created.

Health care organizations—including hospitals, clinics, skilled nursing facilities, and nursing homes—are complex institutions that provide many different services and handle crises and life-and-death situations routinely. In addition, these organizations are regulated by state, federal, local, and accrediting agencies. These pressures can increase the chances of making mistakes, and the rules and penalties that health care organizations often impose on their employees can increase fear and stress among employees. To break this vicious circle—pressure, mistake, penalty, increased pressure, increased mistakes, increased penalties—health care organizations must create more constructive and supportive work environments that include increased training and crisis intervention, rather than attempting to punish and correct actions and errors on an individual basis.

Management should consider using employee focus groups and surveys to help determine which procedures and interventions can help create a respectful and fear-free work environment focused on problem solving and constructive risk taking. In terms of workforce diversity, specific initiatives, including employee discussion groups, in-service training, and work-group training, should explore how diversity can affect and contribute to a fearful work environment. These initiatives will probably need to be repeated periodically, because habits, prejudices, fears, and misunderstandings do not disappear quickly.

Interdepartmental Antagonism

In addition to fear and disrespect, interdepartmental antagonism is identified by Deming as a major barrier to quality and success. Just as members of individual work groups and departments must learn to work together, so too must individual departments of a health care organization learn to reduce interdepartmental conflicts and antagonism and work together as a team.

Caste systems result when an organization's culture seems to value certain departments, such as nursing, over others, such as housekeeping or building services. In many health care organizations, operating departments are formally or informally considered to be more important and of higher status than support departments, an attitude that is communicated both verbally and nonverbally. The authors have interviewed many operating managers who openly believe that their functions should be accorded more organizational influence and consideration than the functions of support departments. These attitudes and resulting caste systems stand in the way of effective teamwork and high-quality patient care.

Contributing to interdepartmental antagonism is the belief, held by many managers, that feedback from managers of other departments is not worth considering. However, because health care organizations are complex, multiple-service entities whose departmental functions are interrelated and interdependent, their managers and departments must work as a team to ensure high-quality patient care and efficient business practices. Managers must consider all input offered, regardless of what department or level of employee it comes from. Interdepartmental input has become even more important as the traditional hierarchical organizational structure of health care organizations has been replaced by diverse, small, and quick-reacting cost-center-type operations. This organizational transformation has created new challenges for health care managers, who must manage a highly diverse environment and continuously obtain balanced input from all levels of the organization.

Interdepartmental antagonism can be minimized, and teamwork promoted, by doing the following:

- Focusing on the overall systems and aims of the institution and reexamining its methods in relation to the potential for interdepartmental antagonism
- Providing for an openness in communication and a promotion of trust to meet common goals
- Treating everyone as a part of the team who is required to get the job done
- Providing an environment for continuous improvement by encouraging new ideas and risk taking

Weak Leadership

A management issue related to interdepartmental antagonism is weak leadership. Often managers are resistant to input from managers who are considered to be weak or ineffective leaders. Deming contends that strong leadership motivates employees to work to their best ability. Following this reasoning, weak leadership is a major barrier to both quality improvement and effective diversity management, which are core organizational values in the health care field of the 1990s.

However, in Deming's lexicon the term *leader* refers to more than those who are called managers and supervisors by virtue of their job description. Deming recognizes that all organizations have people who, regardless of job title, are respected opinion shapers, role models, and leaders. These leaders communicate to workers what the organization accepts and values, as well as what the organization reflects and disapproves of. Such leaders are looked to particularly when the organization fails to formally or informally communicate its value system and sends mixed signals to employees.

Ineffective communication feeds employees' perceptions that the organization's leadership is weak and/or ineffective. In many health care organizations, the authors have found that leadership perceived to be weak or ineffective is one of the greatest employee concerns. Whether the leaders are in fact weak or ineffective hardly matters; if they are perceived as such by the employees, they cannot lead effectively. Perceived weakness in leadership is especially unfortunate in the diverse health care workforce, because leadership perceived to be weak or wavering in its commitment to valuing diversity cannot hope to effectively *manage* a diverse workforce.

A health care organization's managers can do several things to demonstrate that they strongly support and value diversity and quality improvement. Managers can take both formal and informal initiatives as long as they demonstrate strong support of and commitment to diversity and quality.

Management by walking around (MBWA) is an especially effective technique to use for diversity and quality management. This popular technique prevents managers from becoming isolated in their offices, exposes managers to work-floor activities, makes managers accessible to staff, and demonstrates that managers are interested in and care about day-to-day frontline operations.

To demonstrate commitment to valuing diversity, managers should sponsor and participate in activities of special interest to workers with diverse backgrounds and abilities. For example, managers could help plan and celebrate special occasions, holidays, and rituals specific to various cultural and ethnic groups. Additionally, managers could sponsor activities and workshops relevant to older workers, women, or the differently abled. Community leaders who represent the organization's diverse groups could be involved in such activities and celebrations, and staff members should be given limited time off to participate in related civic activities.

Perhaps the best way for managers to demonstrate support for workforce diversity and quality improvement is to establish a mentoring program. The purpose of the mentoring program is to foster leadership qualities in top performers and develop all employees from each of the organization's diverse groups. Such a program legitimizes leaders in each cultural group and provides opportunities for feedback concerning how the organization can better respond to the workplace needs of its diverse employees. An effective mentoring program should have the following elements:

- Specific objectives that relate to an organizationwide program for developing leadership skills and preparing future managers and mentors
- Involvement of rotating groups of employees who represent each area of the organization and each element of its diverse workforce
- Pairing of each employee with a respected manager (or with a higher-level manager if the protege is a manager himself or herself)
- Regular meetings, preferably over a period of several years, in which mentor and protege discuss work-related issues, career development and enhancement, and any other topics that will help encourage the protege's performance and advancement
- Organizational recognition of *all* participants in the mentoring program

Mentors, proteges, and the organizations they work for benefit from well-run mentoring programs in many ways. Mentors and proteges form bonds that strengthen organizational teamwork and communication. The organization grooms future managers who are likely to feel intense loyalty to their mentors and their organization. Additionally, mentors and proteges enhance their careers, demonstrate their leadership skills, and often are placed on the organization's fast track.

Approaches to Education and Self-Improvement

After identifying and addressing barriers to full organizational partnership in quality and diversity management, health care organizations should examine approaches to enhancing organizational partnership in those management areas, especially in terms of educational and self-improvement strategies. To ensure full support of and partnership in improved quality management, managers and employees will need to learn about and focus on teamwork, cultural diversity, and workforce empowerment, as well as CQI. Accomplishing these goals will require health care organizations to create and implement extensive education and training programs. This educational effort must receive full management support and will likely necessitate significant investments of time, effort, and money.

Learning about new trends and practices in CQI can best be accomplished through an integrated two-phase approach. Phase one focuses on changing attitudes toward quality management and introduces the new quality-related concepts and practices in a constructive and nonthreatening manner. Phase two trains and educates students of quality to integrate the new attitudes and practices into the organization's culture and structure while, at the same time, ensuring continuity.

Many resources are available to educate health care institutions about CQI, and it is beyond the scope of this book to address this topic in detail. However, organizations engaging in quality-related educational efforts generally focus on the following areas, which comprise phase one:

- Shifting of paradigms affecting quality management, that is, focusing on the future and what can be done to optimize performance rather than dwelling on the way things have been done in the past.
- Creation of new organizational vision and mission statements, that is, focusing on strategies and new structures supporting what the organization wants to become.
- Examination of culture and diversity issues relating to quality improvement initiatives, that is, applying what has been learned about the organization's diversity to develop aims and methods for quality improvement along with specific actions to achieve it.
- Building of work teams, that is, building upon the aims and methods for quality improvement to assemble work teams from appropriate departments across the organization to focus on key issues.
- Empowerment of staff, that is, opening the communication channels throughout the organization to ensure that ideas, solutions, and efficiencies can come from all employees without fear. To help open such channels, staff need to be trained in the arts of solving problems and taking risks.
- Redefinition of roles, responsibilities, and authority, that is, articulating to everyone the dramatic changes in the roles of management and staff to reinforce the fact that the work environment has changed (for example, helping everyone to understand that managers are now characterized as facilitators and coaches who help those on the front lines to get their jobs done as effectively and efficiently as possible).

Education in these areas will help managers and staff members understand and accept the changes needed to make CQI possible.

The educational process comprising phase one cannot be defined precisely in terms of length, scope, and structure, nor should it be. Organizations can differ widely in their approaches to phase one according to their size, complexity, acceptance of management, and so forth. Each of the aforementioned areas needs to be worked through systematically according to the institution's ability to digest its changes. Because change is not only organizational but cultural, institutions should progress through phase one slowly rather than at too fast a pace.

Phase two helps ensure that CQI efforts create lasting benefits and also focuses on diversity issues. The major topics of phase two include the following:

- Reinforcing topics presented in phase one
- Implementing CQI in a diverse environment
- Solving problems as a team
- Improving work processes through group discussion
- Communicating and providing feedback
- Integrating changes into daily activities in a diverse environment
- Determining how to orient new staff members to CQI and diversity issues

Phase two helps the organization to ensure the continuity of the changes begun in phase one. The seven items in phase two must help to define a new approach to managing the institution on an ongoing basis, thereby replacing the more traditional management roles.

The Transformational Leader

Although the two-phase educational program described in the preceding section will help managers and staff members become full partners in effective quality and diversity management, this process is so challenging and complex that it requires a new kind of leader. In their book *The Transformational Leader*, Noel Tichy and Mary Anne Devanna argue that the term *leadership* must be redefined for diverse organizations. The authors identify seven characteristics that the new leaders (whom they call the *transformational leaders*) will need if they are to manage a diverse workforce.[4]

1. *Transformational leaders identify themselves as agents of change.* Change is part of every health care worker's vocabulary, no matter what level of the organization they occupy. Transformational leaders realize that the methods, tools, and procedures of yesterday are obsolete and that they must pave the way for change. This realization is especially important when creating CQI initiatives. However, it is important to remember that the drive for quality must start at the top levels of the organization. Organizational agents of change must not forget to educate workers about the stress health care organizations are facing due to financial constraints, labor shortages, and increased customer demands when implementing a quality program.
2. *Transformational leaders are courageous.* These leaders are intellectually and emotionally courageous in telling employees the sometimes unpleasant truth about changes in the health care field.
3. *Transformational leaders believe in people.* They believe in the worth of all people, and this quality is especially important in the increasingly diverse workforce. In the eyes of transformational leaders, all employees are entitled to workplace opportunities and are capable of top performance.
4. *Transformational leaders are value driven.* Transformational leaders articulate their organization's core values and inculcate them throughout the organization by supporting policies, practices, and systems that support these values. To promote quality and diversity as organizational values and yet maintain an organizational culture that supports neither—that is, to preach one thing and practice another—only pays lip service to the two most critical determinants of future organizational success.
5. *Transformational leaders are lifelong learners.* These leaders view mistakes as learning experiences rather than problems that must be eradicated or hidden. They practice MBWA and have an open-door policy that helps them learn from employees which quality-of-service and quality-of-work life issues should be addressed.

6. *Transformational leaders can cope with complexity, ambiguity, and uncertainty.* Transformational leaders formulate theories, articulate principles, examine values and practices, and analyze assumptions, which are all necessary skills in the increasingly complex health care field.
7. *Transformational leaders are visionaries.* Transformational leaders not only create organizational vision but also transform the vision into goals and objectives that employees can strive toward in a spirit of teamwork.

The managerial training program described in chapter 4 can help managers become transformational leaders and enable them to take the next step in building a full partnership between diversity and quality management.

Team Building

The team-building process, as traditionally practiced in the United States, consists of two elements: task and relationship. Often a task is given top priority unless a special or crisis situation makes the relationship of team members more crucial. Teams are formed to accomplish many different tasks, for example, to win a ball game, to create a new product, to evaluate a service, or to determine a diagnosis. In cultures outside the United States, relationship building is the key motivation for building a team. A team is formed to nurture relationships among its members, which will then lead to the accomplishment of specific tasks. This cultural difference in priorities is significant, because, in a diverse workforce, difference in priorities often leads to confusion and ineffective teams.

In *Managing Diversity*, Lee Gardenswartz and Anita Rowe examine team-building attitudes that conflict with various cultural values. These conflicting attitudes, which inhibit efforts to improve product or service quality, include lack of sensitivity to the desire for harmony, lack of sensitivity to social status and family, lack of sensitivity to the expectation for inclusion, and lack of sensitivity to the belief in predestination.[5]

Insensitivity to the Desire for Harmony

American work culture has, over the years, come to accept disharmony within work teams as a fact of life and therefore has learned to value resolving conflict more than ensuring harmony. Other cultures, however, strive to avoid conflict in their work teams at all costs in order to maintain a personal ideal of harmony. Additionally, some women are socially conditioned to be peacemakers and may try to avoid seeming aggressive or confrontational in teamwork situations.

Much decision making and problem solving in U.S. organizations results from what traditional managers consider to be healthy debate. However, this healthy debate sometimes becomes heated and participants are often challenged to defend their views. In many organizations, these debates are the preferred method for making management decisions requiring knowledge or input from a variety of resources and departments within the organization. How managers perform in these debates is often a key criterion in deciding whether they have what it takes to achieve organizational success and advancement.

Without training in diversity issues, most organizations remain unaware that this practice discriminates against female managers and managers from cultural or ethnic backgrounds that value harmony and avoid overt conflict with peers. In many cases, women and members of these cultural and ethnic groups have had to adapt to difficult and uncomfortable communication styles that conflict with their innate value systems. Employees who did not or could not adapt to this style could either quit the organization or resign themselves to low-level jobs.

An unwillingness or inability to adapt to a confrontational management style is not merely employee stubbornness. Certain cultures inculcate harmony as a core value during the rearing of children, throughout the family structure, and in the workplace. In these cultures, those who are unable to accept and practice this harmonious philosophy are ostracized. To adapt to the confrontational method of group decision making found in the United States not only is difficult but also can be destructive to an individual's self-image and even inhibit the ability to function.

Until the recent acceptance of TQM and CQI concepts by health care and other organizations, there was no sound mechanism for changing organizational culture. Although organizations cannot be expected to adjust to every workforce idiosyncrasy, a central tenet of CQI and TQM provides a useful guideline. As was discussed earlier in this chapter, in order to improve quality, organizations must obtain optimum performance from each employee as an individual and as a team member. To achieve optimum performance, organizations must create an atmosphere in which each employee feels respected and free from fear. Valuing diversity, which makes *all* employees feel like valued members of the organization, is a key part of creating an atmosphere of optimum performance.

Insensitivity to Social Status and Family

The American work culture purports to value egalitarianism and therefore consciously de-emphasizes social and family status in the workplace. Organizational promotions depend, at least in theory, on education, training, skill, and performance, as opposed to family background and social class. However, members of certain cultures are direct about their belief in distinctions based on social class, education, and family background. Creative and well-thought-out quality improvement programs have found effective ways to address social and family differences while at the same time encouraging workplace teamwork and respect.

For example, a large, culturally diverse health care institution in Chicago has developed a variety of organizationwide functions aimed at motivating employees (and their families) from different cultures to interact socially. The organization formally sponsors several functions each year for employees and their families and publicizes numerous employees-only social functions.

Because of cost constraints, many health care organizations have recently had to reduce the number of employee and employee–family functions they provide. This reduction often symbolizes (in the eyes of employees) a lack of organizational commitment to employees. However, organizations committed to implementing CQI programs are increasing the number of employee and employee–family functions they sponsor, recognizing that these functions demonstrate that employees and their families are valued by the organization. In addition, such functions help family members to support employee commitment to the organization.

Insensitivity to the Expectation for Inclusion

Work practices in the United States tend to dictate that only those staff members directly involved in a project or in quality improvement initiatives should be included on work teams. Workers excluded from work teams sometimes become offended. For example, people from some European and western cultures have strong group beliefs that cause them to want to be included in virtually all workplace meetings and discussions that involve their friends or associates.

This sense of exclusion can make employees feel anxious and unvalued by the organization and can negatively affect organizational morale and efficiency. To avoid these problems, managers and administrators should carefully explain to all employees the process and rationale for employee participation in particular meetings and decision-making processes, a participation that ought to be rotational and available to everyone. Organizations should also ensure that important decisions and the results of all meetings are quickly and thoroughly communicated to employees to prevent feelings of exclusion or the possibility that employees learn such information by accident or as a result of secondhand information.

Insensitivity to the Belief in Predestination

American work culture (and Americans in general) tends to display a "we-can-do-it" attitude. Workers from other cultures, however, may have a strong belief in fate and predestination that precludes the belief that all things are possible through hard work. Workers from cultures that have strong attitudes toward what is and is not possible or meant to be may seem to impede quality improvement efforts in organizations that are not sensitive to such cultural backgrounds. These cultures may have philosophical beliefs about why certain jobs or processes cannot be improved (that is, performed more efficiently or accurately) or performed at all.

Accommodating such ingrained cultural resistance to change without compromising an organization's commitment to progress and quality improvement requires patience and understanding on the part of health care organizations. Employees with these cultural backgrounds who seem resistant to change or quality improvement efforts should not be viewed as poor performers or workers with limited potential.

One of the most effective ways to encourage such employees to participate in quality improvement efforts and adjust to change is by developing inclusive systems that appeal to those particular employees along with the rest of the workforce. Although it requires some research, granting organizationwide rewards that are culturally accepted and valued by a work group's culture can produce positive results. Culturally appropriate rewards can help workers who are culturally resistant to change and quality improvement efforts to embrace the American "can-do" spirit.

The importance of effective team building in a diverse workforce cannot be overstated—it is a fundamental element that enables a diverse workforce to buy into and feel part of an organization and its quality improvement efforts. Team building is also an important step in diversity management and quality improvement strategies, which are detailed elsewhere in this book.

Two Key Steps toward Diversity Management and Quality Improvement

There are two key steps toward effective diversity management and quality improvement. These steps provide organizations with a proper perspective for the implementation of new strategies and encourage the acceptance of these strategies by a diverse workforce. The first step, conducting an institutional audit to identify cultural barriers that prevent employee partnership in quality improvement initiatives, is discussed in chapter 3, although in a slightly different context. The second step, using work teams effectively, will expand upon the previous section to focus on helping work teams to reach maximum effectiveness in a diverse work environment.

Institutional Audits

Institutional audits (called environmental assessments in chapter 3) of complex organizations such as health care institutions are themselves quite complex and must be tailored to each organization. Performing an institutional audit to determine an organization's cultural barriers to quality improvement is an intricate process that must be carefully thought out. These audits are more qualitative than quantitative, and their results can be difficult to analyze and interpret. Furthermore, institutional audits examine sensitive issues that can cause managers and employees alike to become defensive and discount the findings. An outside organization or consulting firm that specializes in this kind of audit can help in this challenging process. (See appendix A for a list of appropriate consultants.)

The objective of the institutional audit is not to conduct an exhaustive review of institutional operations but to focus on key areas that exhibit organizationwide problems. This focus enables organizations to generally identify major problems without getting overly involved in the specifics of problems. The following areas should be examined in the audit:

- Attitudes and morale
- Communication
- Organizational openness
- Teamwork (among operating departments and among administrative and operating departments)
- Labor–management relations
- Management mix, promotions, and turnover
- Hiring practices
- Training and development of management and staff

These topics are discussed in the following subsections. Information relevant to these topics may already be available in recent management reports or accessible in various organizational databases. It is critical that all possible information be gathered concerning each of these areas before management begins to identify cultural barriers to quality improvement and formulate the interventions necessary to develop an organizationwide program that addresses problem areas.

Attitudes and Morale

Attitude survey instruments are commercially available from a number of sources to help health care organizations gauge the feelings and concerns of their workforces. However, these instruments must be chosen carefully to meet the needs of each organization. The following criteria must be met if an attitude survey instrument is to provide the proper information:

- The survey questions should address morale issues specific to the various cultures found in the workplace.
- The instrument should be designed so that its results can be measured for statistical significance.
- Management should agree that the instrument addresses organizational needs.
- Survey terminology should be recognizable to the institution's various nationalities and cultures.
- Usage of the instrument should only disrupt the workforce to a small extent.
- The amount of time required to complete the survey should be reasonable enough to ensure that workers will be able to fill it out carefully and completely without feeling pressured or rushed.

Communication

To pinpoint cultural barriers to quality improvement initiatives, the institutional audit must assess the effectiveness of the organization's overall communication. This assessment can be performed by conducting employee focus groups or by other less-formal means, as described in chapter 3. Effective communication, essential to all successful organizations, is especially essential to the success of quality improvement initiatives.

Organizational Openness

Organizational openness is critical to determining how effectively an organization will deal with CQI, cultural diversity, teamwork, current change, and future organizational change. Such openness can be characterized by good communication throughout the organization as well as frequent feedback, high levels of trust, and free sharing of information and ideas, particularly with regard to the search for better ways of doing things.

The degree of organizational openness can be partially determined by an attitude survey and then supported by either focus groups or a review of how the organization dealt with the implementation of major changes in the recent past. For example, how the organization implemented a new accounting system, decentralized or centralized its operations, or automated various operations can help determine its organizational openness.

Teamwork

One of the greatest barriers to the success and growth of any organization is disharmony among functions and departments. The degree of organizational disharmony or teamwork can be assessed easily through discussions with individual managers and first-line supervisors throughout a cross section of the organization. Most employees will provide frank and honest information on this topic because disharmony prevents them from doing *their* jobs.

Labor–Management Relations

Three groups must be examined when auditing labor–management relations: top-level management; middle-level management and first-line supervisors; and unions. Any one of these three or a combination of these groups can be the source of serious labor–management problems.

Top-level management usually sets the tone for labor–management relations. Even though top-level management is ostensibly in control of the organization, if the union feels that top-level management is abusing their relationship, the union can take many "unofficial" steps that will negatively affect morale and efficiency. In so doing, unions can prevent the organization from making changes and improving itself. Middle-level management and first-line supervisors often feel threatened by change and can impede the implementation of top-level management programs to improve the labor–management climate. To assess these attitudes and defuse potential problems requires a well-designed attitude survey and informal discussions with members of all three groups. (Middle-level managers, first-line supervisors, and union leaders usually will readily share their frank opinions.)

Management Mix, Promotions, and Turnover

Most organizations have data on management mix, promotions, and turnover readily available on their human resources information systems. Data can also be obtained from periodic human resources reports. This information can be used to measure how strong a commitment the institution has made to cultural diversity, how many promotions have occurred among various cultural groups, and how successfully the institution has retained its best workers.

Hiring Practices

Analysis of an institution's hiring practices can reveal problems that often are easily preventable. Information on hiring practices is readily available through the organization's human resources department. The organization's hiring practices should show a commitment to workforce diversity and should reflect the organization's direction in terms of management mix, promotion, and retention.

Training and Development of Management and Staff

All health care organizations should have extensive training and development programs for management and staff. In order to target management and staff training needs and formulate plans to address those needs, training and development programs should be coordinated with the professional development process. Here again, the human resources department should have information on existing training and development programs, making it a simple task to determine which programs meet the needs of the institution. The knowledge of an institution's human resources professionals will also enable management to determine the adequacy of the current programs, review the staging of various programs, and assess additional needs.

Effective Work Teams

After performing an institutional audit to obtain a clear picture of what needs to be done to overcome an organization's cultural barriers to quality improvement and enhance the acceptance of cultural diversity, the next step is to create effective work teams. The effective use of work teams is one of the most important considerations in obtaining full employee partnership in quality improvement initiatives and management of workforce diversity. Health care organizations have used various types of teams over the years to study problems and complete special projects, but building effective work teams in a diverse workforce requires training and sensitivity.

It is at the work-team level that the connection must be made between knowing and understanding quality improvement concepts and actually using these concepts to create change, whether the change involves TQM, CQI, or other quality initiatives. Because health care organizations have diverse workforces, their work teams are likely to consist of a mix of cultures. The following seven steps will help ensure the effectiveness of diverse health care work teams:

1. The work-team approach and philosophy toward quality improvement must be clearly communicated to all team members. This communication is often provided in training sessions, using handouts that include exercises, references, and examples. Training that utilizes real-life examples and case studies is most effective.[6]
2. Work teams must have reasonable objectives that can be easily understood by all team members. Expected results should be clearly outlined and, most important of all, should be achievable.
3. Work-team objectives should be prioritized in order of importance to provide a direction or focus for team members' actions. As quality improvement programs progress, work teams are often transformed into CQI teams to identify and assess which problems should be the focus of future quality improvement efforts.
4. Once quality problems are identified, work-team members should be chosen by the appropriate managers to reflect the range of diversity and knowledge necessary to fully address those problems.
5. Work teams should be given clear objectives and timetables for obtaining expected results toward the established aims. Management should solicit regular feedback from the teams and should be ready to provide the necessary support for teams that have difficulties.
6. Work teams should make final reports to management that detail the problems being addressed and potential solutions to those problems. Management should respond to reports by stating which actions it will take and the time frame for those actions.
7. Management should implement the work team's solutions as soon as possible. Formal recognition must be given to work-team participants. Recognition will also be given in the form of staff members who will informally measure improvements in quality efforts resulting from the work team's recommendations.

Reasons for the Failure of Quality Initiatives

Studies have shown that quality efforts are more likely to fail than succeed. In *The Only Thing That Matters*, Karl Albrecht refers to this failure as "the fizzle factor."[7] Albrecht's research has identified six common fizzle factors:

1. *Little commitment from management:* This factor occurs when employees fail to find sufficient evidence that management, especially top-level management, is strongly committed to quality improvement initiatives.
2. *Giving up when times get tough:* During times of health care downsizing, restructuring, and wage freezes, quality improvement efforts may be moved to the back burner, especially if management and employees view quality and service improvement as a high-cost item.
3. *Failure to engage middle-level management:* Middle-level managers are the backbone of health care organizations. They are the ones who "make it happen." Quality improvement and diversity management initiatives should target middle-level managers (rather than administrators) for leadership roles. Top-level management should help ensure middle-management "buy-in" by determining which issues, needs, and concerns are most important to this crucial constituency.
4. *Failure to win hearts and minds:* Health care organizations should determine whether its employees are sincerely committed to quality initiatives or whether employees perceive them to be the latest management fad. Organizations should also determine whether top-level management has undertaken the education and communication efforts necessary to ensure organizationwide commitment. Health care organizations should avoid jumping on the quality bandwagon before their organizational culture is prepared. If major morale problems exist, if employees are cynical because changes have not addressed their issues or concerns, or if diversity is not valued by the organization and its employees, the organization is not ready to begin a full-blown quality improvement initiative.
5. *Use of old management styles:* If management still views its role as to define employees' output and ensure that employees meet that output, quality efforts are doomed to failure. This outdated management concept was created by Frederick Taylor in his 1911 book, *The Principles of Scientific Management.*[8] Surprisingly, most American management styles are still based on Taylor's methodology.

    New management methods that view employees as intelligent and capable of making sound decisions are most appropriate for quality improvement and diversity management efforts. This new methodology maintains that the manager's role is to lead and support employees' efforts—providing a customer-service orientation where management serves rather than controls the customer (that is, the employee). This concept also relates to employee empowerment, which not only gives employees a few more "volts of power" but also involves employees in goal setting and decision making. Employee empowerment ensures that employees have sufficient information, skills, and understanding to accomplish organizational quality improvement efforts.

6. *Creation of a measurement psychosis:* Quality efforts have spawned paperwork nightmares that emphasize the measurement and tabulation of individual behaviors rather than focus on quality improvement strategies. These paperwork nightmares not only discourage employees and managers from following through on quality initiatives, but they also obscure quality improvement goals, preventing employees from seeing the forest for the trees.

   Karl Albrecht explains the difference between focusing on behavior and focusing on strategy by using the example of a hotel clerk. When the focus is on behavior, the quality improvement process may stipulate that a hotel desk clerk say a guest's name twice during the check-in process. When the focus is on strategy, the clerk must ensure that the guest has received high-quality service when he or she accepts the key and proceeds to his or her hotel room. In the second case, the emphasis is not on measuring how many times the clerk smiled or addressed the guest by name, but on ensuring that the check-in process goes smoothly and meets the guest's needs.[9]

There are other reasons why quality initiatives may fail, but the preceding six reasons provide a quick checklist that health care organizations can use to assess organizational readiness and the appropriateness of the quality improvement program's design.

References

1. Thomas, R. R., Jr. *Beyond Race and Gender.* New York City: AMACOM, 1991.

2. Scherkenbach, W. W. *The Deming Route to Quality and Productivity.* Washington, DC: CEEPress, 1988.

3. Walton, M. *Deming Management at Work.* New York City: G. P. Putnam's Sons, 1990.

4. Tichy, N., and Devanna, M. A. *The Transformational Leader.* New York City: John Wiley & Sons, 1986.

5. Gardenswartz, L., and Rowe, A. *Managing Diversity.* Chapter 4. Homewood, IL: Business One-Irwin, 1993.

6. For further information, see Leebov, W., and Ersoz, C. J. *The Health Care Manager's Guide to Continuous Quality Improvement.* Chicago: American Hospital Publishing, 1991; and Melum, M. M., and Sinioris, M. K. *Total Quality Management: The Health Care Pioneers.* Chicago: American Hospital Publishing, 1992.

7. Albrecht, K. *The Only Thing That Matters.* New York City: Harper Business, 1992.

8. Taylor, F. *The Principles of Scientific Management.* Easton, PA: Hive Publishing, 1982. (Originally published in 1911.)

9. Albrecht.

Chapter Six

Retaining and Recruiting Health Care Workers

As was discussed in earlier chapters, workforce demographics have changed enough that health care employers can no longer count on having an ample supply of qualified employees. Now more than ever before, it is crucial that health care organizations understand and adapt to workforce trends. As was also discussed earlier, health care is one of the nation's fastest-growing fields of employment, and it is already experiencing difficulty in finding qualified applicants. To make things even more difficult, hospitals currently are under rigorous scrutiny by outside organizations that are charged with measuring the quality of the care hospitals provide. The Joint Commission on Accreditation of Healthcare Organizations (JCAHO) is moving toward the standardization of quality assessment processes. And quality of service, quality of care, and quality of products are all directly related to the caliber of an institution's employees. The effects of staff shortages also are being exacerbated by greater-than-ever strains on the national health care system, including the AIDS epidemic, the needs of an aging population, the growing number of uninsured patients, the increasing numbers of drug-dependent patients, the resurgence of such diseases as tuberculosis, and new health hazards in the workplace (such as adverse reactions to chemicals and carpal tunnel syndrome).

These factors have made the retention and recruitment of qualified workers a top priority in health care organizations. Because the workforce has become increasingly diverse, effective management of that diversity is a crucial factor in successful retention and recruitment policies. This chapter will present strategies for attracting and keeping qualified workers in a seller's market. Because employers invest a lot of time, effort, and expense in their workforces, the chapter begins with a discussion of how to avoid losing that investment.

The Challenge of Employee Retention

In today's environment, health care organizations are being challenged to find the best-qualified applicants for vacant or new positions at the same time they are working to retain the experienced and qualified workers already on their staffs. Successfully retaining employees involves five processes: reducing employee turnover, adapting to changing attitudes toward work, keeping and challenging current employees, adapting to a changing workforce, and becoming an employer of choice.

Reducing Employee Turnover

Reducing employee turnover concerns all health care organizations. In fact, never before has control of turnover been more critical. Nationwide, turnover costs amount to millions of dollars per year.

In *Managing Employee Turnover*, Francis L. Ulschak and Sharon M. SnowAntle provide a useful formula for determining an institution's turnover cost:

Total separation costs + total replacement costs + total training costs + total net differential performance between leavers and replacements = Total turnover cost[1]

Reducing current rates of employee turnover in health care institutions will soften the impact of the impending labor crisis. Ulschak and SnowAntle point out several job-related factors that affect employee turnover:[2]

- Job satisfaction
- Satisfaction of personal needs
- Job expectations
- Role ambiguities
- Nature of the job interview
- Orientation to the job and the organization
- Commitment
- Supervisor–employee exchange
- Participation in decision making
- Effectiveness of communication
- Equity perceptions
- Stress
- Job vacancies
- Absenteeism
- Job tenure
- Size of the organization
- Type of position

These factors also influence job performance and the overall quality of care provided by an organization. Of these factors, improvements in four specific areas are especially important in reducing employee turnover: promoting job satisfaction, satisfying personal needs, fostering positive supervisor–employee relationships, and encouraging participation in decision making.

Job Satisfaction

The more satisfied employees are with their jobs, the less likely they are to leave them. That much is obvious, but the term *job satisfaction* can be defined in many ways. For many baby boomers (people over 30 years old in today's labor force), it involves working long hours and achieving a quick ascent up the corporate ladder. For the younger workers who will dominate the workforce in the future, however, job satisfaction often means attaining a high quality of life at home as well as at work. Long hours at work and stressful jobs may not equal job satisfaction for them. For example, a 1990 article in *Fortune* magazine told of a 1987 college graduate who took a fast-track job with the New York office of Merrill Lynch, a huge brokerage firm. He described it as "a nonsensical, 100-hour week, cram-it-down-your-throat, no-social-life world" that he quit after a year, despite assurances of a promotion, to take a job with a smaller investment firm. He explained his decision this way: "I want to be happy and fulfilled—socially and culturally—and to progress in the work world to the point where I'm happy with myself. I'm not shooting for a title. Titles are bunk. Our generation is much less political in the workplace than the ones that preceded us."[3] His outlook is very different from the prevailing view of many baby boomers.

Many factors other than age affect concepts of job satisfaction in a diverse workforce. As discussed in chapter 2, some cultures prize personal relationships, on and off the job, and money, prestige, and titles may be less meaningful to employees from such cultures. Consequently, supervisors and executives cannot assume that all employees share their concept of what constitutes job satisfaction. They must ask questions and listen to employees' diverse responses and, if necessary, modify policies and procedures to maximize job satisfaction.

Satisfaction of Personal Needs

Related to an employee's sense of job satisfaction is the sense that his or her personal needs are being satisfied by his or her work. Ulschak and SnowAntle list some key "job satisfiers" that maximize employees' sense that their employers acknowledge their contributions and attempt to accommodate their personal needs, including feeling recognition for their job performance through management feedback and performance appraisals, sensing their own accomplishment and competence in fulfilling work responsibilities, believing that their work is important and that they are making meaningful contributions to the organization, and being able to integrate the demands of work with those of their lives outside the workplace.[4] An increasingly diverse workforce has increasingly diverse personal needs; health care institutions that recognize and accommodate employees' personal and family obligations will retain the maximum number of employees and protect their most vital resource—people.

Positive Supervisor–Employee Relationships

Studies have shown that the supervisor–employee relationship is one of the most significant factors in determining an employee's level of job satisfaction.[5] Training supervisors to understand and manage a diverse workforce will be crucial in establishing and maintaining positive supervisor–employee relationships. Properly trained managers acknowledge, understand, and respect the individual needs of, and differences among, their employees. (Chapter 4 outlines a training program in this area.)

Towers Perrin, a large management consulting firm, and the Hudson Institute conducted a survey of corporate response to demographic and labor force trends. They found that 55 percent of the responding companies gave the highest priority to training supervisors to motivate and communicate with a diverse group of employees.[6]

Participation in Decision Making

Ulschak and SnowAntle, the authors of *Managing Employee Turnover*, report that "the more opportunity an employee has to be involved in meaningful decision making about issues that affect him or her, the more likely it is that he or she will remain with the organization for an extended tenure."[7] But in order to involve employees in the decision-making process, managers must fully accept the validity of their participation. In a diverse workplace, this means that managers must accept and respect employees who may be different from themselves and may have different goals and priorities. Chapter 9 presents a case study of how an international corporation coped with the realization that its minority employees were hesitant to discuss differences and take advantage of opportunities to participate in decision making.

Adapting to Changing Attitudes toward Work

The preceding subsection discussed aspects of work life that can help reduce the likelihood that individual employees will leave the organization. In order to retain employees, however, organizations must also recognize and adapt to the fact that the overall attitudes toward work have shifted over the past few decades in the United States.

In the past, health care and other employers seldom worried about having enough qualified employees. People who had been forced to delay starting families until after World War II made up for lost time by creating a "baby boom" of births between 1945 and 1964. The baby boom coincided with a period of extraordinary growth in industry, which provided a wealth of employment and advancement opportunities for this bumper crop of Americans. Then, in the mid-1970s, industrial growth began to slow. By the mid-1980s, when workers born between the years of 1967 and 1975 began coming of age, mergers, acquisitions, bankruptcies, global competition, and corporate restructuring drastically changed the American business climate and reduced employment opportunities. Current managers clung to their positions, and reduced opportunities for advancement caused workers to hit plateaus relatively early in their careers. Working hard, being loyal to the company, and keeping the boss happy by agreeing with his or her rules no longer automatically resulted in stable, long-term employment and regular promotions. Nearing retirement, the ideal "organization man" of the 1950s and 1960s was being replaced by employees with new agendas.

The workers of the 1990s and beyond will be loyal, not to their employers, but to themselves and to their occupations. They believe that career longevity and advancement will result from hard work, expertise, and loyalty to oneself and one's profession. And such loyalties sometimes mean challenging the established rules and practices of employers.

These changes were effectively summarized in a newspaper article by William H. Whyte, who in 1956 published a landmark study of corporate employees, *The Organization Man*. In 1991, Whyte interviewed some of the people he had profiled in his study and learned that some had taken early retirement as a result of the uncertainties of the 1980s, others had been fired as a result of corporate downsizing, and still others had been demoted. Whyte was struck by the fact that the children of these organization men did not want to follow in their fathers' footsteps. The children wanted to work to live, not live to work. Whyte described these new workers as follows: "Celebrated as sensitive souls or castigated as yuppies, they have followed self-fulfillment with abandon. Many took those values into the workplace, demanding that these jobs fulfill their needs for self-expression. Many made work the center of their lives. But unlike their fathers, they refused to give loyalty to any one organization."[8]

The workers of the 1990s and beyond are more concerned than workers of past eras with quality-of-life issues. This is true for a variety of reasons: because of their parents' experiences, because they come from cultures that value family relationships, because both parents are now deeply involved in their children's daily activities, and because they are caring for aged parents, among other reasons. Health care organizations that recognize and adapt to employees' changing attitudes toward work and changing priorities in life stand the best chance of retaining that increasingly valuable resource—qualified, trained employees.

The changing workforce has already begun to change the workplace. New styles of leadership and communication exhibited by workers from diverse backgrounds and with diverse abilities have created new challenges for employers who seek to retain workers.

Keeping and Challenging the Best Employees

Managing a diverse workforce challenges past management assumptions. (Chapter 4 outlines the new management attitudes and skills that will be needed to communicate with, develop, and motivate workers in the 1990s and beyond.)

Companies that are touted in the media as "excellent" companies for which to work are continually conducting organizational assessments, surveys of employee attitudes, and surveys of customer satisfaction in an ongoing effort to improve their efforts and to adapt to change. Such organizations recognize that change will not be just the watchword of the future, it will be the future.

According to *The New American Boom,* published by the staff of the *Kiplinger Washington Letter,* "The swiftness of change will put an extra premium on agility and quickness of response. Companies both enormous and tiny will re-tune their command structures to fit new ways of doing business and stimulating innovation, while keeping step with the needs and demands of new generations of employees."[9] Addressing employee expectations will no longer be a "soft" human resource issue; it will become a "hard" bottom-line initiative. Benefits, salaries, promotion policies, performance evaluations, and other human resource issues must accommodate the changing workforce.

James L. Ketelsen, chairman and chief executive officer of Tenneco, recommends the following five strategies to keep and challenge the best employees in a changing workforce and to meet changing worker expectations:

- "Make a commitment to creating advancement opportunities for all workers by selecting and promoting managers who believe in advancement opportunities for women and minorities."
- "Increase the involvement of women and minorities in formulating policies and programs by using active advisory councils. Empower them and listen to them."
- "Link executive bonuses to successful hiring and promoting of women and minorities."
- "Design family-friendly benefits to meet the needs of the new workforce. If employees are not forced to choose between family obligations and career opportunities, they will be better able to meet both personal and company goals."
- "Maximize opportunities for women and minorities by providing them with training and development and, most importantly, with line positions with profit-and-loss responsibility. Do not pigeonhole nontraditional employees in staff jobs and then declare them unprepared for greater responsibility."[10]

Following these strategies will help organizations adapt to change on an ongoing basis and maximize their ability to keep and challenge workers.

Adapting to a Changing Workforce

Effective adaptation to changes in the workforce presents many new challenges to organizations. In the recent past, as the workforce became increasingly diversified, members of new or "different" groups had to do most of the adapting; that is, they had to "go along to get along."

Women, for example, learned how to strike a balance between assertiveness and femininity. They could not afford to be perceived as either too aggressive or too soft if they wanted to get ahead. Workers from Asian cultures learned how to be more direct and outspoken in their interactions on the job. African-American workers often had to modify their mode of communicating to match that of the white majority. In *Black and White, Styles in Conflict*, Thomas Kochman describes differences in communication styles between African-Americans and whites: "The black mode is high-keyed; animated, interpersonal and confrontational. The white mode is relatively low-keyed; dispassionate, impersonal and non-challenging. The first is characteristic of involvement; it is heated, loud and generates affect. The second is characteristic of detachment and is cool, quiet, and without affect."[11]

Gays and lesbians learned to hide their sexuality because "coming out" could lead to discrimination on the job, which could go as far as losing their jobs, particularly for teachers and members of the armed forces. Differently abled employees learned to find their own ways of adapting to the workplace because requests for better signage, wheelchair access, and the like were often viewed as asking for "special treatment." Nonnative speakers learned that speaking languages other than English on the job was often viewed by managers and coworkers as "conspiratorial."[12]

Today, however, the preponderance of "different" employees has shifted the balance. The workplace must now change to adapt to a diverse workforce. The leaders and managers of the future will come from this diverse workforce, and standards and definitions of leadership will have to change to accommodate them. The following paragraphs offer considerations for a redefinition of leadership.

Most studies and concepts of corporate leadership were based on the goals and behavior of white men, who have traditionally dominated the leadership ranks. As the workforce becomes more diverse, however, concepts of leadership will need to be redefined to take into account differences in leadership style in the many groups. Because women will account for the majority of new entrants into the workforce, and therefore into management, an examination of how their leadership styles differ will highlight the kinds of differences organizations can expect in the coming years.

In *The Nature of Managerial Work*, a study of male managers by Henry Mitzberg, the author summarizes his subjects as follows:

1. They worked at an unrelenting pace and took no breaks.
2. They viewed unscheduled tasks and encounters as unwelcome interruptions that caused discontinuity and fragmentation.
3. They spared little time for activities not directly related to their work.
4. They preferred face-to-face interactions to dealing with paperwork.
5. They maintained a complex network of relationships with people outside their organizations.

6. Immersed in the day-to-day need to keep the company going, they lacked time for reflection.
7. Their self-identity was tied almost completely to their jobs.
8. They had difficulty sharing information.[13]

Contrast this with the picture of women leaders described by Sally Helgesen in *The Female Advantage:*

1. "The women worked at a steady pace, but with small breaks scheduled in throughout the day."
2. "The women did not view unscheduled tasks and encounters as interruptions."
3. "The women made time for activities not directly related to their work."
4. "The women preferred live action encounters, but scheduled time to attend to mail."
5. "They maintained a complex network of relationships with people outside their organizations."
6. "They focused on the ecology of leadership rather than being overly absorbed in the day-to-day tasks of management."
7. "They saw their own identities as complex and multifaceted."
8. "The women scheduled in time for sharing information."[14]

As a group, the women managers exhibited more flexibility, a more multi-dimensional self-identity, and a greater ability to share than did the male managers. These traits are in sync with the needs and goals of the newly diverse workforce of the 1990s and beyond. In *Megatrends 2000*, John Naisbitt and Patricia Aburdene characterize the new leadership that is emerging as nurturing, noncoercive, and nonhierarchical. According to Naisbitt and Aburdene, "The female manager is a natural for this, and will not be a 'manager' in the old sense, but a leader by power of example. To be a leader in business today, it is no longer an advantage to have been socialized as a male. Women may have an advantage over men who will have to unlearn old authoritarian behaviors."[15]

The change in leadership style that has been precipitated by changes in the workforce has required organizations to become more sensitive to employee concerns such as family leave, day care and elder care, and discrimination on the job. In effect, it has helped humanize the workplace. This humanization is leading to organizationwide changes that can reduce turnover, enhance recruitment strategies, and position an organization as the employer of choice for the diminishing pool of qualified workers.

Becoming the Employer of Choice

The term *employer of choice* was coined in the late 1980s at about the same time that studies began to predict future labor shortages. The term recognizes that during periods characterized by a low supply of labor, companies tend to increase salary and benefit packages to competitive levels and it becomes harder to distinguish among companies based on compensation criteria alone. To become an employer of choice, an organization must create an overall work environment that appeals to employees in a seller's market. In the 1990s and beyond, employers of choice will adapt the work environment to accommodate and value workforce diversity. For example, to become an employer of choice, Lotus was one of the first organizations to change its benefit policies to cover "significant others," regardless of sexual orientation, in addition to legal spouses. This enhanced Lotus's ability to recruit applicants who have nontraditional family relationships.

Becoming an employer of choice necessitates examining the existing organizational culture (as discussed in chapter 3). The organization's culture affects virtually every aspect of life in the organization, from how and why people are hired and move through the organization to whether employees dining in the cafeteria tend to remove their plates from the tray before eating.

According to the authors of *The Feminization of America*, "The better a culture functions, the less awareness its members have of its power over them, because much of [that power] is unconscious [and] its dictates operate through the individual psyche. Culture is identified by what people say and do, the objects they invent, the symbols with which they present and interpret themselves, [and] the social relationships provided for and prohibited."[16] Assessment and adjustment of organizational culture to become an employer of choice not only helps retain workers, it enhances an organization's ability to recruit new workers. However, in addition to an appropriate corporate culture, to recruit effectively in a seller's market of increasingly diverse workers, organizations must develop new and effective approaches to recruitment.

Innovative Approaches to Employee Recruitment

With the coming increase in jobs and shortage of qualified workers, health care organizations must develop innovative approaches to recruitment; they can no longer rely on classified advertisements in local or national papers, word of mouth, and walk-in applicants. According to a survey by the American Hospital Association in 1989, labor shortages forced 25 percent of responding hospitals to cut services; in addition, 15 percent closed beds or units, and almost 13 percent sent patients to other hospitals.[17] The respondents reported shortages of physical therapists, occupational therapists, certified nurse anesthetists, clinical perfusionists, speech pathologists, respiratory therapists, and pharmacists. Many of these jobs have been identified by the Bureau of Labor Statistics (BLS) and various studies as high-growth areas for the future.

This chapter has already discussed the importance of reducing employee turnover in health care organizations, and earlier chapters have touched on some innovative recruitment techniques that were used to cope with the shortage of nurses in the 1980s. Even more creative strategies will be needed to cope with labor shortages in the future. Health care must now look at recruiting from a marketing perspective.

Many of the jobs that are projected to have the greatest growth are already experiencing high vacancy rates, and the pool of qualified applicants is not growing. For example, the U.S. Department of Labor projects a 57 percent increase in jobs for physician assistants by the year 2000. Today, newly graduated physician assistants receive an average of seven job offers, according to a recent study.[18] Yet, despite widespread unemployment in the United States, interest in health care careers appears to be waning at a time when opportunities are the greatest.

To what can this apparent lack of interest be attributed? Part of the problem may be a general lack of information about the wide range of careers in health care. One need not qualify for medical school or nursing school to have a career in health care. Health care institutions that are on the leading edge of recruitment are reaching out to secondary and even elementary schools to familiarize students early on with the wide variety of careers in health care and the broad range of skills and training they require. Examples of these outreach efforts include health care career days for grade school students and health care job fairs for high school students.

Other innovative recruitment strategies include using contract or temporary workers and offering prospective employees flexible scheduling and on-call pool staffing. Health care organizations have also stepped up their efforts to recruit qualified workers from other countries.

Case Study

The following case study shows how a group of hospitals in the Twin Cities of Minneapolis and St. Paul, Minnesota, developed an innovative strategy and action plan to deal with a labor shortage of crisis proportions.

In 1989, health care organizations in the Twin Cities were experiencing problems common to many health care organizations in the United States—a shortage of nurses and shrinking enrollments in nursing schools. A 1989 study by the Minnesota Department of Health identified personnel shortages in 14 health occupations and pinpointed several causes:

- There were fewer first-time entrants to the workforce than in previous years. Those entering were choosing careers in engineering, computer science, law, and tool and die making over health care.
- The local workforce was becoming more diverse. To attract people to health care careers, it was necessary to develop an understanding of the needs and demands of new populations.
- Recent observations at career day programs in Minnesota high schools suggested that student interest in health care careers was declining, just as a

greater variety of careers was becoming available. For example, at career days, there were no requests for information about careers as radiologic technologists, respiratory therapists, medical records technicians, pediatric nurse practitioners, or many other health care careers. One high school counselor reported that in the past five years no one in her school had requested information on any health care career. Visibility clearly was a major problem.[19]

To solve the nursing crisis, Health Employers Inc. (HEI), the Minnesota Association of Colleges of Nursing, the Minnesota Community College System, and the Coalition on Nursing decided to pool their efforts and resources by forming a consortium. Health Employers Inc. is a nonprofit association comprised of Minnesota hospitals that originally joined together to negotiate labor contracts. In this effort the HEI's role was expanded to include not only negotiations and labor relations but also human resource forecasting, data analysis, recruitment and retention information, and labor education and training. Another partner in the consortium, the Minnesota Association of Colleges of Nursing, is a nonprofit organization representing the 14 baccalaureate nursing programs in Minnesota. The third partner, the Coalition on Nursing, was established in 1989 as a joint venture between hospital administrators and various organizations representing sectors of the nursing profession. The fourth partner, the Community College System, includes the 18 two-year public colleges in Minnesota.

The consortium determined that in order to solve the labor crisis, three areas needed immediate attention: (1) the nursing shortage had reached critical proportions for hospitals, and the consortium recognized that new approaches were needed to solve the problem; (2) enrollment in Minnesota's nursing schools was continuing to decline, nursing schools were closing, and colleges were dropping nursing programs; and (3) students were not aware of the wide range of opportunities in nursing. (They perceived nursing as a demanding career that had long hours and low pay. Nursing programs also had a high dropout rate.)

After extensive research, several key findings emerged:

- Statewide, vacancy rates for registered nurses in hospitals were averaging 10 percent, and the shortage was affecting both metropolitan and rural hospitals, although rural hospitals were harder hit.
- The traditional source of new entrants to the nursing profession, women aged 18 to 34, was not adequate to meet the growing demand. Efforts to attract nontraditional recruits (that is, men and workers making midcareer changes) were showing signs of success, however.
- There were very few unemployed registered nurses who were qualified or who wished to return to nursing. Therefore, hospitals needed to strive to retain current nursing employees.
- Current nursing employees expressed dissatisfaction with their work environment. Hospitals therefore needed to restructure to provide nurses with

increased career opportunities and a greater voice in the organization and delivery of health care.
• Both the health care delivery system and the nursing profession were undergoing extensive transformation. Therefore, the roles and responsibilities of nursing needed to be redefined to match the new environment.

The consortium made 24 recommendations, including the establishment of the Higher Education Research Foundation (HERF), to address these issues. However, the consortium was still faced with the problem of ensuring a pool of future nurses. The six community colleges in the Twin Cities metropolitan area were the major providers of professional nurses. At that time, they admitted approximately 570 students per year from associate degree professional nursing programs, but the programs had a high attrition rate and were not graduating enough nurses to meet the staffing needs of area hospitals. Clearly, enrollments needed to be increased and attrition rates needed to be reduced. (This is the same problem of recruitment and retention faced by health care organizations in general.)

To solve the problem, the Minnesota Community College System and the HEI established a joint financial arrangement to increase the number of slots in nursing classes to 780 over the next two years. In addition, the 20 HEI hospitals established scholarships to be awarded to individual nursing students. "We are very enthusiastic about it," said Clarence Harris, vice-president for human resources at Abbott-Northwestern Hospital in Minneapolis, one of the members of the HEI. "It is the type of collaborative effort which will guarantee that the health care industry gets the type of people it needs while at the same time guaranteeing that students will have jobs."[20] The HEI also worked with its 20 member hospitals to ensure that nursing salaries were made more competitive with other professions and that work schedules were made more flexible.

In making plans for the future, the consortium took into account nursing executives' requests for more nurses with baccalaureate degrees. In a 1987 survey by the American Hospital Association, 55 percent of responding nursing executives reported that they wanted the majority of their staff nurses to have baccalaureate degrees.[21] To address this growing demand, the HEI and Minnesota's four-year nursing programs joined forces to increase the number of registered nurses with baccalaureate degrees. Health Employers Inc. hospitals made scholarship money available to qualified colleges and universities to award to qualified nursing students. Through its collaboration with the nursing programs, the HEI devised a program to provide 8 to 10 applicants for each vacant nursing position.

Members of the HEI also recognized that a recruiting crisis existed for medical laboratory technicians, radiologic technicians, respiratory therapists, and physical therapists. In response, the organization joined with educational institutions in programs similar to their efforts in nursing to encourage and enable people to prepare for careers in those fields.

The strategies and actions described in this case study go beyond such traditional methods of dealing with health care shortages as flexible scheduling, staffing studies, advanced skill training, cross-training, and internal promotions. The result is the development of long-term solutions by increasing the supply of qualified workers and creating ongoing interest in pursuing health care careers.[22]

Exploring Nontraditional Sources of Labor

In addition to expanding interest in health care occupations, long-term solutions to labor shortages may be found by exploring nontraditional sources of applicants. During labor shortages, organizations become more open to recruiting nontraditional applicants. This strategy meshes well with changing workforce demographics, which also have made organizations, particularly in health care, consider nontraditional sources of labor. (Such nontraditional groups are discussed in chapter 1.) However, nontraditional sources of labor may bring with them new challenges for employers. Some nontraditional sources of labor and the challenges they may present are explored briefly in the subsections that follow.

Minority Youth

The high rates of unemployment among African-American and Hispanic youth and the high interest in this population in stable, decent-paying, long-term employment with opportunities for advancement make this group a highly viable source of workers for health care organizations. However, because many of these young people have never held steady jobs or had steadily employed role models, employers may need to supplement training in job skills with training in the fundamentals of functioning in the world of work. Taking the time and effort to provide such training when needed will help ensure a steady supply of young workers to fill future employment needs. Recruitment programs can be set up through neighborhood centers, minority advocacy groups, and local high schools.

Older Workers

As the number of workers under age 40 declines, many organizations are turning to older workers to fill openings. Fears that older workers may be resistant to change or unable to master new technologies have proved to be largely unfounded. In fact, such workers make valuable contributions. Television campaigns, newspaper advertisements, and local senior organizations are effective recruitment channels for older workers.

Differently Abled Workers

As discussed in chapter 2, the enactment in July 1991 of the Americans with Disabilities Act (ADA) provided a silver lining in the cloud of workforce shortages.

Although differently abled workers may require some adjustment of facilities and procedures, the cost involved is usually less than expected. Furthermore, the ADA requires many organizations to make adjustments in any case to accommodate disabled patrons and members of the general public. The fact that such changes open the workplace to differently abled workers is value added.

Aliens

In 1993, aliens represented approximately 7 percent of new employees in the workforce; by the year 2000, however, they will comprise 21 percent, or more than one-fifth of new entrants. By adapting policies, practices, attitudes, and behaviors to accept and attract alien workers, organizations can begin right away to tap this increasingly important source of workers.

Women

Women are already a major component in the labor pool. In the years to come they will play an increasingly important role. Organizations will need to continue to make progress—willingly or not—in providing opportunities for advancement to women and in addressing women's concerns in the workplace.

Even the nontraditional labor resources may not be adequate to provide skilled, qualified workers quickly enough to meet the needs of health care organizations. Increasing the skills of current workers is an option that many health care organizations are exploring.

Development of Multiskilled Practitioners

Encouraging current employees to develop additional skills—that is, to become *multiskilled*—is becoming an increasingly popular method of alleviating shortages, at least temporarily. A multiskilled health practitioner, as opposed to a single-skilled specialist, is "a person who has been cross-trained to provide more than one function, often in more than one discipline. These combined functions can be found in a broad spectrum of health-related jobs ranging in complexity from the nonprofessional to the professional level, including both clinical and management functions. The additional functions added to the original health care worker's job may be of a higher, lower, or parallel level."[23] An innovative approach to the use of multiskilled practitioners taken by Methodist Hospital of Indiana (in Indianapolis) provides an interesting example of how effective such workers can be.

ADD-A-COMP (Add-a-Competency) is Methodist Hospital of Indiana's educational program designed to develop multiskilled health care professionals. Through the program, workers with training and experience in specific areas of health care (such as technologists, therapists, nurses, medical assistants, and emergency medical service personnel) apply for admission into one or more of the program's modules to acquire additional skills in a new or related area. The following three aspects of the ADD-A-COMP program make it especially notable:

- *Directed, self-learning packets:* These packets are used as an alternative to traditional classroom-based instruction. This approach has allowed the hospital to implement and expand the ADD-A-COMP program without having to add full-time employees. All packets correlate theoretical learning with clinical instruction, assess knowledge and competencies, and guide participants through a step-by-step learning process.
- *Reduced training time:* The use of learning packets with condensed, intensive clinical experience allows students to be trained in a relatively short period of time, reducing the amount of time they must be away from the work site.
- *Maximum flexibility in skill combinations:* The program offers maximum flexibility in creating individualized skill combinations.

A report on the success of Methodist Hospital's ADD-A-COMP program made the following recommendations to organizations considering the establishment of a multiskilled practitioner program:

1. Learn as much as possible about the multiskilled concept before making the commitment to set up the program.
2. Recognize that embarking upon a paradigm shift will require people to see things in new and different ways.
3. Start building support for the program during its infancy. Continue building support and soliciting input throughout the project.
4. Conduct an informal needs assessment to identify current problems and determine the goals of the multiskilled practitioner program. Useful questions include: What skills need to be combined? Who has the time and aptitude to learn more and perform in more than one area?
5. Assess the environment and climate for change. Determine what obstacles are there and how can they be overcome.
6. Form a committee that includes representatives from administration, education, clinical services, human resources, and employee groups that are likely to be affected.
7. Select an educational approach that is tailored to the institution's environment.
8. Obtain benchmark statistics for goals for the multiskilled practitioner program from other organizations with similar programs.
9. Carefully select the first group to be cross-trained and position it for success.
10. Develop an ongoing assessment and evaluation process.[24]

Although the use of multiskilled practitioners is not a new concept, new and innovative applications such as this can help alleviate labor shortages. To cite some examples, historically very specialized jobs can be transformed so that a radiographer can perform basic laboratory procedures, a respiratory therapist can obtain EKGs, and a nurse can conduct obstetrical sonography examinations. In addition, multiskilled practitioner programs, which are an area of employee development and enhance employees' skills and abilities as well as their self-esteem, can aid in retaining and attracting good workers.

Multiskilled practitioner programs that enhance workers' skills is one aspect of coping with the coming shortage of qualified workers. Another approach is to attempt to supply would-be workers with the necessary skills.

The Skills Gap

Health care organizations not only face numerical shortages of workers, they also must cope with a shortage of applicants with the requisite skills to fill the jobs being created. Health care jobs require increasingly higher levels of education and special credentials or certifications, but the skills of the labor force have not kept pace. Increasingly, organizations are finding that potential applicants lack even basic literacy skills, making it harder for employers to provide on-the-job training for unskilled workers.

Redefining Basic Training

Rage and indignation swept through the United States in 1992 when Yoshio Sakurauchi, speaker of the lower house of the Japanese parliament, reportedly said that about 30 percent of U.S. workers are illiterate and insinuated that the U.S. workforce is lazy and uneducated. Unfortunately, so far as illiteracy is concerned, Sakurauchi was right. According to a well-researched study entitled *Closing the Literacy Gap in American Business*, 30 percent of unskilled workers, 29 percent of semiskilled workers, and 11 percent of managerial, professional, and technical employees are functionally illiterate.[25] To further complicate matters, a survey of 3,400 adults over the age of 20 by the U.S. Census Bureau and the U.S. Department of Education revealed that one in eight (about 13 percent) could not read.[26] Illiteracy is "the broken cog in the American economic machine" and is a serious threat to U.S. economic survival in a global economy.[27] Employers are beginning to grapple with the problem of illiteracy, which is estimated to rob the economy of $140 to $300 billion per year in productivity.[28]

The authors of *Closing the Literacy Gap in American Business* present a number of examples that highlight the problem of illiteracy in the U.S. workforce. For example:

• The Midwest-based Campbell-Mithun-Esty Advertising reported that only 1 applicant in 11 met minimum literacy standards for mail-clerk jobs.

- A New York-based insurance company estimated that 70 percent of dictated correspondence must be redone at least once because of human error.
- Swift Textiles of Columbus, Georgia, installed computerized looms that many of its workers simply could not operate because they lacked the basic reading and simple math skills necessary.[29]

The authors suggest that the gap between skills and job demands is widening because "jobs in the service, information and manufacturing sectors continue to grow more complex, while the majority of our schools are structured to support the agrarian and grunt-labor/basic skills jobs of the pre-1960's."[30]

Functional illiteracy affects more than the ability to read and write; it also reflects the ability to process information and apply it to specific tasks. Most experts would agree that a person must be able to process information and apply it to tasks at no lower than a sixth-grade level to be considered functionally literate. But according to a study by the U.S. Departments of Education and Labor, "Some 75% of the workforce in the year 2000 is on the job now, and one in eight of these workers reads below the 6th grade level. Today, workers need to be able to read materials written between the 9th and 12th grade level. Jobs in the future will require even greater skills."[31]

In an effort to bridge the skills gap, corporate training programs have become (and are likely to remain) big business involving billions of dollars. The health care field has been hit with labor shortages in numerous areas, ranging from nursing to housekeeping, security, and data processing. In the past, training efforts in health care organizations have been skill based and focused on mastering new techniques and technologies. The large number of functionally illiterate workers has forced organizations to consider offering programs that will combat illiteracy and offer basic remedial training.

Case Study: Greater Southeast Healthcare System

The Greater Southeast Healthcare System in Washington, DC, was one of the first health care organizations to aggressively address both the problem of illiteracy and the need to upgrade employees' skills. It has developed programs aimed at employees as well as high school and college students. The programs for students introduce them to health care careers through education, training, and work experience. To ensure that entry-level workers from such programs have the requisite literacy skills, Greater Southeast formed a joint venture with the District of Columbia School System. Students who are not college bound can participate in work–study programs at Greater Southeast Community Hospital. Through its Stay in School Program, which targets high school seniors, participants work afternoons for nine months in different hospital departments, assisting in clerical and administrative tasks and attending classes in basic workplace skills.

Another program offered by Greater Southeast Community Hospital is the Skills for Effectiveness and Success (SES) program, which helps employees acquire basic skills. The goals of SES are to:

- Improve the work performance of entry-level employees
- Provide employees with the skills they need to advance their careers, resulting in decreased frustration and increased retention, as well as greater numbers of qualified internal candidates for skilled positions within the system
- Serve the community by providing training in basic skills to people who have been rejected for jobs at Greater Southeast.

The curriculum, which was determined by the results of a needs-assessment study, teaches:

- Techniques for learning, changing, and adapting in a work environment
- Basic reading, writing, and computation skills
- Communication skills
- Creative thinking and problem-solving skills
- Personal management skills, such as time management
- Group effectiveness skills, including interpersonal, conflict resolution, and teamwork skills
- Organizational effectiveness and leadership skills

Greater Southeast Community Hospital presently requires all new employees to have at least a high school diploma. For those few current employees who lack a high school diploma or general educational development (GED) certificate, Greater Southeast established an on-site GED class that is available to employees and members of the community. This innovative approach will help provide a pool of workers ready to pursue the additional training needed to qualify for hard-to-fill positions in health care.

Another initiative undertaken by Greater Southeast is to provide tuition assistance to students at the University of the District of Columbia who are enrolled in programs in nursing, respiratory therapy, and radiologic technology. Every academic year, the hospital provides as many as 12 students with up to two years' tuition support. In exchange, the students agree to work at Greater Southeast after graduation, although there is no specific length of service required.

Greater Southeast also uses two additional educational programs to help its employees develop the skills needed to advance in today's health care positions. These are the Basic Academic Skills for Employment (BASE) program and the Training Alternatives Program (TAP). The BASE program, a computer-directed study program available from Educational Technologies, Inc., helps employees master the academic skills required by specific jobs, allowing them to proceed at their own pace.[32] The program includes 254 lessons, 39 quizzes, and 41 tests in the following 15 subject areas:

- Reading
  - Reading comprehension
  - Vocabulary
  - Work knowledge
- Language
  - Grammar and usage
  - Spelling
  - Punctuation
  - Capitalization
- Mathematics
  - Computation
  - Concepts
  - Word problems
  - Introduction to algebra and geometry
- Writing
  - Language mechanics
  - Language usage
  - Sentences
  - Paragraphs

The Training Alternatives Program (TAP) is another self-directed study program. Developed by the human resources staff of Greater Southeast Community Hospital, TAP uses books, video cassettes, and audio cassettes.[33] Topics include stress management, communications, conflict resolution, problem solving, public speaking, leadership, and supervisory and management skills, as well as opportunities to continue career development.

Greater Southeast Community Hospital is active in dealing with workforce shortages and educational issues on a national level through its participation in the Secretary's Commission on Achieving Necessary Skills (SCANS). The commission was established by the Secretaries of Labor and Education and seeks to identify the skills needed to survive in the workplace and techniques for effectively measuring skill levels. It is committed to improving the school-to-work transition for millions of young people entering the job market. Greater Southeast's innovative and effective multilevel workforce educational program will enable it to bridge the skills gap and alleviate the shortage of skilled workers that faces the health care community.[34]

Developing a Workforce Educational Program

The Greater Southeast Community Hospital's multilevel program is an excellent example of an effective workforce educational program. However, organizations are not rushing to follow in the footsteps of Greater Southeast and other pioneers. A 1990 study by the Commission on the Skills of the American Workforce found that fewer than 10 percent of businesses plan to increase output by reorganization or growth that requires better-educated employees. Only 15 percent worry about the present and future shortage of skilled workers. Fewer than 30 percent are planning any special programs for aliens, women, and minorities, who will make up 85 percent of the new entrants into the workforce by the year 2000. However, the recent estimate that U.S. productivity has declined by $300 billion annually because of ill-educated workers is getting attention from businesses.[35]

The educational shortcomings of the American workforce have been a factor in the decisions of many U.S. firms to move overseas. They also have increased the foreign acquisition of American business. The number of corporate bankruptcies is up, in part because there are too few adequately educated workers to help companies compete successfully in the increasingly aggressive world marketplace.[36]

Although establishing a workforce educational program is costly in terms of both economic and human resources, educational expenses can easily be justified. An effective workforce educational program can:

- Decrease hiring costs
- Decrease training costs
- Decrease the number of accidents on the job
- Increase operational efficiencies by reducing errors, reducing the time supervisors spend answering basic questions, increasing production levels, improving employees' troubleshooting abilities, increasing employees' interest in job advancement, and increasing employees' problem-solving skills[37]

The Future Labor Shortage

The shortage of qualified workers is already creating problems for health care organizations and U.S. businesses in general. Not only is there a shortage of workers, the available labor pool is sadly lacking in basic skills. The public school system is often unable to provide workers with the skills needed to function effectively in the workplace. For example, nearly 60 percent of Chicago public high schools ranked in the bottom 1 percent of the nation on the ACT college entrance exam in 1991.[38]

It seems obvious that America needs a second educational revolution similar to the one that took place during the years 1890 to 1914 that established the present public school system. But such revolutions cannot occur overnight. And employers need to develop strategies to face present and future shortages of workers. Health care organizations in particular must develop strategies that will enable them to retain current workers, attract new workers, and ensure that all workers have the skills needed to do their jobs. The Greater Southeast Healthcare System, the HEI, and Methodist Hospital of Indiana provide blueprints for retaining, recruiting, and training workers for the demanding health care workplace of the present and the future.

References

1. Ulschak, F. L., and SnowAntle, S. M. *Managing Employee Turnover.* Chicago: American Hospital Publishing, 1992, pp. 1–16.

2. Ulschak and SnowAntle, pp. 20–22.

3. Deutschman, A. What 25 year-olds want. *Fortune,* Aug. 27, 1990, p. 47.

4. Ulschak and SnowAntle, pp. 133–34.

5. The Hay Group. *Aligning New Employee Attitudes and Values to Improve Productivity, Cost, and Quality.* New York City: The Hay Group, 1989.

6. Towers Perrin, Hudson Institute. *Workforce 2000, Competing in a Seller's Market: Is Corporate America Prepared?* New York City: Towers Perrin, 1991.

7. Ulschak and SnowAntle, p. 21.

8. Whyte, W. H. The sun sets on the silent generation. *New York Times,* Aug. 4, 1991.

9. The Kiplinger Washington Editors. *The New American Boom.* Washington, DC: Kiplinger, 1986.

10. Managing the changing workforce. *Chicago Tribune,* October 20, 1990.

11. Kochman, T. *Black and White, Styles in Conflict.* Chicago: University of Chicago Press, 1981. See especially chapter 2, "Classroom Modalities."

12. Loden, M., and Rosener, J. *Workforce America.* Homewood, IL: Business One-Irwin, 1991.

13. Mitzberg, H. *The Nature of Managerial Work.* New York City: Harper & Row, 1973.

14. Helgesen, S. *The Female Advantage.* New York City: Doubleday Currency, 1990, pp. 10–27.

15. Naisbitt, J., and Aburdene, P. *Megatrends 2000.* New York City: William Morrow, 1990.

16. Lenz and Myerhoff. *The Feminization of America.* New York City: St. Martin's, 1985.

17. American Hospital Association, quoted in McGee, L. Innovative labor shortage solutions. *Personnel Administrator,* Dec. 1989, p. 57.

18. *Chicago Tribune,* April 18, 1993, Section 8, p. 1.

19. Trautman, D. Healthcare personnel shortages: reversing the trend. *The Strategist,* [Metropolitan Council, St. Paul, MN] 1990, pp. A-1–A-3.

20. Harris, C. Interview with author. Minneapolis, Aug. 3, 1992.

21. American Hospital Association. *Report of the Hospital Nursing Personnel Survey.* Chicago: AHA, 1987.

22. Harris, C. Interview with author.

23. What are multiskilled health practitioners? *Newsletter of the National Multiskilled Health Practitioner Clearinghouse,* [University of Alabama, Birmingham] 1988.

24. Hospital Research and Educational Trust. *The ADD-A-COMP Program: Multiskilled Practitioner Education at Methodist Hospital of Indiana, Inc.* Chicago: HRET, 1992.

25. Gordon, E., Ponticell, J., and Morgan, R. *Closing the Literacy Gap in American Business.* New York City: Quorum Books, 1991, p. 1.

26. U.S. Census Bureau and U.S. Department of Education, quoted in Gordon and others, p. 1.

27. Gordon and others, chapter 1.

28. U.S. Department of Commerce, quoted in *Chicago Tribune*, August 5, 1988, Section 3, p. 3.

29. Gordon and others, p. 3.

30. Gordon and others, p. 5.

31. U.S. Departments of Education and Labor.

32. The telephone number for Educational Technologies, Inc., is (609) 882-2668.

33. Information about the Training Alternative Program can be obtained from the human resources staff of Greater Southeast Community Hospital, Washington, DC, at (202) 574-6780.

34. Kurtz, J. A., Taylor, P., and Odyniec, B. Interview with author. Washington, DC, August 26, 1992.

35. Commission on the Skills of the American Workforce, quoted in Gordon and others, p. 120.

36. Gordon and others, chapter 8.

37. Gordon and others, chapter 8.

38. City's grades keep sliding. *Chicago Sun-Times*, Nov. 30, 1992, p. 1.

Chapter Seven

Managing Diversity in the Volunteer Workforce

Former president George Bush referred to volunteers as "a thousand points of light." According to a 1989 survey conducted by the Gallup Organization for the Independent Section, however, about 98 million American adults did volunteer work in 1989.[1] For health care organizations plagued by rising costs and severe staff shortages, volunteers provide hours of dedicated labor and in many cases are crucial to the organizations' provision of high-quality care and even their viability. Without volunteers, hospitals would need to hire more paid employees. Assuming that such employees could be found—and, as has been discussed in earlier chapters, qualified health care workers are likely to remain in short supply—adding paid staff would further tax the financial resources of many health care organizations and drive costs up even higher.

Earlier chapters have discussed how the makeup of the overall population of the United States has changed and will continue to change in the decades to come. The U.S. population has aged and become increasingly diverse ethnically and culturally. In addition, new laws, technological advances, and changing mores have helped differently abled people to become more active and visible participants in everyday life. This newly diverse general population makes up the pool from which volunteers are drawn. Health care organizations can help alleviate drastic shortages of personnel and money by learning how to effectively recruit, train, and retain a culturally diverse corps of volunteers. This chapter will outline strategies for managing diversity in the increasingly crucial volunteer workforce.

The Tradition of Volunteerism in America

Americans like to think of themselves as a nation of volunteers. They join teams, social and service clubs, civic groups, political parties, parent–teacher associations, and religious organizations. And, as part of these affiliations, Americans provide volunteer services to the community. In a 1981 speech before the National Alliance of Business, former president Ronald Reagan used a passage from the classic Gary Cooper movie *Mr. Deeds Goes to Town* to explain the American concept of volunteerism:

From what I see, there will always be leaders and always be followers. It's like the road out in front of my house. It's on a steep hill. And every day I watch the cars climbing up. Some go lickety-split up that hill on high—some have to shift into second—and some sputter and shake and slip back to the bottom again. Same cars—same gasoline—yet some make it and some don't. And I say the fellow who can make the hill on high should stop once in a while and help those who can't.[2]

Many Americans seem to share Mr. Deeds's view and are willing to help those in need.

Even in a pressure-cooker world, where balancing the demands of family, work, and economic survival is a challenge, many people still choose to volunteer. Understanding what motivates them can help health care organizations to plan their recruitment and training programs to attract a committed volunteer workforce.

In *The Good Heart Book*, author David Driver summarizes the key reasons that lead people to volunteer:[3]

- *To find fulfillment:* Helping people in need gives volunteers a sense of purpose; by doing something worthwhile, volunteers build self-respect. Baby boomers seem to be especially interested in giving something back to the society that has given so much to them. Volunteering helps them feel that they are part of the solution to society's problems, that they are making a difference.
- *To develop new skills:* Volunteering gives people an opportunity to develop new skills. Some organizations, such as the American Red Cross, do not differentiate between paid staff and volunteer staff in making assignments. Volunteers in such organizations are not relegated to occupying figurehead roles on advisory boards or performing menial tasks; they receive the necessary training to allow them to work at all levels and departments of the organization. In the process, they have the opportunity to learn and practice new skills.
- *To make new friends:* Through volunteering, people meet and work with others. Often volunteers can broaden their horizons by interacting with people from different neighborhoods, cultures, socioeconomic groups, and ethnic groups and with people with different physical and mental abilities. In the process, volunteers often form lasting friendships.
- *To develop new outlooks:* Volunteering often provides people with firsthand knowledge about, and new perspectives on, a wide range of health and social issues such as child abuse, the AIDS epidemic, and inadequate access to medical care, to name three.
- *To enhance one's career:* Volunteering often provides opportunities to take on responsibilities that are not readily available in one's day-to-day work life. For example, serving as an officer or committee chair in a volunteer organization

can provide valuable experience in handling budgets, raising funds, speaking in public, and planning and running an organization. In addition, leaders (or other participants) of volunteer groups often enjoy high visibility in the community and can develop contacts with local civic and business leaders who might otherwise have been inaccessible to them. Volunteering also offers the opportunity to explore new careers without leaving one's current field. For example, a teacher interested in becoming a speech therapist could volunteer in the speech pathology department of a health care facility to gain first-hand knowledge of the field before switching careers.

As the preceding summary of reasons for volunteering indicates, volunteers can gain much more than a good feeling from their experience. Health care organizations should certainly emphasize these benefits in their recruiting efforts. In addition, they must apply recruiting methods similar to the ones they use to recruit and retain paid employees, such as maximizing job satisfaction and applying the new golden rule of diversity ("Do unto others as they would like you to do unto them").

The major difference between recruiting and retaining a volunteer workforce and recruiting and training a paid workforce is *incentives*. Directors of volunteer services and frontline supervisors of volunteers must manage and maintain a viable pool of volunteers without using traditional incentives and disincentives. For volunteers, there are no salaries, merit pay increases, traditional promotions and advancements, or reward systems. Thus, understanding the needs and motivations of volunteer workers is crucial for the success of many health care organizations. It is no exaggeration to say that the number and quality of the volunteer staff can make or break a hospital.

The Redefinition of the Volunteer Worker

As discussed earlier, a more diverse general population has led to a more diverse pool from which volunteers are drawn. Organizations that rely on volunteers, such as health care organizations, must expand and adjust their definitions of who volunteer workers are to include many nontraditional groups.

According to the Current Population Survey (CPS) conducted in May 1989, one in every five Americans does some volunteer work for religious groups, schools, or other organizations.[4] Who are these volunteers? Where and for whom do they volunteer, and how much time do they spend in these unpaid activities? The CPS survey found that about 38 million people—about 20 percent of the civilian population aged 16 and over—did volunteer work. The Gallup Poll mentioned earlier used a different methodology and arrived at an even higher number. It found that over 54 percent of Americans aged 18 and over did volunteer work.[5] Both estimates are impressively high.

A 1991 study reported in *The Monthly Labor Review* found that volunteerism varies with demographic and economic characteristics. Persons aged

35 to 44 were more likely than those who were younger or older to have done some volunteer work. Whites were much more likely than African-Americans or Hispanics to report that they had done volunteer work. College graduates were more likely than those with less schooling to have served as volunteers.[6] (See table 7-1.) The study also found that volunteers were more likely to work for religious organizations than for any other type of organization and that equal proportions of men and women reported working for religious organizations as their primary volunteer activity. Secondary volunteer activities differed along gender lines: men were more likely to volunteer for work in civic, political, sports, or recreational organizations, whereas women were more likely to volunteer for work in educational or health care organizations. The average amount of time spent volunteering was less than five hours per week.[7]

These 1991 numbers show a reliance on traditional sources of volunteer labor—whites, women, and college graduates. However, as an increasingly diverse and nontraditional population becomes the main source of volunteers, organizations will be forced to expand their concepts of who volunteers are and discover ways to tap nontraditional sources. This will be especially true for health care organizations, which have traditionally depended on women as volunteers. As the next section discusses, however, women are and will continue to be less available as volunteers today and in the future than they were in the past.

Shifting Away from Reliance on Female Volunteers

The strong tradition of volunteerism among American women is rooted in the nineteenth century, when the United States moved from an agrarian economy to an industrial one. Men were the main beneficiaries of the new system that offered wages for work in industry and manufacturing. Women were expected to perform the unpaid labor of running the home, caring for the family, and serving the community. Volunteer work was an acceptable way for women to utilize their skills and energy without intruding into the male domain of paid employment by taking jobs away from husbands or sons. Volunteering was considered to be especially appropriate for married women in that it did not conflict with their duties as wives and mothers. Women could arrange their volunteer schedules so that they were home in time to care for their children after school, do the housework, and prepare meals.[8]

When women entered the workforce in great numbers, whether by choice or by necessity, in the 1970s and 1980s, their participation in volunteer service changed drastically. As one scholar noted in a speech aptly titled "Crisis Time for the Non-Profits": "The two-wage-earner families will reduce substantially both the number of women volunteers and the number of hours which they will allocate for volunteer work. Inasmuch as the traditional and major source of volunteers has been women, the change will have a major impact."[9] The organizations that traditionally have relied on women to make up the majority of their volunteer corps, such as health care organizations, have been faced with

Table 7-1. Unpaid Volunteer Work in 1989

Characteristic	Both sexes		Men		Women	
	Volunteer workers	Volunteers as percent of population	Volunteer workers	Volunteers as percent of population	Volunteer workers	Volunteers as percent of population
Total	38,042	20.4	16,681	18.8	21,361	21.9
Age						
16 to 24 years old	3,966	12.3	1,814	11.4	2,152	13.1
16 to 19	1,902	13.4	879	12.3	1,023	14.4
20 to 24	2,064	11.4	935	10.6	1,129	12.1
25 to 34 years old	8,680	20.2	3,678	17.4	5,002	23.0
35 to 44 years old	10,337	28.9	4,683	26.8	5,655	30.9
45 to 54 years old	5,670	23.0	2,601	21.8	3,069	24.1
55 to 64 years old	4,455	20.8	1,987	19.8	2,468	21.8
65 years old and over	4,934	16.9	1,917	15.8	3,016	17.7
Race and Hispanic origin						
White	34,823	21.9	15,273	20.0	19,550	23.6
Black	2,505	11.9	1,082	11.5	1,423	12.3
Hispanic origin	1,289	9.4	587	8.6	702	10.1
Marital status						
Never married	6,327	13.7	3,102	12.4	3,225	15.3
Married, spouse present	26,344	24.8	12,131	22.8	14,213	26.9
Married, spouse absent	765	13.2	275	12.1	489	14.0
Divorced	2,510	17.3	908	15.3	1,602	18.6
Widowed	2,096	15.3	266	11.9	1,831	16.0
Years of school completed by persons 25 years old and over						
0 to 11 years	2,939	8.3	1,295	7.8	1,644	8.8
12 years only	11,105	18.8	4,120	16.0	6,985	20.9
13 to 15 years	7,572	28.1	3,042	24.0	4,531	31.6
16 years or more	12,459	38.4	6,410	36.0	6,049	41.4
Employment status						
In labor force	27,284	22.1	14,094	20.9	13,190	23.6
Employed	26,439	22.6	13,734	21.4	12,705	24.0
Full time	21,182	21.9	12,541	21.8	8,641	22.0
Part time	5,257	26.0	1,193	18.0	4,064	29.9
Unemployed	845	13.8	360	11.1	485	16.8
Not in labor force	10,758	17.1	2,587	12.2	8,171	19.6

Note: This table lists persons who performed unpaid volunteer work at some time during the year ended May 1989. Numbers of volunteer workers are in thousands.

Source: Monthly Labor Review, Feb. 1991, p. 18.

a reduction in the numbers of women volunteers as well as the numbers of hours they work. It is likely that this reduction is permanent. As has been noted in earlier chapters, predictions are that the percentage of women of working age who are actively involved in the workforce will continue to grow. Thus, it is especially important that hospitals and other health care organizations develop strategies to effectively recruit and manage volunteers from nontraditional sources.

Exploring Nontraditional Sources of Volunteer Labor

In order to maintain a viable volunteer labor pool, health care organizations must explore nontraditional sources of volunteers. A 1990 Gallup Poll identified four major groups of people who were willing to volunteer and were underrepresented in and underutilized by volunteer programs: African-Americans, Hispanics, persons with incomes of less than $20,000, and youths aged 18 to 24, especially young African-American males.[10]

Two other groups that should be added are differently abled and older persons. Differently abled people have the highest unemployment rate of any group and therefore are likely to have the time to volunteer and the interest to do so, making them a valuable and largely untapped resource. Older persons who have not been forced to remain in or return to the paid workforce by financial constraints are another group that is likely to have the time to volunteer and an interest in doing so.

Note that these groups are some of the same groups that are expected to make up a significant part of the paid workforce by the year 2000. As the labor shortages intensify and large U.S. businesses step up their efforts to recruit members of these groups for their paid workforce, health care organizations will need to develop increasingly innovative and effective volunteer recruitment strategies. Before effective recruitment strategies can be devised, however, organizations must become aware of barriers to volunteering that may confront potential volunteers from nontraditional groups.

Overcoming Barriers to Volunteer Work

People from diverse cultures and backgrounds, older people, and differently abled people are all potentially dedicated volunteers. However, unless health care organizations make special efforts to recognize and overcome a number of potential barriers, the barriers may prevent such people from volunteering. Those barriers can be classified by category as conceptual/linguistic, economic, physical, and time barriers.

Conceptual/Linguistic Barriers

An equivalent of the American concept of volunteering does not exist or is not easily expressed in some cultures or languages. The concept of recruiting people to volunteer in established institutions that have paid staff may also be absent in some cultures. Certain aspects of volunteering, such as working outside of one's own neighborhood or community, may be difficult for people from some cultures. And some cultures may consider it an embarrassment or a "loss of face" to have to turn to outside groups for assistance.

For example, in Hispanic culture it is traditional to keep problems, issues, and concerns inside the family. Mujeres Latinas en Accion (Latin Women in Action) is one of a few agencies dedicated to providing leadership training to Hispanic women in an effort to get them more involved in the community. "The idea that women need to do for themselves and take care of themselves is contrary to the pervasive cultural dynamic in which the woman is in the role of the helper," said Sylvia Puenta, board chair of Mujeres Latinas en Accion. "It's a stereotype, but it also is a cultural reality that the family comes first."[11]

Language barriers can also be a major problem whenever Hispanics or members of some other minorities volunteer outside their immediate communities (or even attempt to interact with city services, schools, and other institutions). The case study of Methodist Hospital presented later in this chapter describes how one hospital successfully overcame such cultural barriers to volunteering.

Economic Barriers

Often people who would like to volunteer cannot afford to do so. Transportation, care for children and other dependents, and even appropriate clothing may be too expensive.

Physical Barriers

Certain neighborhoods may be considered too difficult to get to or too dangerous by some potential volunteers. For example, many of the women in Mujeres Latinas cited fear of gangs as one of the tangible barriers to getting involved in their communities. Directors of volunteer services will need to identify creative, innovative approaches to combat these everyday problems. Potential volunteers who are afraid of physical harm could be provided with additional security when using parking facilities. In addition, car pooling or other special arrangements could be arranged for persons who may have difficulty with transportation to and from a volunteer site.

Time Barriers

As discussed earlier, the days of volunteer pools consisting primarily of women who were not part of the paid workforce are over. The hours that health care organizations need volunteers often coincide with the normal workday, which prevents members of the workforce from volunteering. The growth of both two-wage-earner and single-parent families has made time spent with families precious to today's workers, who may be reluctant to spend leisure hours away from home doing volunteer work. Opportunities to volunteer as a family unit—that is, to involve all family members in the volunteer effort—may be appealing to such people.

These barriers, although challenging, are far from insurmountable. The following case study describes how one hospital overcame a cultural barrier and created a successful volunteer program.

Case Study: How Methodist Hospital Reached Out to a Changing Community

Methodist Hospital is located in Arcadia, California, a city that, like the state of California itself, is rapidly becoming multiethnic. The Asian population in the San Gabriel Valley, where Arcadia is located, rose from 77,300 in 1980 to 180,000 in 1987. In a single decade (1980 to 1990), Arcadia's population changed from being almost all white to being 25 percent Chinese. In its effort to continue to serve its community, Methodist Hospital started to explore ways to reach out to the growing Chinese population. A number of cultural factors contributed to the fact that nationwide the Chinese have not been active volunteers in American health care organizations.[12]

The hospital soon realized that Chinese culture looks at illness and health very differently than does American culture. Chinese medicine teaches that to have good health one must be in a state of spiritual and physical harmony with nature. Illness is the result of disturbing the balance of nature in a precisely ordered universe. In ancient China, the best physicians were those who prevented illness, not those who cured it. Physicians who did not prevent illness and thus had to cure it were considered second-rate. Physicians were paid by patients who remained healthy; when patients became ill, not only did the payment stop, but physicians had to pay for the needed medicine.[13]

Many Chinese today prefer traditional Chinese medicine to Western medicine. Some aspects of Western medicine are extremely distasteful to the Chinese, such as diagnostic tests, especially those that require drawing blood. Many Chinese believe that the body cannot regenerate blood that is lost. They also believe that a good physician should be able to make a diagnosis simply by examining a person, and they do not react well to the sometimes painful diagnostic procedures common in Western medicine. In Chinese culture, one's body is not one's personal property but a gift from one's ancestors that must be properly cared for and maintained. Because of their deep respect for their bodies, Chinese people often refuse surgery, believing that it is better to die with their bodies intact. To sum up, a Western hospital is an alien place for many Chinese. Not only are the customs and practices strange to them, but the language barrier can add to feelings of helplessness. When hospitalized, Chinese patients rarely complain, and these seemingly exemplary patients often endure great fear and discomfort in silence.

In addition to the cultural differences in views toward illness and health, Methodist Hospital also found that the American concept of volunteerism was unfamiliar in Chinese culture, which values privacy and self-sufficiency. The Chinese community needed to be convinced of the need for services within the community and how Chinese residents could fill those needs through volunteering. Methodist developed an educational program to communicate the needs of the community and how volunteers from the community could meet those needs.

Methodist then found that its usual recruitment methods—volunteer fairs and promotional literature—were not successful in attracting Chinese volunteers. The hospital decided to seek the support of the leaders in the Chinese community, who became linchpins in the hospital's community outreach efforts. The community leaders recommended that the hospital try one-on-one recruitment. Magically, the barriers began to fall, and one-on-one recruitment became Methodist's most successful recruitment strategy within the Chinese community.

Once volunteers were recruited, Methodist set about creating projects that used those volunteers in outreach efforts in the community. Examples included health fairs to acquaint the Chinese community with the hospital's needs and show potential volunteers how important their services would be both to the hospital and to the community at large. Another project that has been very successful is the Chinese Information Line, through which Chinese volunteers provide callers with information about the hospital. Yet another highly successful project has been the junior volunteer program. Many Chinese adults who cannot or will not volunteer themselves encourage their children to volunteer both because it helps the children to assimilate into American society and because they are interested in having their children become physicians, nurses, and other health care professionals. These junior volunteers not only provide valuable services to the hospital, they are the link in the chain of future generations of volunteers in the Chinese community.

Methodist Hospital's Chinese volunteer program has become extremely successful. The hospital credits this success to several factors. First, it thoroughly researched the health care needs of the Chinese community. It reviewed hospital discharge data to identify the hospital services used most frequently by Chinese patients. It also contacted the intercultural committee of the Arcadia Chamber of Commerce and the Arcadia School District to learn what services the Chinese population wanted as well as to gain a better understanding of the traditional medical practices of the Chinese community.

Second, the hospital conferred with Asian employees, physicians, and outside cultural consultants to learn more about Chinese customs and attitudes about time, work ethics, medicine, and privacy. Armed with these data, the hospital developed a training program to sensitize employees to the needs of people from different cultures.

Third, the hospital built and solidified its relationships with leaders of the Chinese community.[14,15] Throughout the process, Methodist Hospital's experience shows the importance of careful research, creativity, open-mindedness, and adaptability in recruiting nontraditional volunteers.

The Training and Management of Culturally Diverse Volunteers

As Methodist Hospital discovered, the increasing diversity of the U.S. population is necessitating changes in how volunteers are recruited, retained, and managed. The volunteers of the 1990s and beyond may not share the long-standing American tradition of volunteer service and may need to overcome barriers to service that were not faced by the traditional pool of volunteers. In addition, because of grave labor shortages in the paid workforce, volunteer services will be facing competition from businesses offering paid employment. Thus, it will be more important than ever before that directors of volunteer services try to maximize volunteers' job satisfaction and feeling that they are making a valuable contribution to the organization. In other words, these directors must provide a sense of value to volunteers who seek more from the experience than a warm feeling inside from doing good. The following considerations, which are important in effectively managing any volunteer group, are especially crucial in managing the increasingly diverse health care volunteer pool of the 1990s and beyond.

Making Careful Service Assignments

With a culturally diverse volunteer corps, special care must be taken in making assignments. Directors of volunteer services must be sensitive to cultural traditions that, for example, may make it difficult for male volunteers to accept supervision by women or older volunteers to accept supervision by younger people. Careful training of supervisory staff can avert many problems in this area.

In working with older people or differently abled people, those making assignments should not prejudge which duties might be too difficult for volunteers. At the same time, directors should be aware of potential problems and take quick action to make diplomatic reassignments when necessary.

In multicultural communities, every effort should be made to prevent or, if necessary, defuse tensions between groups. Problems may arise when volunteers from one culture are assigned to work with patients, employees, or other volunteers from another culture with which there may be a tradition of mistrust or friction.

Organizations must also try to find meaningful assignments for volunteers and explain how volunteers' duties fit into the organization's big picture. Full-time workers who are squeezing time to volunteer out of busy schedules are no longer willing to spend hours stuffing envelopes. For example, the American Heart Association, where envelope stuffing was a key volunteer activity several years ago, now hires people to do this and gives its volunteers more meaningful assignments. The United Way Voluntary Action Centers have a skill bank that helps organizations match volunteers' skills to the organizations' needs. To professionalize the volunteer experience and clarify mutual expectations, many volunteer organizations sign a written contract with volunteers that specifies what the volunteer has agreed to do and how that work will benefit the organization.

Conducting Timely Performance Appraisals

Like all other workers, paid or unpaid, volunteers are entitled to sensitive, constructive feedback on how they are performing their duties. In providing appraisals to a diverse volunteer corps, supervisors should be sensitive to cultural traditions that are more or less confrontational than the American norm, and they should choose their words carefully. Supervisors must also be sensitive to the needs of volunteers from cultures in which women do not evaluate men or younger people do not evaluate their elders.

The appraisal process also gives volunteers an opportunity to provide information on problems or needs—such as transportation problems, schedule conflicts, or problems with the volunteer assignments—and feedback on how the organization can improve the volunteer experience. Health care organizations cannot afford to lose valuable volunteers because their personal needs are not being addressed.

Providing Effective Training

Effective training programs are essential factors in the retention and motivation of volunteers. During orientation, trainers should make sure that volunteers understand the crucial role they play in helping the organization to meet its service mission. After basic orientation, volunteers, like all valued workers, need careful, effective training. An effective training program not only helps ensure the success of the volunteer program, it also gives volunteers new skills and experiences that can benefit them in other areas of their lives, including their paid employment. This perhaps unexpected benefit can serve to deepen their commitment to the organization for which they volunteer.

When training a diverse volunteer workforce, supervisors must be prepared to fill gaps in volunteers' skills and education. Nonnative speakers of English may need language training, for example, and people who have been out of the workforce for a while may need training in the use of computers or other electronic equipment. Trainers must carefully assess volunteers' needs and be supportive and diplomatic when suggesting any additional skills enhancement.

Providing Suitable Recognition

A crucial element of any effective volunteer program is a process for providing suitable recognition. Recognition is important in any business, of course, but it is the only real way for organizations to reward and thank unpaid workers. If volunteers do not feel appreciated, they are likely to quit. Daily and weekly compliments and recognition are essential and more personal than annual dinners, service pins, plaques, and letters. Organizations can show appreciation to volunteers by sending stories and pictures to local papers and thank-you letters to volunteers' employers outlining their value to the organization.

In some organizations, such as the Girl Scouts of America, recognition of volunteers takes on almost religious implications. The importance of giving volunteers suitable recognition is stressed in the organization's management programs, and managers are encouraged to be innovative and creative in recognizing volunteers. To show appreciation for a troop leader, for example, one district manager created a sign that read "A Special Girl Scout Leader Lives Here" and placed it outside the troop leader's home. For a nominal cost, the district manager was able to make her appreciation known throughout the neighborhood.

The reader should be aware, however, that some cultural values can have an impact on how appreciation should be expressed to certain volunteers. For example, the value of saving face is central to the cultural norms of many Asian, Middle Eastern, and Hispanic volunteers. This value may result in a volunteer's feeling some discomfort when being complimented in front of others. Other values—such as not calling attention to the individual, or valuing the group over the individual—could cause discomfort among many members of the above-mentioned cultures, particularly when those volunteers are praised publicly or excessively, or when they are singled out for individual achievement. Remember, however, that not all individuals from these cultures will share the same values; each individual must be treated uniquely.[16] Many of these issues are also crucial to the effective management of diversity in the paid workforce, but they are of vital importance in working with unpaid workers who, lacking salaries and the other benefits of paid employment, must feel that their volunteer experiences are satisfying and worthwhile and that their efforts are necessary and appreciated if they are to remain part of the volunteer pool.

Ten Steps to Success in Recruiting, Training, and Retaining Volunteers

As this chapter has discussed, it has become harder than ever before for health care organizations to successfully recruit, train, and retain a viable and responsive volunteer staff. The principles of diversity management discussed throughout this book can be meaningfully applied to managing culturally diverse volunteers in the following action strategies:

1. *Recruitment:* Recruitment efforts should seek to increase the diversity of the volunteer pool through improved college relations programs, recruitment through cross-cultural community outreach programs, and research into and exploration of innovative recruitment methods.

2. *Career development:* Organizations should give people from diverse ethnic and cultural backgrounds, older people, and differently abled people the same opportunities for advancement that are offered to more traditional volunteers.
3. *Diversity training:* Employees, supervisors of volunteers, and the volunteers themselves should be given careful training that addresses myths, stereotypes, organizational barriers, and cultural differences. The training should increase all parties' diversity sensitivity and maximize effective interaction.
4. *Upward mobility:* Organizations should strive to break the glass ceiling and increase the numbers of people from nontraditional backgrounds and groups in positions of leadership in the volunteer ranks.
5. *Input and feedback:* Organizations should move from asking managers and volunteer leaders what they think an increasingly diverse volunteer pool wants to asking the volunteers themselves.
6. *Self-help:* Organizations should encourage the development of multicultural networks and support groups. These groups not only foster interaction and cooperation among volunteer workers, they can help volunteers find solutions to problems, such as with transportation or child care, that otherwise might affect their ability to volunteer.
7. *Accountability:* Managers should be held accountable for the successful training, development, and retention of the volunteers assigned to them.
8. *Systems accommodations:* Organizations should recognize and support diversity by recognizing and accommodating the religious holidays, dietary restrictions, and physical limitations of members of a diverse volunteer workforce.
9. *Outreach:* Organizations should strive to develop reputations as leaders in respecting and nurturing multiculturalism and diversity. By supporting diverse and multicultural organizations, vendors, events, programs, and services, organizations can position themselves as employers of choice for both volunteers and paid workers.
10. *Community representation:* To deliver essential health and human services, an organization's volunteer pool must mirror the diversity of the community, much the way Methodist Hospital altered its volunteer pool to match its changed demographics.[17]

References

1. Mergenbagen, P. A new breed of volunteer. *American Demographics,* June 1991, p. 54.
2. Reagan, R. Address to the National Alliance of Business, Washington, DC, Oct. 5, 1981.
3. Driver, D. E. *The Good Heart Book.* Chicago: Noble Press, 1989, chapter 2.
4. U.S. Bureau of Labor Statistics and U.S. Bureau of the Census. Current Population Survey, May 1989. The sample included about 60,000 households that were

scientifically selected to represent the civilian noninstitutional population (sixteen years old and older) in the fifty states and the District of Columbia. Information was collected on more than 150,000 persons living in those households.

5. Mergenbagen.

6. Hayghe, H. V. Volunteers in the U.S.: who donates the time? *Monthly Labor Review*, Feb. 1991, p. 17.

7. Hayghe, p. 21.

8. Kamier, W. *Women Volunteering.* Garden City, NY: Anchor Press, 1984.

9. Wyle, F. W. Crisis time for the non-profits. Speech delivered at the Board Retreat of the San Fernando Valley Unit of the American Cancer Society, San Fernando, CA, Sept. 10, 1988.

10. The Gallup Organization. *The 1990 Gallup Survey of Giving and Volunteering.* Princeton, NJ: The Gallup Organization, 1991. The survey's sample consisted of 2,727 persons eighteen years old and older who were selected to be representative of the U.S. population. Included were oversamples of African-Americans, Hispanics, and those with household incomes of more than $60,000 to improve the reliability of survey results for these smaller populations. Respondents to the Gallup survey were given a clear definition of volunteer activities and were prompted to recall infrequent or brief incidents of volunteering by responding to a list of seventeen possible volunteer activities.

11. Garza, M. Hispanics find help breaking cultural taboos. *Chicago Tribune*, Sept. 26, 1993, Section 6, p. 1.

12. Spector, R. E. *Cultural Diversity in Health and Illness.* Norwalk, CT: Appleton-Century-Crofts, 1985.

13. Mann, F. *Acupuncture.* New York City: Vintage Books, 1972.

14. A Chinese volunteer program. *Volunteer Leader*, Summer 1991.

15. Jackson, M. Telephone conversation with author, Aug. 7, 1992.

16. Thiederman, S. *Profiting in America's Multicultural Marketplace.* New York City: Lexington Books, 1991, pp. 229–30.

17. Nestor, L. Managing cultural diversity in volunteer organizations. *Voluntary Action Leadership*, Winter 1991, p. 19. These ten steps were adapted from Lennie Copeland of Copeland Griggs Productions.

Implementing the Change Plan

A key determinant of an organization's success is its ability to adapt to and creatively deal with change. In order to adapt to and successfully manage the major changes caused by workforce diversity, health care organizations must be able to manage large-scale change, which requires a viable change plan. In order to effectively implement a change plan, health care managers must understand the nature and concept of organizational change and be familiar with techniques for implementing organizational change. This chapter provides a road map for implementing a viable change plan, especially in relation to the management of workforce diversity.

The Challenges of Organizational Change

Change can be difficult in health care organizations. Health care organizations are made up of people, and resisting change is part of human nature. The implementation of organizational change, if mismanaged, can upset the normal rhythm of the organization, feed feelings of insecurity among staff, and do more harm than good. Organizational change is accomplished most easily when employees are convinced that the new ways of doing things are part of a carefully planned strategy devised by competent leaders. Organizational change is also abetted when employees believe that the changes will significantly benefit them and the organization.

Comparing Diversity Change to Organizational Change

Organizational change focuses on new ways of doing things throughout an organization—affecting every employee at every level—in order to improve overall productivity, efficiency, morale, and working conditions. The underlying assumption of organizational change is that organizations owe their success to people rather than to systems.[1] Organizational change is pervasive. It affects decision making, leadership, trust, communication, individual and group roles and responsibilities, and empowerment. This type of change requires support and reinforcement throughout the organization.[2]

Diversity change, which results from diversity management, is even more intense than organizational change. Whereas organizational change reengineers how people work together to increase productivity, *diversity change* focuses more specifically on how people perceive other people. Diversity change should help people overcome personal and group prejudices about those who are different, and the diversity change process may even alter the way people feel about themselves.

It is important to remember that, as noted in chapter 4, diversity management is not merely achieving affirmative action goals in hiring and promotion or fostering an understanding of the value of differences among people of different races, cultures, genders, ethnicities, ages, physical abilities, and lifestyles.[3] Nor does diversity management attempt to treat all groups and constituencies in the same way. Instead, effective diversity management accommodates differences and distinctiveness among diverse groups and individuals while creating an atmosphere in which everyone can perform to his or her best ability. Diversity thus becomes a constructive force in the workplace.[4,5]

Because it affects how people think about themselves and others, diversity change may be more difficult and require more time than organizational change. Diversity change must overcome the stereotyping and prejudices that are integral parts of the socialization process, and it must support and reinforce employees as they assess themselves and modify their behavior accordingly.[6] Although diversity change can be considered part of the overall organizational change process, given the increasing workforce diversity in health care organizations, diversity management may in fact be the driving force behind overall organizational change.

Implementing Change

Implementing change means putting new strategies and plans to work in an organization's day-to-day operations. Although implementing change seems simple or obvious, it requires careful planning, good organizational communication, effective work teams, managers who can act as facilitators, reinforcement of staff efforts, and the belief, held by employees throughout the organization, that change is good and necessary.

When a health care organization begins the change process, it attempts to effect major behavioral change among its employees. After the change process is implemented, change becomes an accepted norm and employees are able to find as much (or more) professional satisfaction in the organization's culture and direction as they find in their own position or department in the organizational structure.[7] Employee interest shifts from personal concerns and issues to organizationwide concerns and issues.

Employees' perceptions and beliefs will determine the successfulness of the change implementation process. A major challenge of the change process is to overcome barriers to employee participation and win acceptance for change.

If employees are to buy in to the change process, managers must first demonstrate, through their behavior and attitudes, that they believe in and support it. Without employee buy in and support, it is impossible to effectively implement the change plan, and an ineffective change plan may even decrease the level of productivity in the organization.[8]

To ensure organizationwide buy in and support, it is important that everyone in the organization understands the change plan's aim and mission from the outset. *Everyone* includes not only employees, supervisors, and managers from all levels of the organization, but also outside parties that affect employees' jobs, such as suppliers, and all of the health care organization's subsystems.[9] Every person or entity interacting with the health care organization must be aware of and understand its change plan.

To help ensure the change plan's success, some measurable results should be evident early in the implementation effort. Success breeds success, and people tend to learn faster from successes than from failures.[10] The lack of evident, measurable results early in the implementation effort probably indicates that something is inherently faulty with the change process itself. If initial signals and indicators are negative, the creators of the change plan should step in immediately and make necessary adjustments. The ability to adjust the change plan on an ongoing basis is essential to implementing and managing the change process.

The Need for Champions of Diversity

Champions of diversity—employees at all levels of an organization who will advocate and facilitate diversity change—are essential to effective change implementation. Because changes in managing health care diversity cannot be totally driven from the top of the organization down, there must be leaders at all levels of the organization, regardless of job title, to win the hearts and minds of employees and get them behind the change plan. These leaders are the champions of diversity.

Identifying Champions of Diversity

Initially, health care organizations must assess and recognize their talent resources when formulating and implementing a diversity change program. Organizations should not rely solely on managerial talent. Problems are often apparent to frontline employees, the people actually involved in providing services to patients, long before managers become aware of the problems.[11] The management group charged with improving diversity management in the organization must look to all levels of the organization to determine how to develop the workforce into champions of diversity. The most likely candidates will be open-minded, team oriented, results oriented, and flexible. Probable champions of diversity will also be good communicators who are committed to the organization and believe that continuous change is good and necessary.

Obtaining Recommendations from Each Major Work Group

Because champions of diversity must have the respect and support of the organization's employees, a first step in identifying appropriate initial candidates is to obtain recommendations from each of the health care organization's major work groups. The organization's employees, no matter what their level (managers, professionals, and staff members), are the first source of information about who among them could—and should—serve as champions of diversity. Employees are the best judges of who in their ranks are respected leaders and role models and can best serve as exemplars of the new corporate norm of valuing differences and accepting and embracing workforce diversity.

Chapter 3 explained how to create a diversity committee of key managers and staff to gather information concerning workforce demographics, coordinate culture and value analyses, and begin to develop diversity management strategies. This same committee, made up of employees who support or promote minorities and women, value diversity, and are viewed as concerned and people-oriented role models should oversee the selection of initial champions of diversity.

The diversity committee should begin its search for diversity champions at the management level and seek recommendations from top-level, middle-level, and first-line managers. The committee should then seek recommendations for diversity champions from professionals from both operations and support areas, focusing on areas of the health care organization with especially diverse workforces. The committee should then solicit recommendations for diversity champions from staff members, who are probably most affected by workforce diversity issues on a daily basis.

Because of the complexity and variety of health care organizations, it is difficult to provide specific guidelines for the number of champions to be selected at the outset of the program. The best guideline is to select enough champions to fully represent the employees at all levels and in each area of the organization. As all employees are eventually trained in diversity issues, other champions will emerge to augment the ranks of the initial champions. In this way, everyone in the organization buys into the program, the value of diversity management is recognized, and true and lasting change will take place.

To obtain recommendations for diversity champions, the diversity committee should meet with employee groups in a familiar and comfortable setting, preferably in the employees' own department. Because health care organizations are usually around-the-clock operations, the committee should meet with groups from all shifts. At the outset of these meetings, the diversity committee should clearly describe the diversity change program, why it is seeking champions of diversity, and the characteristics of the people who will serve as champions of diversity. At that time, the committee should explain that, although the recommendations of the various work groups are an important part of the champion selection process, the final decision will be based on several criteria, and the committee cannot guarantee that any specific group's nominee will be chosen in the final selection process. This is important to emphasize to avoid misunderstandings and feelings of betrayal if a particular group's nominee is not selected. Depending on the makeup of an organization's workforce, interpreters may be necessary to ensure that the committee's explanations are understood by nonnative speakers of English. After the explanations, the committee should ask whether employees have questions, and these questions should be answered fully and frankly. (Interpreters may be needed for this part of the meeting as well.) Although the process of soliciting recommendations should be open and vigorous discussion should be encouraged, the actual recommending of champions by employees should be done by secret ballot or other confidential means. This confidentiality avoids pressure, coercion, hurt feelings, or any other dynamics that prevent employees from exercising their best and most honest judgment in making recommendations.

Once all work groups have made their recommendations, the diversity committee should evaluate them carefully and select candidates from all key work groups, cultures, and shifts. An important part of the selection process is evaluating candidates in terms of leadership traits.

Balancing Different Concepts of Leadership

Leadership is an elusive concept, especially in terms of workforce diversity, because the concept of leadership often differs among various cultures. In some cultures the leadership ranks are dominated by men; in others, women predominate. Some cultures have autocratic leadership styles. In other cultures the main concern of leadership may be avoiding embarrassment or saving face. Still other cultures believe that leaders can only come from certain social classes. Additionally, members of some cultural or ethnic groups may object to or resist leaders from certain other groups.

To avoid leadership conflicts, the organization's management, and preferably its diversity committee, should know what kind of leadership is best suited to the organization's goals and objectives. Champions of diversity are leaders, and the diversity committee should select champions who will be respected and supported by the organization's diverse groups. The committee should ensure that the champions' concepts of leadership will not subvert, however unconsciously, the organization's overall diversity management goals.

Identifying "Ideal" Champions

As the diversity committee reviews recommendations from the various work groups, it should evaluate the recommendations in terms of the characteristics of "ideal" champions of diversity. In terms of cultural diversity, ideal champions should represent the various cultural and ethnic groups in the organization's workforce. Such champions may be members of nonwhite racial or ethnic groups, speak a language other than English that is prevalent in the workforce, and/or have one or more parents from one of the ethnic or racial groups prevalent in the workforce. In addition, ideal champions may have grown up in a multicultural community, have lived abroad, or have other characteristics that indicate that they will be good leaders and role models in a diverse workforce.

In terms of other types of diversity, ideal champions may be women, older workers, gays or lesbians, or differently abled, again depending on the specific groups in the organization's workforce. In terms of personal characteristics, ideal champions of diversity should be respected by their peers; able to lead by example; diplomatic, sensitive, and empathetic; willing to learn about and work with people from diverse groups; and strongly oriented toward helping others. The diversity committee should ensure that all of the various groups and constituencies found in the organization's diverse workforce are represented by the selected champions of diversity.

Making the Final Selection

In making the final selection of champions of diversity, the diversity committee should carefully interview each candidate to assess his or her understanding of the importance of diversity in the organization, as well as his or her understanding of the champion of diversity's role within the organization. Final interviews should also ensure that candidates understand and are enthusiastic about the level of commitment necessary to be a champion of diversity.

Interviewing Candidates

The interview process is a key step in selecting champions of diversity. Up to half of those recommended by the work groups will be weeded out during the interview process. Therefore, the interviews must be conducted with special care and sensitivity so that those who are not selected do not become negative influences on the diversity change plan.

The diversity committee should meet with each candidate individually. Candidates should be reassured that the discussion will be kept strictly confidential and that, whether or not the candidate is selected, the committee and the health care organization greatly appreciate the candidate's willingness to serve. Each interview should follow the same overall format, including an explanation of the change plan, the role of the diversity champion, and the selection process. The candidate should be given ample opportunities to ask questions, and the committee should answer them openly and honestly. At the end of the interview, the committee should prepare a written summary to document the interview process.

The discussion of the change plan and the role of the diversity champion is probably the most important aspect of the interview. The committee should ensure that the candidate understands what is meant by workforce diversity, as well as the role of champions of diversity. The discussion should touch on, but need not be limited to, information provided by the internal and external environmental assessments (see chapter 3) concerning major issues and problems related to the organization's workforce diversity, the objectives of the organization's change plan, the plan's expected results, and the plan's time frame for accomplishing diversity change.

The diversity committee should also explain the duties and responsibilities of the champions of diversity. These duties and responsibilities include serving as a role model for other employees; supporting and helping to implement the diversity change plan; serving on a team that will address diversity-related problems; reporting periodically to the diversity committee; alerting the diversity committee to problems and concerns related to workforce diversity; receiving specialized training in workforce diversity issues; and participating in the training of other employees.

The committee should take care to ascertain that candidates who continue in the selection process fully understand and support the role of champion of diversity and are willing and able to fulfill the role. However, the diversity committee should assure candidates that there will be absolutely no negative repercussions if they decide that they do not wish to be diversity champions. Candidates should be given a chance to withdraw from consideration at the end of the interview and should be assured that they can think their decision over and withdraw at any time within the next few days with no negative consequences. The diversity committee should then communicate the organization's gratitude for their participation to date in the process.

Choosing the Champions

Once all candidates have been interviewed, the diversity committee must choose the champions. The committee should consider each candidate by evaluating the summaries of the interviews and, if necessary, contacting candidates to ask additional questions. Those candidates who make the final cut should be interviewed one more time to make sure that they are still interested in being diversity champions. The committee should choose some backup candidates to compensate for those who drop out.

When the committee has made its final selections, the candidates selected should be gathered, told of their selection, and asked to make a formal commitment to serving as champions of diversity. It is then time to announce the selections to the rest of the health care organization and begin to prepare the champions for their roles.

The Strategy of Marketing Change

Marketing the change plan is possibly the most important aspect of an organization's entire change process. For many employees, the plan will create major changes in their work culture. In fact, many employees at all levels of the organization may never have had to think about and adapt to workforce diversity. Therefore, in presenting the diversity change plan, management must be careful to get things off to a good start. The organization's champions of diversity are key players in this process.

Preparing the Champions of Diversity

The organization's champions of diversity, although they represent the organization's many cultures and work groups, should see themselves as a team. The initial meetings of this group are crucial to establishing a sense of teamwork.

The first meeting after the selection of champions has been announced should emphasize getting acquainted and building enthusiasm for their new roles as champions of diversity. Each champion should be invited to discuss why he or she chose to be a part of the diversity change process and which diversity-related issues concern his or her department.

At a second meeting, which should be held within a week, the group should discuss objectives, strategies, and time frames (discussed in the next three subsections). It is important that the meeting be held within a week, because a week is enough time for the champions to begin to discuss the change plan within their own departments and cultural groups, but it is not enough time for enthusiasm to dissipate.

Building and maintaining enthusiasm among the organization's champions and other employees is essential to the success of the diversity change plan. Frequently, the earliest supporters of innovation and change will be lower-level employees; managers and supervisors tend to adopt a wait-and-see attitude toward change or wait for a consensus among their peers.[12] The enthusiasm and efforts of the champions of diversity not only provide initial support for the change process, but also help provide the necessary motivation to inspire other employees to hop on the change bandwagon. Top-level managers should be enthusiastic sponsors and initial organizers, but they should not seem to be the only supporters of the change plan. Positive pressure for change should come from top-level management down, from low-level staff up, and from side-to-side among peers.

Reviewing the Objectives

In order to improve organizationwide handling of workforce diversity and its related issues, everyone in the organization, especially the champions of diversity, must have a clear idea of the goals and objectives of the change plan. Only then can the goals and objectives be supported by specific and meaningful programs and enforced as part of the overall organizational change plan. In other words, all employees at all levels of the organization must understand and accept that they and the organization will benefit by supporting workforce diversity and that the organization will not tolerate poor treatment of fellow workers. The change plan's workforce diversity objectives should emphasize establishing a commitment to teamwork, providing a productive work environment for all employees, fostering respect for individuals' values and rights, giving all employees opportunities for promotion and career development, and providing top-quality patient care.

Such objectives provide a new basis for evaluating services and how services are provided throughout the organization, particularly in relation to quality. Recall that chapter 5 discussed the parallels between diversity management and quality management that R. Roosevelt Thomas, Jr., pointed out in *Beyond Race and Gender:*[13]

- Both involve employee involvement and empowerment.
- Both require cultural changes for full implementation.
- Both require a long-term commitment.

Diversity change objectives also demonstrate that the health care organization recognizes that its employees are its most important asset and that attracting and retaining good employees is essential to long-term success.[14]

The organization's diversity change objectives, as well as its mission and goals, should be summarized and distributed at the second group meeting of the champions of diversity. The champions of diversity will in turn distribute this information to friends and fellow workers. The champions should feel free to ask questions and discuss the objectives at this second meeting. The second meeting is an excellent time for the diversity committee to remind the champions that their role is to sponsor change and improve teamwork, openness, quality, service, and cultural symbiosis. The diversity committee should communicate that, in effect, the champions are the catalysts of change in the organization.

Reviewing the Strategy

At the second meeting of the diversity champions, the diversity committee should also review the strategy for implementing diversity change. The strategy should incorporate the organization's objectives, philosophy, and ideals into a plan that can be embraced by employees. The plan should appear straightforward and achievable, emphasize management's desire to do things differently, and show management's respect and concern for employees. In addition, the plan should provide a clear rationale that employees will understand and readily support in terms of adjusting their behavior in the workplace. Finally, the plan should have both long-term and short-term goals and should be able to demonstrate visible results.

If the diversity committee seems committed and enthused when presenting the change plan and is open to questions and suggestions from the champions of diversity, the champions should come away from the second meeting with a sense of enthusiasm about the plan. They should also come away with the understanding that although they are key factors in the plan's success, their most important function is to help others in the organization accept and actively support the plan.

Outlining Events and Timetables

Also at the second meeting, the diversity committee should inform the champions of diversity, and through them the entire organization, of the diversity change plan's schedule of events and timetable. The implementation of the diversity change process has two phases. Phase one is the introduction of the program and the initial training of managers, diversity champions, and employees in general. Phase two ensures the ongoing continuity of the program, providing reinforcement and support for the belief system needed to maintain effective diversity management.

Phase One: Introduction and Initial Training

During the time the diversity committee conducts the first two meetings of the champions of diversity, the committee should also meet with the health care organization's managers to ensure that they are up-to-date. (Chapter 4 discusses preparing management to accept workforce diversity.) Both managers and diversity champions should be briefed on the training and orientation sessions that they will be asked to attend over the next 30 days. Chapter 4 presents an outline of a model one-day training program for managers. Appendix F provides an outline of a model five-day training program for champions of diversity. Many organizations opt to bring in professional trainers who specialize in diversity training to run the initial training programs. (See appendix A for suggested professionals.) Once they have been trained, managers and champions of diversity can serve as trainers for the rest of the organization, at least during phase one.

Phase Two: Ongoing Continuity of the Program

Managers and diversity champions will need ongoing support and training to ensure the ongoing success of the diversity change plan. They will also need safe forums in which to vent their emotions, discuss problems, and brainstorm ideas. An outside consultant can be helpful, especially in the initial parts of phase two (which presumably lasts indefinitely), in facilitating and guiding the exchange of ideas in the safe forum.

Regularly scheduled meetings will help ensure the success of these support and training efforts. At least every 60 days the diversity committee should meet with managers and champions, sometimes separately, sometimes together. If outside consultants are involved in the change plan as trainers or facilitators, they should be present at these meetings so that they can remain aware of the problems and successes of the managers and champions.

Creating a Sense of Change Plan Ownership among Managers

If the diversity change plan is to be successful, it must have the total support of everyone in the organization, but managers especially should have a sense of ownership in the change plan. Chapter 4 presents a development plan for managers that focuses on diversity management. Some managers resist change because they fear that they will lose authority, have to change their management style, or be forced to clean up messes or problems that result from a new program, among other reasons. To overcome such resistance and build a sense of management ownership, top-level management should help managers understand how the diversity change plan benefits them and the organization as a whole. Managers should also be helped to understand the necessity of making the change. As Peter M. Senge writes in his book *The Fifth Discipline*, "people learn what they need to learn, not what someone else thinks they need to learn."[15]

Supporting Managers during the Change Process

In order to develop a sense of ownership in the change plan by managers, managers must be assured that top-level management supports them and recognizes that change can be difficult. Top-level management should discuss the change plan and its ramifications with managers over a two- or three-month period, perhaps as a part of regular managers' meetings.

In addition, managers should participate in group and individual sessions that discuss the specific objectives that they should achieve under the diversity change plan. These sessions should be run by a skilled facilitator either from within the organization, such as a human resources specialist skilled in open-group discussions and training and development, or from a consulting firm that specializes in diversity management. The sessions should be organized around sound training principles that emphasize the objectives, mission, and goals of the change plan. Managers will also require training for their new roles as diversity facilitators, sponsors, coaches, team members, and mentors.

Top-level management's discussions with managers should explain the change plan's time frame and detail the entire change program, including the role of the champions of diversity. If managers are to buy into the change process, they must understand and accept the time frame, the total change plan, and the fact that their participation is essential to the plan's success. Top-level management should explain that it will provide private, one-on-one support and guidance to managers who have difficulty embracing the change process. Top-level management should also stress the importance of managers coming forward with problems and concerns early on so that they can be handled with a minimum of trouble and disruption to the change plan. Only when managers feel that top-level management understands how difficult change can be and supports managers in their efforts to achieve change will managers have a sense of ownership of the change process.

Showing Managers How the Change Plan Affects Them

New practices ushered in by the diversity change plan will probably allow employees to have more latitude to study problems and work out solutions themselves. Some managers may view this new empowerment of employees as pushing managers into the background rather than letting them manage and lead.[16] Although this is an inaccurate picture, it is true that the diversity change plan will create a totally new framework for how managers supervise employees. Under the change plan, managers do not simply tell employees what to do; instead, they give them ideas to consider. Management by walking around (MBWA), discussed in chapter 5, is a key management technique for staying in touch with employees and troubleshooting problems with them.

Another new aspect of managing under the diversity change plan is cross-departmental communications and problem solving. The change plan requires that managers build relationships with their counterparts in other departments and share ideas and problems rather than compete. Such requirements may intimidate some managers. However, the organization, through its information sessions and training programs, can reassure managers that these changes will help the organization adapt to changes in the workforce, the business environment, and society in general and ensure the organization's—and their own—continued success in the 1990s and beyond.

Announcing the Changes to the Entire Organization

As managers and champions of diversity participate in numerous meetings and training and brainstorming sessions, it is likely that some information about upcoming changes will spread informally to most employees through the organization's grapevine. However, the organization has the responsibility to formally communicate the diversity change plan to all employees. Formal announcements, which should be in written and oral (that is, announced at a special meeting) form, should state the purpose and rationale of the change plan, its benefits to the organization and its employees, and its positive influence on quality and customer satisfaction, as well as who will oversee the implementation and what the timetable for plan implementation will be. Because the goal of formal and informal communication processes is to minimize uninformed gossip, speculation, and rumor, employees should be encouraged to discuss the change plan and its ramifications with their supervisor or diversity champion, who should be readily accessible for such discussions.

Formal program announcements should be carefully coordinated to be made in rapid succession to all employees on all shifts. Management should not forget employees who may be on vacation, out sick, or between schedules and should notify such employees as soon as possible. The following is an outline of a workable timetable for formally announcing a diversity change plan to employees:

- *Day 1*: Management meets with the champions of diversity.
- *Day 2*: Group meetings with all staff on all shifts are conducted. Letters go out to those on vacation. The meetings and letters identify each group's diversity champion and discuss the overall program.
- *Day 3*: Smaller staff and departmental meetings with managers and champions take place. Managers and champions outline more details of the program and training schedules.
- *Day 5*: A memo from the chief executive officer is distributed to all staff expressing his or her encouragement and appreciation.
- *Day 7*: Management and champions meet for a joint discussion of the plan and for questions and answers.

Once the change plan has been announced, the organization can expect to encounter some resistance from employees. The following section discusses strategies for overcoming resistance to change.

Overcoming Resistance to Change

Like managers, employees may at first be resistant to change, especially the sweeping organizational and behavioral changes recommended by the diversity change plan. Most employees have developed certain work practices and routines over the years that are familiar, comfortable, and second nature. Quite naturally, employees resist shaking things up unless they see a clear reason and advantage to doing so. Especially in diverse workforces that comprise a multitude of different cultures, races, and interest groups, major changes in how people from diverse groups interact can be difficult to achieve. However, health care organizations must overcome resistance to these changes if they are to survive in the diverse workplace of the 1990s and beyond.

The most important factor in overcoming employee resistance is to convince employees that change is an ongoing process that is integral to the overall goals of the organization. Employees usually react badly to what they perceive as change for the sake of change (for example, management adopting the latest fad in managerial techniques). However, if management demonstrates that the change plan is integral to the organization's overall goals of enhancing its success and improving its work environment, and if management demonstrates that employees and the overall organization will benefit from the diversity change plan in terms of increased employee empowerment, less conflict, and improved working conditions, quality, and customer service, then employees are less likely to resist. In addition, if employees understand that management is truly committed to improving workforce diversity management as part of creating a work environment where all employees are able to do the best job possible and strive for career development and promotions, employees are likely to embrace the change.

In order to maintain improvement and change, employees must perceive that there is not a single level or objective that needs to be achieved, but that the organization must evolve and change on an ongoing basis along with its employees and its environments. Health care employees should be helped to recognize that in the years to come, employee and customer diversity will only increase, and employees must be prepared to adjust to this fact. Viewing change as an ongoing process helps encourage long-term commitment, a willingness to look at problems and services in new ways, flexibility and adaptability, and interpersonal and interdepartmental cooperation and problem solving. Acceptance of ongoing diversity change encourages respect for others, equal access for all groups to career development and advancement based on merit, and a lessening of fear, anxiety, and stress for all workers.

Maintenance of the Change Process

Maintaining the change process is just as important as implementing the change process. Management must gather the commitment and momentum necessary to maintain the change process over a period of six months to a year while new habits and methods of doing things become entrenched in the organization's culture and old ways begin to seem uncomfortable or ineffective.

Finding Solutions to Problems

After the most major and overt diversity problems have been dealt with, management must maintain the impetus for change so that employees are not tempted to rest on their laurels. Fortunately, by the time the most overt problems are on their way to being solved, employees will be much more adept at recognizing problems, which will enable deeper and more pivotal workplace problems to come to the surface. To resolve deep-seated, pivotal problems, management must ensure that the atmosphere of openness, interdepartmental cooperation, teamwork, and free communication is maintained.

As a result of the change process, problems often can be solved by staff members, interdepartmental teams, managers within or among departments, champions of diversity within or among departments, or combinations of these people and teams. Top-level management is rarely involved in problem solving because solutions to problems are more effective when those who are closest to the problems devise the solutions.[17] The intense involvement of employees in solving the problems that most affect them and the knowledge that they will have such empowerment on an ongoing basis are powerful impetuses to maintaining change.

Reducing Costs

Staff members and managers who are empowered by the change plan and have a sense of ownership of the change process will do a better job of controlling costs than traditional management ever could. This is because they feel more a part of the organization and its policies and practices than they did before the change plan and view the ability to keep costs in line as a good reflection on their ability to be effective, efficient, and productive. It is important to note that the concept of costs extends beyond dollars to encompass saving staff time and labor, improving use of systems, and minimizing ineffective processes. This has a significant effect on the bottom line because in most health care organizations profitability relies upon efficient use of the most valuable resource—employees, both staff members and managers. Success in reducing and controlling costs reinforces the importance of effective diversity management because improved diversity management results in a more productive, cost-effective organization whose employees are able to see concrete, positive results, thus providing further impetus and momentum to carry the diversity management program forward.

Encouraging Creativity and Innovation

Creativity and innovation are essential to finding new and better ways to run an organization and are the hallmarks of effective change and diversity management. Successes, large and small, in improving efficiency, productivity, quality of care, customer service, and work environment encourage further creativity and innovation by motivating staff to take well-thought-out risks and try new approaches. In implementing the change plan, top-level management should expect the best from employees and give them the training and support they need to make this expectation a reality.[18] This is especially relevant to improved diversity management in that under the diversity change plan, biases and prejudices about certain groups—minorities, women, the differently abled, and the like—are replaced by an appreciation that all employees should be given the chance to reach their maximum potential.

Reconfiguring the Organization

To succeed in the 1990s and beyond, health care organizations will have to give up the traditional vertical organizational configuration in favor of flattening the organization to make it more effective and efficient.[19] To achieve this flattening, staff members should be empowered to take a broader, more responsible role in running the organization, and management must take the broader role of facilitating and leading by example. Diversity management is an integral part of flattening the organization; when employee empowerment becomes the norm, previously powerless groups will benefit.

Encouraging Appropriate Organizational Growth

Organizational growth should occur one step at a time and should not be rushed. As Rosabeth Moss Kanter writes in *The Change Masters:* "Time is one of the first requirements for significant long-term organizational changes. There has to be sufficient calendar time to make it work, as well as enough available participant time to engage in planning, communication, and reflection about the appropriateness of job and project activities."[20]

Organizations should stay with strategies until goals are met and understand that it might be impossible to achieve all goals simultaneously or even within the original time frame. If an organization must solve major problems first, it should take the time to do just that and nothing else. Undertaking major growth initiatives will probably only exacerbate existing problems.

At the same time, however, organizations must not use the need to stabilize as an excuse to delay the planning or implementation of changes in diversity management. Instead, organizations should realize that more effective diversity management will help efforts to stabilize and grow.

Staff members cannot be ordered or required by management to buy in to a program for organizational growth that does not have their commitment. The real potential for growth comes when the staff members voluntarily and enthusiastically grasp the new program and make it their own. This ownership requires an understanding and acceptance of diversity management as an integral part of the change process.

The Need for Improved Diversity Management throughout the Organization

Although it is vital that health care organizations emphasize to managers and staff members that managing diversity is an important goal and an integral part of the organization's overall change plan, it is even more important to emphasize the necessity of consistent attention to diversity management in every aspect of planning and operations. In other words, organizations must merge diversity management with change methodology. For instance, if an organization attempts to foster improved diversity management in its staff development activities, yet fails to include diversity management in the new business strategy and marketing plans it develops through change processes, the end result will be counterproductive to the institution's overall goals.

It is especially critical that health care organizations ensure that improved management of workforce diversity is a key component of the organization's overall business strategy. For example, if the organization's overall business strategy is to increase its clientele in a particular geographical area, it must ensure that it has the appropriate development programs to train its diverse staff members to best serve the needs of the target clientele.

From the starting point of business strategy, improved diversity management should factor into plans for operations, marketing, finance, and their various subsets—organizational design, individual job design, performance measures, personnel selection and development, reward systems, and so on—and the subsets of the subsets.

In all of these effects, improved management of workforce diversity is not a mere gimmick to publicize the organization's affirmative action performance, but rather a demonstration of how the organization's much-valued workforce diversity benefits the ultimate consumers—patients and the organization's other "publics." This same diversity principle applies to the financial arena as the organization uses its effective diversity management to attract public and private funding support and contracts. Thus, to achieve and maintain organizational success in the 1990s and beyond, health care organizations must implement effective management of workforce diversity, using a diversity change plan, throughout the entire organization.

References

1. Kanter, R. M. *The Change Masters.* New York City: Simon and Schuster, 1989, pp. 17–18.

2. Byham, W. C., and Cox, J. *Zapp! The Lightning of Empowerment.* New York City: Fawcett Columbine, 1992.

3. Thomas, R. R., Jr. *Beyond Race and Gender.* New York City: AMACOM, 1991, pp. 23–27.

4. Thomas, p. 27.

5. Loden, M., and Rosener, J. *Workforce America.* Homewood, IL: Business One-Irwin, 1991, pp. 26–27.

6. Loden and Rosener, pp. 70–71.

7. Kanter, p. 133.

8. Kanter, p. 125.

9. Byham and Cox, p. 165.

10. Byham and Cox, p. 118.

11. Senge, P. M. *The Fifth Discipline.* New York City: Doubleday Currency, 1990, p. 17.

12. Kanter, pp. 222–23.

13. Thomas, pp. 164–65.

14. Senge, pp. 143–45.

15. Senge, p. 345.

16. Byham and Cox, pp. 95–97.

17. Senge, pp. 275–76.

18. Ziglar, Z. *Top Performance*. New York City: Berkeley, 1986, chapter 4.

19. Byham and Cox, p. 176.

20. Kanter, p. 122.

Chapter Nine

Diversity in Action:
The Baxter Story

This chapter will examine how the change plans and diversity management strategies discussed in preceding chapters were put into practice at Baxter Healthcare Corporation, a major health care organization. Baxter has become an industry leader in the management of workforce diversity and has developed effective techniques that it has woven into the fabric of its operations. Baxter recognizes that diversity management is an ongoing process, not a quick fix; a journey, not a destination. Its leaders realize that they cannot say, in effect, "Great, we have figured out how to manage workforce diversity. Let's check that objective off and move on." In *Beyond Race and Gender*, R. Roosevelt Thomas, Jr., states that culture change, which is caused by diversity management, takes 15 or 20 years of consistent and conscientious effort before it becomes naturally sustainable.[1] Thomas's description of culture change likens an organization to a tree. The behavior of an organization is like a tree's branches; that is, one can see it. The roots, the invisible part, are the underlying corporate culture that nourishes and shapes the branches.[2] Determining how an organization's roots—its corporate culture—must change in order to adapt to an increasingly diverse workforce requires extensive organizationwide soul-searching and analysis.

Challenging Assumptions

In order to change its culture, an organization must challenge the assumptions behind its practices, behaviors, and norms. For example, many organizations claim, "At this institution, the cream rises to the top." In assessing whether this assertion is true, one must examine that "cream," that is, the organization's top-level management. Are top-level managers predominantly white males, or do women, minorities, older workers, and the differently abled have equal access to development and promotional opportunities?

Another claim that many organizations make is, "We are a family at XYZ institution." But are all members of the "family" treated fairly, keeping in mind that fair treatment is not necessarily the same as equal treatment? How are those who do not look, act, or behave like the rest of the family treated? Most organizations have norms that were established many years ago, when the work-force was much more homogeneous than today's workforce.

In 1990, Baxter Healthcare Corporation of Deerfield, Illinois, recognized that the challenge of effective diversity management was a difficult one. Its management dedicated considerable time, money, energy, and other resources to examining, diagnosing, monitoring, and evaluating their cultural norms.

The process of soliciting, analyzing, and assessing employee feedback on work-related issues was not new to Baxter. Conducting surveys, focus groups, and feedback sessions is an important part of Baxter's operational philosophy. The information gathered by those practices has created an enviable work environment at Baxter and has enhanced the perception in the health care industry that Baxter employees are highly competent and well respected. Furthermore, Baxter is recognized in the health care field for excellence in anticipating and meeting its customers' quality expectations in the products and services it provides.

Baxter has long been a leader in health care through its affirmative action and equal employment opportunity (EEO) efforts and is recognized as one of the best companies for women and minorities in terms of career mobility and enhancement. This is partly due to the fact that Baxter chairman Vernon R. Loucks, Jr., has made a personal commitment to creating and sustaining an environment where women and minorities are given opportunities to rise to the executive ranks of the organization. In 1990, *Business Week* identified Baxter Healthcare Corporation as one of the "up and comers" in its list of the best companies for women to work for.[3] One criterion used to identify women-friendly companies was the number of women in key executive positions and on the board of directors. Another criterion was sensitivity toward work and family issues. In this area, Baxter was a finalist for the 1991 Catalyst Award. (Catalyst is a nonprofit organization dedicated to working with top U.S. corporations on women's issues and the advancement of women in management.)

In October 1993 Baxter was again recognized for its commitment to diversity, this time by *Working Mother* magazine, which named the corporation as one of the best 100 companies for working mothers.[4] It was the third consecutive year Baxter Healthcare Corporation had been named to this prestigious list. The magazine cited the company's record of promoting women; the creation of Baxter Women Inc., a networking group; the strength of the company's work and family benefit programs; and the company's willingness to adopt job sharing, flextime, and compressed work weeks. "We very much value this recognition of our efforts to make Baxter a great place to work," said Barbara Young Morris, senior vice-president, human resources, in response to the recognition. "It's our goal to provide an environment that is attractive, supportive, and fair to all individuals, and that means we must recognize the unique needs of our employees."[5]

Given that Baxter was already an industry leader in providing opportunities for women and minorities, one wonders why it decided to "upset the applecart" by embarking upon a massive change process toward more effective diversity management in 1990. Although Baxter's EEO count looked good compared to many other health care organizations, the organization was not yet where it felt it should be, especially given the rapidly changing demographics and diversity of the workforce of the 1990s. Baxter began by examining the issues involved in valuing differences.

Valuing Differences

Instituting a process that values differences is the next logical step after implementing affirmative action mandates, which are basically government requirements that ensure that organizations fill their social and legal responsibilities, especially when working on government-funded projects. In emphasizing the valuing of differences, an organization encourages awareness of and respect for people who are different from mainstream American society.

In most American organizations, *mainstream* means the predominantly white male workforce, for whom most organizational practices, norms, and cultures were established. Women, people of color, the differently abled, older employees, and gays and lesbians tend to disrupt the traditional organization's practices, policies, and politics, especially when the organization does not actively value these employees' differences. Members of those groups cannot contribute fully to the organization's mission, goals, and objectives in such a traditional organization. Before an organization can launch a change process aimed at more effective diversity management, it has no other choice but to accept valuing differences as a norm.

Baxter's valuing-differences process eventually went beyond valuing employees of different races and genders to include nationality, age, physical ability, and sexual orientation in the types of differences the organization would actively value. These additional categories of diversity were identified when Baxter conducted focus groups of employees at various levels of the organization. Baxter also addressed the issue of caste systems, which exist in most corporations. As discussed in chapter 5, a caste system exists when an organization appears to devalue, explicitly or implicitly, certain types of jobs, such as staff jobs, clerical jobs, or technical jobs. Although caste systems are rarely explicit, they send very clear messages about the perceived value of certain job categories.

At the request of Vernon R. Loucks, Jr., the top-level management at Baxter spent about six months discussing how differences can affect a person's ability to contribute fully to an organization. In addressing each of the various issues of valuing differences, the Baxter management asked, "Why should we be concerned about this issue?" In answering its questions, Baxter arrived at the following reasons for valuing differences:

- To respond to a business environment of labor and skill shortages and changing demographics and workforce values. The work environment, as Baxter knew it, was changing, and this was not just a blip on the horizon but a new paradigm in the making.

- To demonstrate to its employees, stockholders, customers, and community that Baxter is a strategically driven, well-managed, quality-focused corporation.
- To prepare Baxter employees to manage and motivate an increasingly diverse workforce. Baxter recognized that traditional approaches to managing a homogeneous workforce would not work in an increasingly diverse work population.
- To enable Baxter to identify, attract, and retain highly skilled and productive employees and suppliers. Before it began its diversity management efforts, Baxter was already a desirable organization for which to work. By addressing workforce diversity, Baxter positioned itself to be the employer of choice in a tight labor market.

In order to continue to attract the most qualified and skilled employees in the tight health care labor market of the 1990s and beyond, Baxter realized that the key would be to recruit a diverse workforce instead of limiting its recruitment efforts to the more traditional white male corporate employees. Baxter recognized that in order to achieve and maintain organizational excellence, it must have a high-quality, well-motivated workforce, regardless of whether it fits the traditional mold. In an organization like Baxter, patents run out, technology gets copied, and desirable markets are crowded by organizations with similar services, but an excellent workforce is a lasting asset that ensures ongoing organizational strength and prosperity. An effective workforce is especially critical to health care customer service, which is heavily influenced by employees and paramount to a health care organization's smooth operation.

Baxter established its rationale for striving for improved diversity management: a recognition that it needed to continue to attract and retain the cream of the crop to remain successful in the increasingly diverse workplace of the decades to come. The next step was for management to ask itself, "How do we shake ourselves up? How do we determine what we need to do and undertake the necessary changes?"

Embarking upon the Change Process

In order to accomplish change, an organization must create a sense of dissatisfaction with the status quo, present an appealing picture of how things can be changed for the better, and then show employees how to accomplish that change. That is exactly what Baxter did to accomplish its diversity management changes. It decided that the first course of action was to have employees define the problem. To obtain this definition, Baxter undertook an internal environmental assessment and culture and value analysis, as described in chapter 3. A survey was designed to explore three basic questions:[6]

1. What must change at Baxter in order to make it a great place for women and minorities to work?
2. What factors prevent effective work relationships among ethnic groups at Baxter?
3. How can Baxter improve working relationships among ethnic groups?

The survey was designed to analyze employees' attitudes *and* behaviors because prior research has shown that attitudes do not necessarily predict behaviors. This was evident in a classic study conducted in the 1960s at the University of Wisconsin. Thirty-four white subjects were asked whether they would be willing to pose for a photograph with an African-American person if the photo were to appear in their hometown newspaper in an ad for the National Association for the Advancement of Colored People. Fifty percent of the subjects verbally expressed a high willingness to pose for such a photograph. The response rate dropped to 24 percent when the subjects were asked to sign an agreement. Only 6 percent agreed to make an appointment to be photographed, and only 3 percent actually showed up for the photo session.[7] This study, and others, strongly suggested that what people say they will be willing to do and how they actually behave are not necessarily the same. With this insight in mind, Baxter divided its survey into two sections: one to determine attitudes and the other to determine behavior.

To determine employees' attitudes, Baxter's survey posed two questions to its employees of various ethnicities and races, differentiating between male and female responses:

1. How comfortable would you be in recommending to a minority friend that he or she join Baxter because it is an excellent place for minorities to work?
2. What would have to change in our corporation to make you feel more comfortable in recommending Baxter as an excellent place for minorities to work?

The rationale for these two questions was to compare, across lines of ethnicity, race, and gender, how attractive Baxter was perceived to be by its current employees. Those conducting the survey hypothesized that if Baxter employees from differing ethnicities, races, and genders feel uncomfortable or unwelcome, they probably will not feel self-confident enough to perform at their peak capacity or be willing to recommend Baxter as an excellent place for others to work.

To determine employees' behavior, Baxter created survey questions that addressed working relationships among people of the opposite sex or from different racial or ethnic backgrounds. The survey was conducted by hypothetically pairing employees from different backgrounds, for example, pairing white workers through a random sampling process with Hispanic, Asian, or African-American coworkers. The paired employees were asked the following questions:

1. What did your coworker do that prevented your working relationship from being as good as it could possibly be?
2. What did you do in your working relationship with your coworker that prevented the relationship from being as good as it could possibly be?
3. What suggestions do you have for improving the working relationship between your ethnic group and your coworker's ethnic group?

Once the questions for the survey were developed and put into final form, the next step was to ensure that enough employees completed the survey. Baxter surveyed over 17,000 employees by mailing a survey instrument to individual work stations. Because the survey asked questions that were potentially difficult and anxiety provoking, those responsible for the survey anticipated that most employees would not complete it. Baxter needed a 10 percent response rate to ensure a meaningful analysis; the actual response rate was 12.5 percent. The respondents represented both genders, a variety of work categories, and all three predominant minority groups at Baxter—Asians, Hispanics, and African-Americans—as well as whites.

Examining the Survey Results

The responses to the survey question, "How comfortable would you be in recommending to a minority friend that he or she join Baxter because it is an excellent place for minorities to work?" seemed positive at first. On a scale of 1 to 10, with 1 being *not comfortable* and 10 being *very comfortable*, the mean score was a high 7.35.[8] Baxter might have decided that this high rating meant that there was no need to change or improve its management of workforce diversity, but Baxter did not take these results at face value. After breaking down the data by the following categories, a different picture emerged:

- *Job classification:* There was no statistically significant difference in responses between hourly and salaried employees, nor between nonexempt employees and managers and professionals. Hourly workers' scores averaged 7.42, salaried workers' scores averaged 7.36, and managers' and professionals' scores averaged 7.29. This meant that whether employees were executives, secretaries, or truck drivers, the comfort level in referring minorities to Baxter was consistently high.
- *Seniority:* There was no statistically significant difference in responses according to employees' length of service, whether it was less than 5 years, between 5 and 15 years, or more than 15 years.
- *Age:* There was a slight difference in responses between employees who were between 30 and 50 years of age and those who were over 50. Employees who were in the 30-to-50-years-of-age category were less comfortable than employees over 50 years of age in referring a minority friend. Employees under 30 years

of age were not statistically different from either of the other two age categories. Those administering the survey hypothesized that the slightly lower mean score for employees between 30 and 50 years of age reflected that group's general desire for change, a trend found in other types of employee surveys.

- *Gender:* This was the first category where a significant statistical difference began to appear. The mean score for males was 7.53; for females it was 7.19. This meant that female employees felt less comfortable referring a minority friend to Baxter based solely on the condition of being a female employee.
- *Ethnicity:* The category of ethnicity was the real eye-opener for Baxter. Breaking down the mean score of 7.35 by ethnic groups produced the following results: whites scored 7.83, Hispanics scored 7.44, Asians scored 7.21, but the mean score for African-Americans significantly dropped to 5.41. Further analysis of the subgroups revealed that 40 percent of the white employees who responded to the survey gave a score of 10 (*most comfortable* with referring a minority job seeker to Baxter), 10 percent gave a score of 9, and 17 percent gave a score of 8. This meant that 67 percent of the white respondents, or 2 out of every 3, felt very comfortable recommending that a minority friend join Baxter because it is an excellent place for minorities to work.

The score of 5.41 from African-Americans was also broken down, revealing a startling difference from the perceptions of whites. Analysis revealed that 16 percent of African-American respondents gave a comfort level score of 10 in referring a minority friend. However, 17 percent gave the lowest comfort level, a score of 1. In addition to this bimodal response, 15 percent of African-American respondents gave a comfort level score of 5. Thus, African-Americans at Baxter were just as likely to heartily recommend Baxter to minority friends as an excellent place for minorities to work as they were to recommend that their friends look elsewhere. Such responses created the organizational discomfort needed to move Baxter's management forward in the quest to increase the corporation's valuing of differences.

When the results of the survey's attitude section, which assessed comfort level ratings, were combined with the results of the survey's behavioral section, which asked employees about their working relationships with people who are different, three recommendations emerged:

1. Baxter needed to dramatically increase its visible commitment to valuing diversity in its workforce.
2. Baxter needed to provide training that focused on valuing differences among employees.
3. Baxter needed to change promotion practices to accelerate the movement of women and minorities into executive-level positions.

In addition to generating the preceding three recommendations, the diversity survey also underscored the following four general observations regarding potential resistance and difficulties that Baxter would face in an attempt to significantly change its diversity management practices:

1. Comfort levels were especially high among older white males who had been with the company for a long time. In order for change to be accomplished, this group had to become dissatisfied with the status quo. Such dissatisfaction could be achieved by highlighting future workforce demographics and the potential for a labor crisis and by appealing to a general concern that all employees should feel comfortable and confident enough to contribute their best efforts on a daily basis.

2. There was an historical tendency to withdraw, especially by minorities, when working relationship problems occurred among ethnic groups. As an organization that tried to empower its workforce to freely identify, raise, and resolve problems, Baxter found this tendency extremely troubling. Employees who find it necessary to withdraw in the face of problems or feel threatened or uncomfortable in addressing cultural differences create roadblocks to the organization's progress and success.

3. Employees manifested a great deal of deflection and denial, as well as a lack of introspection. The behavioral section of the survey revealed that employees were ready to "point the finger" when asked what their partner did to impair their working relationship, but they accepted little personal responsibility for those problems. Employees simply focused on others' problems instead of using positive and constructive communication methods.

4. Based on the data from the survey respondents, Baxter anticipated much passive resistance in addressing the challenges of valuing differences and improving acceptance of workforce diversity. A major initiative would be required to overcome resistant attitudes, which sometimes took the form of remarks such as, "This is not as big a problem as we made it out to be" and "We have other, more immediate priorities."

Now that Baxter had a clear picture of its key diversity management problems and a set of recommendations, its next step was to create an action plan.

Creating the Action Plan

Baxter's action plan began by identifying and formally selecting the necessary champions of diversity, following the process discussed in chapter 8. Because Baxter recognized that improved valuing of diversity cannot be achieved without commitment from top levels of the organization, its chairman, Vernon R. Loucks, Jr., spearheaded the diversity change effort. Loucks appointed three task forces to focus on the three basic questions asked by the survey. Each task force was chaired by a corporate officer and consisted of approximately nine members of Baxter's executive team. (This is an important point: *Top-level management was involved in the process from the very outset, empowering the initiative to* improve the organization's valuing of diversity.) The first task force's objective was to devise a plan of action to dramatically increase the visibility of the organization's commitment to improved management of workforce diversity. The objective of the second task force was to tackle the issues of diversity training. The third task force was assigned to review selection and promotion practices at Baxter. The following three sections summarize the work of these task forces.

Increasing Visible Commitment to Workforce Diversity

As a starting point for increasing the organization's visible commitment to workforce diversity, the first task force composed the following organizational mission statement for all employees to read and understand:

- Baxter International believes that a multicultural employee population is essential to the company's leadership in health care around the world.
- This means *respecting* every individual and recognizing that individual self-esteem is important to performance.
- It means *valuing* people's diverse backgrounds, skills, and capabilities.
- It means *challenging* and providing development opportunities for each employee to achieve his or her fullest potential.
- Baxter managers must understand diversity and effectively manage their diverse employee population.

The first task force also defined degrees of diversity management on a scale from complying to managing to valuing. (See figure 9-1.) *Complying* with diversity management was defined as reacting to an outside pressure, such as affirmative action mandates, rather than actual work-climate issues. *Managing* diversity was defined as creating a successful business by attracting the best people, regardless of age, race, gender, background, physical ability, culture, or ethnicity. The task force defined *valuing* diversity as recognizing that individual self-esteem is important to performance and that people who feel comfortable in their work environment are more likely to feel confident in their ability to contribute to the organization.

Finally, the first task force also developed a communication plan to keep the various organizational units updated on Baxter's progress in diversity efforts. The communication plan specified the periodic distribution of update memos on issues and initiatives related to diversity management from the three task force chairpersons, as well as the publication of several articles on diversity issues in *PACE*, Baxter's internationally distributed internal publication.

Implementing Diversity Training

Outside diversity consultants worked with the second task force to design a comprehensive training program that focused on valuing differences and employee development. The program, entitled "Diversity Is the Issue, Development Is the

Figure 9-1. Conceptual Model of Diversity

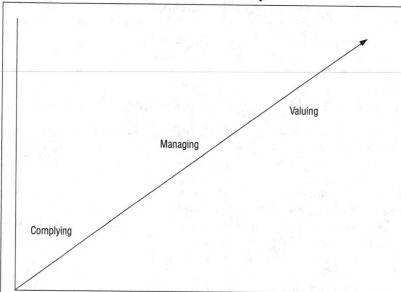

Attitudes of Complying with Diversity

- React to pressure, not the problem, let alone the opportunity.
- Emphasize compliance and obligation.
- Keep the "law" out of our business.
- Practice situational ethics.
- Avoid legal consequences.

Attitudes of Managing Diversity

- Diversity is important as a competitive business practice, and we are here to run a business.
- We need to attract the best people.
- Job stability and continuity are important to success.
- Turnover costs money.

Attitudes of Valuing Diversity

- Individual self-esteem is important to performance.
- People who feel comfortable in their work environment are more likely to feel confident in their ability to contribute.
- Business, social, and moral values are one and the same.
- Your job is a part of life, not vice versa.
- The more productive people are those who feel valued for who they are.
- Productive people = a high-performance organization.

Answer," was based on the premise that Baxter could benefit its employees most through helping them build confidence in their ability to perform constructively and productively.

The training program was initiated by the 28 corporate officers' participation in a two-day version of the program, followed by the participation of the rest of the organization's managers. All Baxter employees would eventually participate in variations of the training program. The one-and-one-half-day basic training program consists of five modules.

Module one, entitled *Introduction*, defines workforce diversity, explains why it is important, and outlines its business implications. Module two, entitled *Challenging Assumptions*, identifies common stereotypes related to employees from diverse backgrounds, helps participants understand their own biases and prejudices, and begins the process of understanding those who are "different." *Analyzing Obstacles* (module three) examines barriers to managing and valuing differences and includes exercises dealing with gender and race issues. Module four, entitled *Developing Potential*, analyzes the manager's role in employee development and the skills needed to manage multicultural teams. Finally, *Action Planning* (module five) addresses methods to accomplish change. Module five concludes by helping participants develop an individual commitment to diversity management with specific goals and objectives that can be incorporated into the management process on a day-to-day basis.

Among the exercises utilized in module three were the "Stop, Start, and Continue" and "Fishbowl" exercises. The Stop, Start, and Continue Exercise is designed to make workshop participants more aware of the differences between various groups and to promote a better understanding of how those differences play out in the workplace. The rules of this exercise are quite simple. Participants are separated into groups, for example, women, men, and minorities. Each group meets to discuss what they want the other group to "stop doing," "start doing," and "continue doing" with regard to work relationships and feedback on behaviors that may be impeding workplace effectiveness. The responding group must then paraphrase what they understand they are to stop, start, and continue; this helps to ensure clarity of issues and eliminate the watering down of those issues. Each group proceeds until all groups have been provided with position feedback on what they need to continue to do to enhance work relationships and feedback. Baxter found this exercise to be extremely effective in promoting communication within and among the various groups.

In the Fishbowl Exercise, workshop participants are separated into subgroups, such as white males, white females, African-American males, African-American females, and so forth. Members of one subgroup at a time move into the middle of the room—as though they were entering a "fishbowl"—and are asked questions by the workshop participants who remain outside the fishbowl. The subgroup within the fishbowl must first discuss the questions among themselves before responding. The ground rules are simple, and the group outside the fishbowl is allowed to ask any questions it wishes. The objective of the exercise is to facilitate communication among the various subgroups and to enhance awareness of how differences impact workplace interactions.

Baxter recognized the importance of having an experienced and trained facilitator present for these and numerous other exercises. The workshops were geared toward assisting participants to change ineffective workplace behaviors but not toward addressing personal issues.

Enhancing Selection, Development, and Promotion Practices

The third task force was charged with keeping Baxter's job pipeline filled with talent rather than merely filling positions as they became available. As a result of this task force's work, developing internal talent among nontraditional employee groups became a key concern at Baxter. Employee development became a participative process among supervisors and subordinates in that employees were asked for input regarding their career directions and skill needs during their performance evaluations.

As a result of this task force's findings and recommendations, Baxter created the position of vice-president for diversity initiatives. The new position demonstrated Baxter's commitment to finding the best people, regardless of whether they come from traditional employee groups such as white males. Baxter began to actively seek, and continues to seek, qualified females and minorities for executive and management positions.

Practicing Diversity

Baxter Healthcare Corporation's quest for more effective diversity management did not stop with its task forces and action plan. Because Baxter is a cutting-edge organization that does not wait for government mandates before it faces the realities of today's workplace, and because Baxter views diversity with a wide-angle lens in its efforts to create a sensitive, caring, responsible, and responsive work environment, Baxter has adjusted its policies to address the changing needs of its workforce.

Family Leave

In January 1991, long before the enactment of the Family and Medical Leave Act of 1993, Baxter instituted a family leave policy. This policy allows employees to take one unpaid leave of absence lasting up to 12 work weeks during a 12-month period. During this leave, the employee's job is held for him or her. The leave of absence may be taken for any of the following reasons:

- The birth of a child to the employee or employee's spouse
- The placement of a child with the employee for adoption or foster care

- The need to care for the employee's child, spouse, parent, mother-in-law, father-in-law, or legal dependent who has a documented serious health condition

Although this leave is unpaid, employees may draw on their accumulated paid sick time.

Work and Family Benefits

Baxter has a full range of benefits to deal with work and family issues. The organization realizes that few American families have a stay-at-home parent to provide child care and elder care and understands that family needs have a direct impact on employees' work lives. Although Baxter's mission statement testifies that the company is "committed to . . . respecting employees as individuals and providing opportunities for their personal development," the mission statement of Baxter's human resource function took this challenge even farther: "To ensure a management environment that emphasizes open communication, respect for the individual, and a healthy balance between work, personal, and family life; and a work environment that ensures that employees derive a sense of accomplishment, contribution, and pride from their association with Baxter."

Baxter recognizes that employees' family lives affect their job performance and that work-related events affect employees' family lives. In an attempt to bring a sense of balance to an employee's world, Baxter's work and family benefits include the following:

- *Resource and informational assistance,* including child care and elder care resource and referral programs, employee assistance programs, career development counseling, and health benefits information.
- *Financial assistance* for costs associated with adoptions and for the education of employees and their dependents. Financial assistance at Baxter also takes the form of an employee credit union, retirement programs, scholarship programs for employees' dependents, and reimbursement accounts for health care and dependent care expenses.
- *Flexibility* in coordinating work and family needs, as evidenced by Baxter's family leave policy and a wide range of flexible benefits that can be selected, depending on individual circumstances. As an example of this flexibility, Baxter has recognized that adoption leave is as important as leave for a natural birth; that men as well as women deserve time to spend with a new child; and that employees should be able to care for a loved one with a serious, long-term illness and still have a job to come back to. Although employees are not paid during these leaves, some of their benefits may continue to be provided by the corporation.

    Another example of Baxter's flexibility is its promotion of job sharing. Although organizations typically view job sharing at a clerical or secretarial level, Baxter has had incredible success with job sharing at the management level. Currently, in one of Baxter's distribution systems, there are two women who share the position of controller. This accommodation was made to assist both employees with managing their family responsibilities.

Baxter's well-designed work and family benefits package makes life easier for its employees and their families and serves as a major step in positioning Baxter as an employer of choice.

Putting Teeth into Diversity Action Plans

The actions taken by Baxter in response to the changing needs of a changing workforce are impressive and forward-looking, and yet the argument can be made that these are all corporate actions to deal with workforce diversity. What is the individual manager's responsibility for effective diversity management at Baxter? Two initiatives, *recognition and reward* and *ongoing measurement and monitoring*, form the foundation for determining the success of individual managers in meeting their responsibility of effective management of workforce diversity.

Recognition and Reward

Baxter's top-level management realized that to achieve effective diversity management, the organization's recognition and reward systems had to change to reflect the importance of workforce diversity. This change has been evident in the awards presented at the annual Chairman's Conference. These awards, presented by Baxter's chairman, are highly coveted within Baxter's corporate culture. In the past, the criteria for meriting an award focused on two objectives: operating excellence and quality. Baxter has recently added a third objective: diversity and employee development. This objective requires creating noteworthy results in the area of valuing diversity and actively embracing employee development. In addition to awards in each of these three categories, Baxter presents the Karl D. Bays Award for best overall performance.[9] To win the Karl D. Bays Award, an operating unit must excel in all three of the preceding objectives.

Ongoing Measurement and Monitoring

To support the recognition process, Baxter has used the data from the original employee surveys to create a Valuing Diversity Index for the ongoing measurement and monitoring of diversity management progress.[10] The Valuing Diversity Index, which has been validated and tested for reliability, measures seven important areas:

1. Organizational climate (how it values differences)
2. Hiring practices

3. Promotion practices
4. Visibility of commitment to diversity
5. Equity and fairness
6. Training and development
7. Workplace politics

Baxter's newsletter *Facets*, which was developed as an ongoing educational medium for addressing diversity issues, recently summarized Baxter's commitment to valuing differences. An article entitled "Figuring the Diversity Equation" provides the following formula to describe the process of valuing diversity at Baxter:[11]

$$VDCI = CA \times AO \times DP \times (Mgmt.Supp. + Comm.)$$

The components of the formula are as follows:

- *VDCI—Valuing Diversity for Continuous Improvement:* VDCI is the bottom-line result of Baxter's commitment to quality, which mandates the best use of the best people. To ensure quality, Baxter must tap its diverse workforce to find innovative and unique ways to survive, prosper, and strive for excellence. This new way of thinking requires changing the old management paradigms that constituted past success, such as the assumption that the path to a successful career meant conformity to "acceptable" norms (which in most cases were the norms of white males).
- *CA—Challenging Assumptions:* It is typical for people to harbor positive and negative assumptions about individuals and groups of people who are different from themselves. These assumptions and stereotypes influence expectations of individual performance and success. Reliance on a predetermined set of assumptions often leads people to expect lackluster performance or failure from others. The concept of challenging assumptions requires Baxter employees to question and understand the personal baggage and stereotypes and prejudices about others that they bring to the workplace.
- *AO—Analyzing Obstacles:* Continuously assessing organizational behaviors and barriers in the corporate culture is part of the road to success in valuing differences at Baxter.
- *DP—Developing Potential:* Developing potential is a strategy for removing workplace obstacles and a way to tap into workforce talent and skills. Developing potential by offering appropriate growth opportunities is the responsibility of every Baxter manager. It is the responsibility of every employee to look for opportunities for job growth and development.
- *Mgmt.Supp. + Comm.—Management Support and Communication:* Management support and communication as a means of maximizing an employee's chance for success is the lifeblood of Baxter's valuing diversity process. This support is made available through workshops and study materials that provide

individuals with new or updated skills, tools, data, or resources for the implementation of needed change. Management support must be communicated to all employees in an atmosphere of mutual trust, honesty, and openness.

Using this diversity equation, along with understanding and acceptance, Baxter continues to promote valuing diversity as a core environmental value. Only when valuing diversity is such a value will the company truly be able to reap the full benefits of the diversity equation.

Studying Baxter's Lessons

As of this writing, Baxter has had time to observe and evaluate the valuing diversity journey it began in 1990. The following five sections discuss valuable lessons Baxter has identified and learned from as a result of living with its valuing diversity initiative on a day-to-day basis.

There Is No Quick Fix to Valuing Diversity

Employee attitudes and behaviors will not change as a result of one or two diversity training sessions. Training is a necessary and continuous intervention to make employees aware of behaviors that create organizational barriers preventing each employee from reaching his or her full potential.

Valuing diversity must be viewed as a long-term process that helps managers and employees internalize the behaviors that help create an environment where differences are not only accepted but valued as an asset in meeting organizational goals. Baxter recognizes and rewards managers who take diversity seriously and incorporate diversity management into their overall business strategies. When such efforts are rewarded and recognized, valuing diversity more readily becomes a part of corporate culture.

Establishing the value of diversity management as a normal part of business culture is a five-step process at Baxter:

1. Baxter provides its managers with education and training geared toward a thorough understanding of diversity from both an internal and external point of view. Educational sessions might, for example, examine the impact of diversity on a changing customer base or discuss how managing diversity can increase workforce productivity.
2. Baxter continues to collect data through the Valuing Diversity Index, surveys, and focus groups to keep managers abreast of changing employee demographics, issues, and concerns. This further emphasizes Baxter's commitment to diversity as a journey, not a destination.

3. By incorporating diversity management into business objectives, Baxter's managers are encouraged to identify one or two diversity objectives for improvement as opposed to using a shotgun approach that tries to attack all of the diversity issues at once.
4. Managers at Baxter are shown how valuing diversity affects their end product. They are more likely to engage in training and change management if they can clearly understand how the culture they create in their own units affects overall employee productivity and customer satisfaction.
5. Managers are recognized and rewarded for implementing initiatives that reinforce the desired behaviors outlined in diversity training and are held accountable for diversity management results.

Effective Workforce Diversity Management Is Not an Isolated Activity

Identifying improved diversity management as a major organizational objective and weaving valuing diversity into the fabric of organizational operations is not a simple or isolated process. In fact, understanding business requirements is critical to valuing diversity. For example, through its just-in-time inventory program, a service initiated to increase customer satisfaction, hospitals may interact with Baxter as often as 10,000 times per month. This service offers clients 10,000 opportunities per month to experience a positive or negative service interaction with Baxter. In the past, hospitals interacted with the white-collar sales staff at Baxter when addressing supply needs. At present, the distribution system is administered predominantly by blue-collar workers in the Baxter warehouses. This change required that blue-collar workers develop skills in communications, problem solving, and customer interaction, and it required an understanding on the part of hospitals that the "supply salesman" of the past had changed. Stereotyped notions of social-class distinctions often got in the way of doing business until both parties realized that successfully meeting customer expectations relied on understanding and teamwork.

Organizations Must Practice What They Preach

Valuing diversity requires a commitment of resources. To demonstrate its commitment, Baxter created a new department solely devoted to valuing diversity. This diversity management department, which reports directly to the chief operating officer, is responsible for identifying the need for, creating, and implementing the organization's various diversity training programs and serves as an internal consultant to the company's various operating units on diversity matters. The advantage of this approach is that the diversity management department, a cohesive group focused only on diversity issues, has developed expertise in working with the organization's various departments to resolve specific diversity issues.

The creation of the new department has been far more effective than adding diversity troubleshooting to someone's already lengthy list of duties.

Baxter views the creation of a diversity department as similar to its earlier quality initiatives. Baxter's quality department began as a separate function focusing only on quality initiatives. As quality became an integral part of Baxter's various business units, the quality department became integrated into the other divisions of the corporation. Baxter anticipates that when diversity management has been embraced and is operating as an integral part of the business units, there will no longer be a need for a separate diversity unit.

In another example of practicing what it preaches, as early as 1987 Baxter formally established its minority and female supplier-development program to identify, develop, and use companies owned by minorities and women. Since the program's introduction, Baxter has increased its purchases from minority-owned businesses by more than 500 percent.

Valuing Diversity Does Not Replace Affirmative Action

Despite receiving some negative press, affirmative action has been a useful intervention in assuring fair access to equal employment opportunities. Although Baxter is committed to a diverse workforce without resorting to a quota system, its valuing of diversity does not preclude the need for affirmative action. Creating access and opportunity for employees who are different is a beginning; creating acceptance and active valuing of their differences is the goal.

Valuing Diversity Is Not a Cookie-Cutter Process

Training programs need to fit an organization's specific diversity issues. The use of focus groups and multicultural teams to develop and recommend diversity management plans is extremely helpful, but teams require time to bond in trust, openness, and respect. Hearts can be in the right place, but egos can get in the way of a team's success when teams are slapped together and rushed. Clear expectations of team and focus group responsibilities must be carefully defined up front. Off-the-shelf training programs can be useful in beginning a discussion of diversity, but these programs will have little organizational impact in bringing about systemic change. Diversity training must be tailored to an organization's specific needs, whether the tailoring is done by current staff or by outside consulting or training groups.[12]

Valuing Diversity at Baxter Today

Baxter has made major strides toward its goals in valuing diversity. However, Baxter views workforce diversity as a long-term process, not a short-term fad or a quick fix. The people who manage Baxter Healthcare Corporation view

themselves as stewards of the organization. Their goal is to create an even better organization for the next generation of stewards, who will then seek to make
Baxter even better. Assuming that succeeding management groups maintain
these same goals, the course that Baxter has charted in the area of workforce
diversity will most assuredly result in a working environment in which differences are naturally sustained. Barriers preventing employees at all levels from
reaching their full potential will be eliminated, not through legislated actions
on the part of governments, but through responsive, caring, and responsible
Baxter management. Eventually, as this cycle continues, valuing differences will
become embedded in the culture at Baxter Healthcare Corporation, making
it even more progressive and effective in the eyes of its employees, stockholders,
and the worldwide communities that it serves.[13,14]

As recently as October 1993, Baxter continued to be recognized for "walking the talk" as it relates to its diversity management efforts when it received
the 1993 Corporate Award for Minority Business Development from the
U.S. Department of Commerce. The Corporate Award is conferred annually
to companies making the greatest impact on the development of minority-owned
businesses. "Baxter is being recognized for its innovation, leadership, and commitment to creating opportunities for minority businesses in the health-care
industry," said Maye Foster-Thompson, executive director of the Chicago Regional
Purchasing Council, which nominated Baxter for the award. "The company
has done an outstanding job of integrating its minority business development
program into its overall corporate goals and strategic plan, underscoring the
company's strong commitment to creating opportunities for minorities."[15]

After Baxter received this prestigious award, Wilfred J. Lucas, Baxter's vice-
president of diversity management, stated:

> Cultural diversity is essential to Baxter's drive to be a world leader in health
> care. Our programs have helped minority-owned businesses enter areas where
> the doors have been closed to them in the past. Since health care affects
> every person in America, it only makes sense that the minority community
> is included in the economic structure of the industry. By expanding our pool
> of vendors, we stand to get better products, services, and prices.[16]

In January 1994 Baxter Healthcare Corporation consolidated and aligned
all of its organizational initiatives under three basic values: Respect, Responsiveness, and Results. The articulation and elaboration of these three values
as they relate to Baxter's employees, customers, and shareholders are intended
to provide an umbrella for further shaping the culture of Baxter as a desirable
place to work, conduct business, and invest.

References

1. Thomas, R. R., Jr. *Beyond Race and Gender.* New York City: AMACOM, 1991, p. 59.

2. Thomas, p. 51.

3. The best companies for women. *Business Week*, Aug. 6, 1990.

4. *Working Mother*, Oct. 1993.

5. Morris, B. Y., quoted in a press release from Baxter Healthcare Corporation, Deerfield, IL, dated Oct. 7, 1993.

6. The initial diversity survey was designed and created by Frank M. J. LaFasto, Ph.D., vice-president, organizational planning and development, Baxter Healthcare Corporation, and Carl E. Larson, Ph.D., professor of speech communication at the University of Denver.

7. Linn, L. S. Verbal attitudes and overt behaviors: a study of racial discrimination. In: Rosnow, R., and Robinson, E., editors. *Experiments in Persuasion*. New York City: Academic Press, 1967.

8. The survey analysis was completed by Omni Research, an independent firm located in Denver, CO.

9. Karl D. Bays was chairman and chief executive officer of the American Hospital Supply Company before the merger that created the Baxter Healthcare Corporation. For a time after the merger took place, Mr. Bays served as chairman of Baxter Healthcare Corporation.

10. *The Diversity Index*, 1992, was sponsored by Baxter Healthcare Corporation and developed by Heidi Brinkman, Ph.D., College of Business Administration, University of Denver; Frank M. J. LaFasto, Ph.D., Baxter Healthcare Corporation; and Carl E. Larson, Ph.D., Department of Speech Communication, University of Denver.

11. Figuring the diversity equation. *Facets*, Summer 1992, p. 1.

12. Lucas, Wilfred (vice-president, diversity management, Baxter Healthcare Corporation). Interview with author. Deerfield, IL, Sept. 23, 1992.

13. LaFasto, Frank M. J. (vice-president, organization planning and development, Baxter Healthcare Corporation). Interview with author. Deerfield, IL, Apr. 13, 1992.

14. Lucas, Wilfred (vice-president, diversity management, Baxter Healthcare Corporation). Interview with author. Deerfield, IL, Apr. 13, 1992.

15. Foster-Thompson, M., quoted in a press release from Baxter Healthcare Corporation, Deerfield, IL, dated Oct. 7, 1993.

16. Lucas, Wilfred (vice-president, diversity management, Baxter Healthcare Corporation), quoted in a press release from Baxter Healthcare Corporation, Deerfield, IL, dated Oct. 7, 1993.

Ensuring Long-Term Success through Effective Diversity Management

Fundamental changes in the American workplace and workforce have created challenges for health care organizations planning for long-term success in managing workforce diversity. The American workplace has evolved from a generally autocratic environment with top-down management to one that is more democratic and participatory. The corporate downsizing and organizational flattening of the late 1980s and early 1990s has accelerated this fundamental change by reducing the numbers of middle managers and levels of bureaucracy and emphasizing the importance of quality and customer service.[1] The pool of potential employees has become increasingly crucial to health care organizations experiencing financial constraints and the effects of a shortage of qualified health care workers. All of these changes have worked together to increase the need for *employee empowerment*, which is the process of management giving all employees the authority and the tools to accomplish the full scope of their responsibilities. In health care organizations that practice diversity management, employee empowerment goes beyond simply enhancing employees' skills and abilities to include eliminating prejudice, intolerance, and stereotypes that prevent employees from diverse groups and cultures from realizing their fullest potential.[2]

Empowering the Diverse Organization

Employee empowerment is a critical part of any program to ensure long-term success in managing a diverse workforce. Although *empowerment* may seem to be simply a buzzword that keeps cropping up in articles and books about management, it is actually one of the least understood and most underestimated of today's business concepts.

For all employees to accomplish the full scope of their responsibilities and realize their full potential, an environment of employee empowerment must accord employees more responsibility while still holding them accountable and must reward all employees for achievements while refraining from penalizing them for their inevitable mistakes. Frederick W. Smith, chairman and president of the

Federal Express Corporation, described this type of management as creating a "power environment" that allows employees to make well-intentioned errors as they try new ways of doing things.[3]

Health care organizations sometimes confuse the considerable autonomy and influence that some workers have in the day-to-day operations of particular areas with true employee empowerment. For example, physicians have a major influence on all aspects of medical care, nurses tend to run day-to-day operations on the floors, and the directors of the dietary, housekeeping, and laundry departments exert considerable influence over their areas. However, such autonomy and influence are actually decentralized control or delegation without coordinated planning or strategy rather than employee empowerment.[4] This ill-conceived, decentralized approach to managing an organization creates obstacles to long-term success in the form of turf conflicts and decisions made in isolation, without consideration of their organizational impact.[5]

In a health care organization where employees are truly empowered, decisions are made by the employees most directly involved with the issues at hand, which frees upper-level management to focus on policy making, overseeing operations, strategic planning, and developing skills to cope with new situations and problems. In *Beyond Race and Gender*, R. Roosevelt Thomas, Jr., refers to this new type of management as the *empowerment model*, which focuses on creating an atmosphere that enables all employees, including those from diverse cultures and backgrounds, of both genders, and of all ages and abilities, to work as effectively and efficiently as possible.[6] Employees working under the empowerment model feel free to work together to take risks, try new ways of doing things, and develop what Peter M. Senge calls a "shared vision" through "creative tension and commitment to the truth that emphasize a reinforcing spiral of enthusiasm and momentum."[7]

Creating a Risk-Taking Environment

Fear is the greatest obstacle to creating the risk-taking environment that is the cornerstone of true employee empowerment, effective management of workforce diversity, and long-term success. In health care organizations, peoples' lives and health are continuously at stake and the potential for liability is almost limitless, making fear a fact of work life. Added to these extraordinary fears are common, day-to-day employee fears that inhibit risk taking, including fear of failure, criticism, demotion or termination, embarrassment, and disappointing peers and supervisors. Diverse health care workforces are likely to include employees who tend to avoid risk or conflict because of their cultural or ethnic backgrounds. Additionally, women and nontraditional employees such as older workers and the differently abled may avoid risk taking out of fear of jeopardizing their newfound place in the organization.

In order to reduce fear and create a work environment that fosters productive risk taking, health care organizations and especially management must understand the realities of risk and reinforce appropriate risk taking. These two steps will particularly help employee groups that are especially risk averse.

Understanding the Realities of Risk

When encouraging employees to overcome fear and take necessary and appropriate risks, health care managers and employees alike should come to understand that risk is a fundamental element of change and the change process. In *Corporate Life Cycles*, Ichak Adizes lists beliefs about risk taking that characterize growing organizations:[8]

- Personal success stems from taking risk.
- Everything is permitted unless expressly forbidden.
- Problems are really opportunities.
- Responsibility is not matched with authority.
- Line people call the shots.

Health care organizations should strive to promote these beliefs in the process of creating a work environment that frees all employees to take necessary and appropriate risks.

Determining and Reinforcing Acceptable and Appropriate Risk Taking

Once health care organizations have begun to institutionalize an understanding of the realities of risk, they should institute procedures for identifying and reinforcing acceptable and appropriate types of risk. In the health care field, ill-advised or inappropriate risk taking can have catastrophic effects.

When determining acceptable and appropriate risks, the goal should be to provide the safest and highest quality care to its customers. For example, it is acceptable and appropriate for a unit head in the emergency department to exceed his or her official authority and, in the absence of a supervisor, approve staff overtime if there is a sudden influx of patients that exceeds the capacity of existing staff to safely handle. Another example of acceptable and appropriate risk taking is when a clerical employee notices that a patient in the waiting room needs immediate help and takes the initiative to summon a doctor or nurse. Still another example is a hospital pharmacist who, while filling a patient's prescription, notes that the patient is already taking medications with which the new medication may interact badly and takes the initiative to discuss the problem with the prescribing physician before filling the prescription. In all of these examples, employees took the risk of exceeding their official authority in order to ensure patients' health and safety. All of these examples demonstrate acceptable, appropriate risk taking by employees who felt secure and empowered enough to act outside of standard operating procedures.

However, many types of risks are unacceptable and inappropriate, including participating in illegal or unethical activities, using questionable or unproven medical techniques, and exposing the organization to unwarranted liability. Although it is impossible and impractical for health care organizations to determine precisely when employees can and cannot take risks, organizations can provide employees with some food for thought on what acceptable limits might be. In training sessions and department meetings, employees might consider the following situations:

- Under what circumstances can nurses fail to carry out the instructions of doctors with whom they disagree without being grievously insubordinate?
- Is it ever appropriate for a purchasing department staff member to choose a vendor on the basis of factors other than low price (for example, quality)?
- Is it ever acceptable for a medical student to challenge an attending surgeon whom the student believes is about to perform an unnecessary operation?

In addition to helping employees determine acceptable and appropriate risks, health care organizations should reinforce acts of acceptable and appropriate risk taking and groom the employees who performed them as role models. This reinforcement can be accomplished by featuring employees in the organization's internal newsletter, creating an employee-of-the-month program, and establishing financial and nonfinancial awards (discussed later in this chapter). As an added incentive to promote acceptable and appropriate risk taking, the supervisors of honored employees and groups should also be acknowledged for supporting and encouraging employee initiative and risk taking.

Building Systems That Encourage and Support a Diverse Workforce

If all health care employees, regardless of their age, gender, sexual orientation, race, culture, or physical ability, are to feel empowered, free from fear, and able to take appropriate risks, health care organizations must build systems that encourage and support a diverse workforce. To build these systems, organizations will need to weave effective management of workforce diversity into every system of the organization.

Because each health care organization has its own unique environment and cultural and diversity makeup, no one standard system blueprint or action plan will work for every institution. Each organization must tailor its own action plan and build and modify its own systems. To accomplish these goals, health care organizations require effective, appropriate *reward systems* to reinforce employee and group attitudes and behaviors that further the organization's overall mission, aim, goals, and *organizationwide involvement* in planning and operational problem solving.

Developing Effective, Appropriate Reward Systems

One of the most significant commitments an organization's management can make to a program is to be willing to reward others for its success. Any kind of reward system will give credibility to management's commitment to a particular program, as well as provide credibility for the program itself. However, often *nonmonetary* rewards can be most satisfying to those recognized and most effective in encouraging strong, long-lasting changes in employee and group attitudes, behaviors, and practices. Nonmonetary rewards, which can be closely tailored to individual or group values, include promotions, plaques and awards, scholarships, publicity in local media, and appointment to key employee committees. After the initial reward, continuing casual recognition of valued employees and groups will have a lasting effect on group performance.

It is important to keep in mind that even well-thought-out reward systems can lose their effectiveness over the long term. Rewards may begin to be viewed by staff members as entitlements, may become too familiar, and may become less effective in reinforcing desired organizational goals such as improved management of workforce diversity. Reward systems are not mechanisms to permanently change behavior; instead, reward systems should initiate change and maintain it long enough for employees to become acclimated to the change and participate in long-term planning to make the change permanent. To ensure that reward systems are effective in encouraging immediate employee interest in improved handling of workforce diversity and other changes, health care organizations should follow several guidelines:

- Determine the behavior to be rewarded.
- Decide whether rewards should go to individuals, groups, or both.
- Establish a reward significant enough to make it worth employees' or groups' time to try to change behavior. It is safer to err on the side of generosity initially because award amounts can be reduced once the desired change is under way.
- Establish a reward committee composed of managers and champions of diversity to evaluate groups and individuals and determine who should receive rewards.
- Review and update reward criteria annually.

These guidelines apply to monetary as well as nonmonetary reward systems.

Special awards programs to recognize, support, and encourage effective diversity management can help reinforce rewards. Such programs should reinforce achievement at all levels of the organization by recognizing outstanding accomplishments in promoting diversity by managers, staff members, and groups or departments. The recognition program can take the form of an awards banquet or dinner, a ceremony in which certificates or plaques are presented, or some other form that the reward committee determines will be most meaningful to the recognized individuals or groups.

In determining reward recipients, the committee should remember that the purpose of the rewards is to recognize agents of change rather than employees and groups who have boosted organizational productivity. The reward committee must use this criterion because initial improvements in diversity management will involve changes in attitude and behavior that are not immediately quantifiable by traditional measures such as improved productivity.[9]

Even the most effective rewards systems must have unwavering commitment and support from top-level management if they are to be successful in reinforcing effective handling of workforce diversity. This pervasive management commitment is sometimes referred to as *walking the talk*, that is, demonstrating to employees through behavior and actions as well as words that management is committed to change and promoting diversity on an ongoing basis for both monetary and moral reasons.[10] A key part of walking the talk is involving employees in setting organizational missions, aims, and goals and planning for organizational action.

Encouraging Involvement in Organizationwide Strategic Planning and Problem Solving

In order for health care organizations to implement diversity change, their change plan must be incorporated into organizational strategic plans and operational solutions. The organization must have a clear, well-thought-out strategy and aim that everyone in the organization can buy in to and support. Although the overall strategy and aim is set by top-level management, once this strategy and aim has been determined, all of the organization's employees should be involved in more detailed strategic planning and operational problem solving. When devising strategies and aims to improve management of workforce diversity, the goal should be to emphasize how these strategies and aims interface with other business issues that affect the organization's long-term success.

To achieve organizationwide involvement in strategic planning, top-level management should hold management sessions and departmental meetings to announce the institution's new overall strategies and aims. Top-level management should then elicit ideas from these management and departmental employee groups on how to refine and implement the strategies and aims through plans and programs. Managers and staff often suggest plans and programs that are fresh and effective.

After these sessions, top-level management should appoint work teams from each of the organization's major departments and units to determine and prioritize issues relevant to accomplishing the strategic plan's objectives. The teams should present these relevant issues to top-level management, which should take no more than a week to approve, reject, or modify the issues delineated. In some cases, top-level management may opt to postpone issues until there is more information or until further study can be done. Whatever actions top-level management takes, it must communicate quickly and clearly with the work teams. At least once a year, top-level management should share information concerning the diversity programs that have been implemented with all employees through summary documents and staff meetings. This initial and ongoing involvement of management and staff in strategic planning and problem solving will facilitate the employee buy in and sense of ownership that leads to successful change.

Reinforcing That the Value of Change Is in the Process

Another key factor in ensuring involvement in organizationwide strategic planning and problem solving is inculcating the concept that the process of change, difficult as it can be, is the key opportunity for learning and growing and that the most valuable part of change is the process itself. More often than not, the greatest organizational changes and learning take place while managers and staff are actually going through the process of diversity change. Although the ability to maintain progress after implementing changes is a key factor in long-term success, the organizationwide learning and changing that takes place during the step-by-step process of making changes and the observing of how new approaches or programs work through every phase of development builds the momentum that fuels the ongoing maintenance and support process.

Reinforcing the value of change processes can be difficult in health care organizations because the processes often seem to add to employees' already intense work pressures. Management and work teams can build employees' enthusiasm and tolerance for the change process by making involvement in the extra activities associated with leadership and participation in the change process into a perk that will lead to organizational rewards and recognition.[11]

Even when initial staff support and enthusiasm have been garnered, months will pass before staff members really begin to feel the positive effects of organizationwide strategic plans and programs to improve management of workforce diversity. Top-level management can accelerate and reinforce the valuing of the diversity change process by taking the following actions:

- Offering support throughout each step of the process
- Establishing an open-door policy so that employees and staff members can ask questions and share ideas at any time
- Encouraging regular employee and staff member meetings, with and without managers
- Developing a sense of ownership in the program and the process among both groups

The diversity change process should unite employees and staff members in the creation and accomplishment of a common set of aims and goals, improve the working environment for all employees and staff members, and increase the quality of service and customer relations.

Fostering Broad Involvement and Commitment

To implement effective long-term change, management and employees and staff members must become so excited about the ways they can change their organization that they become invested in and committed to participating in the change process. To reach this point of enthusiasm, management and employees and staff members must have a high level of emotional involvement in the process and a strong belief that they can make a difference. Additionally, they must participate actively in setting and accomplishing the organization's goals.

Health care organizations have an advantage in obtaining the emotional commitment of their workforces because most of their employees chose health care careers out of a desire to help others. This concern for others can be a strong motivation for employees to accomplish change, especially when the change has the potential to improve the organization's ability to serve its patients and community. An organization that practices diversity management strengthens the process of developing commitment because it integrates the goals, aims, and needs of the diverse workforce into the organization's overall objectives and strategies.

However, managers sometimes stand in the way of fostering broad-based commitment because they cannot or will not share responsibility and authority with staff members. Such managers have not accepted the fact that market forces, shortages of qualified workers, and increasingly informed and diverse workforces require them to change the way they operate. Once managers accept that the question is not whether they should change but rather how they should change, they will be able to share responsibility and authority with staff members and help foster broad-based commitment.

Supporting the View That Change Is a Continuous Process

The old cliche, "If you are not changing, then you are dying," certainly applies to the health care environment of the 1990s and beyond. Productive, carefully managed diversity change has many positive results, including the following:

- It encourages all staff members and managers to come up with new ideas to improve organizational efficiency and productivity and enhance patient care and customer relations.
- It motivates all staff members and managers to be more involved in achieving organizational mission, aims, plans, and objectives because they helped determine those objectives and truly share them.
- It improves morale because employees feel valued, participate in the running of the organization, and enjoy a work environment that is free of fear, prejudice, and bias.
- It helps improve poor performers through role modeling and peer pressure rather than through penalties and fear.

- It increases the recruitment and retention of high-quality employees by improving morale and working conditions and making the organization an employer of choice.

Because change is ongoing and pervasive in all areas of health care, including patient care, medical technology, management, information systems, and customer relations, it is critical to practice continuous quality improvement. *Continuous quality improvement* (CQI) is a methodology that views change and improvement as perpetual, ongoing processes. There is no one level of quality or objective that, once achieved, is the ultimate accomplishment. The goal of CQI is for the organization and its employees to strive to accommodate an ever-changing world and always make things better for the organization and its employees, customers, and community. Improved management of workforce diversity is a key element of CQI because it provides an environment in which employees from diverse groups can realize their fullest potential.

Management bears the primary responsibility for reinforcing the belief that the organization must adapt, change, and improve on an ongoing basis, and strong management commitment to perpetual change and CQI is essential. As Philip B. Crosby writes in *Quality Is Free,* "People perform to the standards of their leaders. If management thinks people don't care, then people won't care."[12] Employees must feel a sense of investment in the organization and its operations before they will go the extra mile to continuously make things better. After all, employees generally get paid the same whether they make the extra effort to continuously improve quality or not.

Measuring the Effects of the Change Process

As Niccolò Machiavelli wrote in *The Prince,* "It must be considered that there is nothing more difficult to carry out, nor more doubtful of success, nor more dangerous to handle, than to initiate a new order of things." The diversity change process often seems difficult, doubtful, and even dangerous because change is not static, but dynamic and ever-changing. Because change is a perpetual state and change strategies and plans need regular modification to accommodate new changes, an effective and efficient system of measurement and evaluation is crucial for successful diversity change.

Obtaining Useful Feedback

If top-level management can obtain useful feedback from employees concerning how the early stages of the change process are progressing, management will be able to uncover the most important staff concerns; minimize conflict, confusion, and miscommunication; and keep channels of communication open. The champions of diversity and the diversity committee can be invaluable in providing feedback on how diversity programs are progressing. In addition, top-level management should conduct feedback sessions with members of a cross section of groups in the organization, including diversity champions, new managers, "old-guard" managers (who are sometimes especially resistant to diversity management changes), all levels of supervisors and managers, and all types of employee groups. These sessions should consist of about 20 participants. (The focus group model found in appendix C can be modified for use in these feedback sessions.)

Top-level management should begin the diversity management plan feedback session by reiterating the overall change plan and listing the specific elements of the plan that will be discussed during the feedback session. Then the floor should be opened to participants and a free and open discussion of progress to date in improving diversity management should be encouraged. If necessary, interpreters should be on hand for employees who have difficulty expressing themselves in English. Top-level management should take special care to inform the group that their feedback will be kept strictly confidential and will be used only to improve the organization's diversity management program. To close the session, top-level management should thank participants for their help and reassure them that nothing they said in the sessions will adversely affect their jobs or career development.

Top-level management can use the feedback from these sessions to determine problem areas or gaps in the diversity management program, target breakdowns in communication, and get a sense of how well employees are responding to and adapting to change. This feedback is part of a more formal evaluation of the diversity change plan to assess progress and determine whether modifications are needed.

Evaluating the Diversity Plan

The key question in evaluating the steps an organization has taken to improve its management of workforce diversity is, "How well has the implementation plan progressed?" Answering this question requires analysis of the diversity change plan's major actions: the announcement of the plan, the selection of diversity champions, the commitment and visibility of senior management, and the communication process (including organizational responsiveness to conflicts, concerns, and issues expressed by organizational units or individuals). To keep the evaluation process manageable, top-level management should evaluate only those elements of the plan that the organization considers to be most crucial to the long-term success of effective diversity management.

Evaluation Criteria

Because the changes required for successful diversity change will not occur overnight, there are a number of progress points along the way that can be evaluated. This process should start with the evaluation of the diversity plan's stated objectives. It is easy to measure the accomplishment of objectives when the objectives contain quantifiable results, for example, "train all management and staff members in valuing differences," "recruit members of underrepresented groups for specific positions," and "incorporate employee development into management performance objectives." Other steps in the evaluation of progress points include:

- Analysis of grievances, conflicts, and management and employee counseling to determine whether conflicts about issues related to workforce diversity are declining
- Analysis of diversity-related employee morale issues to determine whether employees who reported feeling workplace discrimination are feeling better about their work environment and whether those who are not part of the workplace mainstream feel more included and exhibit more willingness to speak up and contribute to organizational success
- Analysis of problem-solving, decision-making, and communication methods to determine whether the diversity plan changes have facilitated progress in these areas
- Analysis of whether the understanding and acceptance of the various issues surrounding diversity have improved
- Analysis of whether diversity is embraced and celebrated within the institution

This evaluation may uncover areas of the change plan that need to be changed or adjusted. Having to change or adjust the plan should not discourage managers or staff members because change and flexibility are integral parts of any change process. The data collected from the evaluation process should be included in a database that measures progress on an ongoing basis.

Maintenance of a Database

An ongoing database that is regularly updated is a crucial element of a successful change process. This database should chart the following data:

- Scheduled dates for implementation of specific steps in the change plan
- Actual dates when various steps in the change plan took place
- Identification of the numbers and types of staff participating in each step of the change plan
- Subjective feedback from staff, broken down by category (for example, departmental methods and procedures, organizational philosophy, working conditions, and relationships with superiors, peers, subordinates)
- Changes implemented as a result of subjective staff feedback
- Objective results, such as changes in absenteeism, union grievances, and profitability, that can be correlated on a time line with specific steps in the change process

All quantitative data should be compiled in a spreadsheet format. (See figures 10-1 and 10-2.) Qualitative data should be broken down into categories to facilitate the referencing and utilizing of the information. (See figure 10-3.) The data should be updated on a regular basis (at least quarterly), and management should consult the data on a quarterly basis to evaluate progress and make any necessary changes in the diversity management program.

Figure 10-1. Sample Time Line Spreadsheet for Measuring Quantitative Progress

Change Plan Action Step	Individual Responsible for Implementation	Scheduled Implementation Date	Actual Implementation Date	Target Completion Date
Adopt decision to engage in a change program for diversity management	Jane Doe, CEO			
Conduct a cultural analysis	José Doe, vice-president, human relations			
Conduct an external environment analysis	Sally Doe, vice-president, community relations			
Perform a gap analysis	John Doe, planning director			
Announce organizational commitment to developing an overall diversity management program	Linda Doe, vice-president, publicity			
Develop and implement a management training program	José Doe, vice-president, human relations			
Select champions of diversity	José Doe, vice-president, human relations			
Conduct legal review	Fred Doe, vice-president, legal department			

Figure 10-2. Sample Format for Recording Objective Business Results

Month	Department	Absenteeism Rate	Union Grievances	Turnover Rate	Impact/Relationship to Progress of Diversity Change Program
June	Nursing	13 days	2	2 nursing assistants	Nursing staff members are missing recent diversity management in-services due to absences; newly hired nursing assistants will have to participate in all diversity management in-services

Note: Results should be recorded on this form at least once per quarter.

Figure 10-3. Sample Format for Recording Subjective Staff Feedback

Staff Level	Unit/Department	Methods/Procedures	Working Conditions	Organizational Philosophy	Working Relationships	Date Comments Received	Follow-Up
Hourly	Clerical		Desires more training in word processing				Survey of staff to ascertain training needed
Hourly	Maintenance	Suggests team approach to cleaning patient rooms rather than maintenance employees working alone			Supervisor seems to treat different employees differently		Consideration when developing training for supervisors
Professional	Medical			Feels that the organization is not sufficiently responsive to community needs			Referral to community services department for response
Professional	Administration			Feels that the organization does not sufficiently value the importance of nonmedical staff			Inclusion in team-building exercises and training
Hourly	Cafeteria				Needs access to multilingual or bilingual staff to assist with non-English-speaking customers		Referral to human relations department for response
Volunteer	Patient Services						
Professional	Nursing	Suggests nurses work with admitting department directly during patient intake to expedite services					Referral to medical department work team for further study

Overcoming Resistance to the Change Process

There are several reasons for health care employees' inherent tendency to resist change, and these reasons manifest themselves in a multitude of attitudes, including the following:

- *Insecurity*: "What will be lost as a result of the change?"
- *Ambiguity*: "Where will I and my unit or department fit into the new organizational picture?"
- *Inertia*: "We have always done it this way."
- *Contentment with the status quo*: "If it ain't broke, don't fix it."

The natural management reaction to resistance is to try to browbeat or penalize the resisters, which only tends to make them more resistant. The most effective way to overcome resistance to changes in diversity management is to market the need for the diversity plan to the employees most likely to support the plan, that is, members of diverse groups within the organization. According to the authors' over 40 years of combined organizational experience, approximately 10 to 15 percent of an organization's members are potentially strong supporters. However, an equal number of an organization's population tends to be hard-core resisters. Another 20 to 25 percent of staff members are usually split between *early adopters* (those who fall in line with the changes easily) and *skeptics* (those who require proof of the need for change). The rest of the organization usually falls in the category of *late adopters*, those who will join the change effort once they see which way the wind is blowing.[13]

Although there are many methods to overcome resistance to change, positive reinforcement of change is the most effective way to overcome resistance. Organizations must recognize, reward, and celebrate those individuals, units, departments, and work teams that have made successful strides in meeting workforce diversity objectives.

Redefining Teamwork and Work Teams for the 1990s and Beyond

Teamwork is not a new concept, and all organizations realize that teamwork is essential to accomplish certain tasks and goals. However, teamwork is becoming an increasingly important component of organizational success in the 1990s and is likely to remain so in the decades to come. A form of teamwork that came to the forefront in the early 1990s is self-managed work teams.[14] A *self-managed work team* is made up of 6 to 18 cross-trained employees who are given complete responsibility and authority to carry out a well-defined function.[15]

Self-managed work teams take the traditional concept of work teams to a higher level. These teams are empowered and given broad authority to study an issue or identify a problem and, often, to either implement needed changes or outline how to make the changes. Self-managed work teams are often composed of a cross section of managers and employees who have specialized knowledge concerning the problem or area to be studied. Organizational issues are often discussed and analyzed in such detail that the self-managed work team meetings provide cross-training to team members, which can help them in obtaining future job promotions.

In general, teamwork is essential to change management, continuous improvement, and diversity management. Changing employees' attitudes, ideas, feelings, commitment, effort, and behavior are integral parts of a successful diversity change plan. These changes are accomplished most effectively through the teamwork process, where employees can exert peer pressure, model desirable behaviors and attitudes, and work together to plan and solve problems.

Redefining teamwork to suit the needs of the workforce and workplace of the 1990s requires the following organizational innovations:

- Open management
- Commitment to change, excellence, and high quality
- Focus on customer service and satisfaction
- Creation of an atmosphere of continuous improvement
- Improved diversity management

Given the increased diversity in health care workforces, it is critical that work teams reflect their organization's levels and areas of diversity. Work teams must transform themselves from groups learning how to work together into cohesive, optimally functioning self-directed units.[16]

Work teams of the 1990s are made up of a diverse and empowered group of employees whose organizational importance has been increased by shortages of qualified workers. These teams operate in all departments and all levels of the organization and are likely to interact with a wide variety of employees throughout the organization's hierarchy. For effective diversity management, the organization's champions of diversity should be represented on all work teams. Although management may interact with and advise work teams, it should not try to run them. In the 1990s and beyond, the work team will be the primary vehicle for supporting continuous change and workforce diversity and building positive momentum in the workplace.

Recognizing, Rewarding, and Valuing Workforce Diversity—Shifting Paradigms

Health care organizations often succeed for reasons that are not easily quantifiable, for example, good patient care, a caring atmosphere, good relations with the surrounding community, or a dedicated workforce. Managers who focus only on financial objectives and productivity ratings often meet with failure. The financial, legal, societal, and practical pressures on today's health care organizations have forced managers to realize that their workforce is their most important asset. Organizational success and viability depend on the ability to mobilize employees to make a commitment to the organization and actively participate in running the organization. Management must empower employees at all levels and from all backgrounds to actively help the organization establish and attain its goals. Investing in workers and allowing each employee to achieve his or her maximum potential are the guidelines for ensuring organizational success and overcoming obstacles. Establishing shared organizational values, modes of communication, and belief systems that respect the diversity of the organization's various groups creates tremendous momentum toward success and gives employees their due as stakeholders in the organization's success or failure.

All of these changes involve a shift in *paradigms*—models or templates of the organization's traditional and current belief systems—to new and continuously changing organizational and workforce standards and ideals. One historical paradigm in U.S. society that has recently shifted is the concept of the melting pot, in which aliens become assimilated or Americanized (also discussed in chapter 2). This melting pot melts or blends away differences so that U.S. society becomes a homogeneous whole. In fact, during the intense immigration periods of the 1800s and 1900s (up until the relatively heavy Hispanic immigration of the past 20 years), many immigrants believed that the American dream was to assimilate and become Americanized. After World War II, the civil rights movement focused on attaining racial integration and equal treatment under the law. The melting pot image began to change, beginning in the late 1960s, with the emergence of a sense of racial and ethnic pride that discounted the desirability of assimilating into mainstream white society. Minorities began to establish their racial and ethnic identities as African-Americans, Native Americans, Asian Americans, and so on. Instead of trying to be invisible, gays and lesbians asserted the right to have an untraditional sexual orientation and take pride in that orientation. Similarly, other groups, including the differently abled, older workers, and women, demanded that society value them and their differences. A paradigm shift occurred that changed the melting pot, which blends and melts differences, into a salad bowl, in which each "ingredient" makes its own distinct contribution. Applied to the workplace, the salad bowl paradigm creates a synergy that allows each employee to maximize his or her individual contributions to the whole rather than being subordinated to a homogenous oneness.

Paradigm shifts are necessary for health care organizations to inspire an institutionwide belief that diversity management is achievable and that such efforts are important preconditions to successful change. An organization's failure to shift paradigms will seriously undermine its long-term change efforts. Two general areas where paradigm shifts often need to occur are within internal and external organizational relationships.

Internal Relationships

An important organizational paradigm is the working relationship between the different departments within a health care organization. There is often some tension between medical staff members and administrators, who for the most part have nonclinical backgrounds. The doctors might disdainfully view administrators as "bean counters" who do not understand the day-to-day functionings of a health care organization. At the same time, administrators may view doctors as arrogant and uncooperative concerning the nonmedical aspects of running the organization. These views create an organizational paradigm in which each group is the other's opponent or obstacle. This paradigm must shift to a belief that all departments and groups are partners that should work together with mutual respect and that this cooperation will cause the organization to improve and prosper. This paradigm shift relates particularly to workforce diversity management because change efforts in this area will be initiated and maintained by the administration. The success of these diversity management efforts requires that the medical staff have a belief system that views the administration as a partner, not an opponent.

External Relationships

In addition to an organization's internal working relationships, paradigm shifts are also important to a health care organization's overall goals and external relationships. For example, a small but modern hospital in a rural but growing town about 30 miles from a major metropolitan area serves a fairly homogeneous population of farmers and tradespeople but virtually no minorities. A current paradigm for this hospital might be that diversity management is not important because diversity is not an element of its patient or employee base. However, as the neighboring metropolitan area continues to spread outward and the town continues to grow, diversity will become a factor in the hospital's organizational culture. If the hospital fails to quickly shift its paradigm, it will be unprepared for the future.

Avoiding Static Equilibrium

Paradigms are self-fulfilling prophesies. For example, if an organization believes it cannot achieve a goal or work with others in a certain way, then that belief will become a reality. This organization would require an organizational paradigm shift to a belief that it can achieve its goals in order to make its goals come true and continually expand its horizons. This fundamental paradigm shift is consistent with the principles of total quality management and continuous change because optimistic, ongoing efforts are required to meet goals and improve the organization. When change efforts are not supported by organizational paradigms, the organization will eventually reach a level of static equilibrium. In effect, no growth or improvement will be sustained beyond the initial efforts of the change program. In the end, an organization in static equilibrium may revert to where it was before change efforts were initiated and executed.

When a health care organization follows the steps outlined in this book for implementing effective diversity management, the result can be visualized as a perpetual motion machine. (See figure 10-4.) Senior management occupies the "north" position on the circle, providing the machine with its initial energy, momentum, and direction. Moving clockwise, the champions of diversity are located in the "east" position, combining their energy with the energy of the rest of the organization, which is located at the "south" position. This combined energy reacts throughout the organization to identify and bring forward

Figure 10-4.   Diversity Management as a Perpetual Motion Machine

all of its diverse elements and to empower the entire staff, which is located at the "west" position. The circle is completed by the increased momentum directed toward senior management by the empowered and diverse staff. This momentum causes the entire motion to repeat itself because change is perpetual. This continued cycle creates more and more success for the organization and causes the circle to grow. This growth is potentially infinite, limited only by the organization's paradigms, which surround the circle.

References

1. Byham, W. C., and Cox, J. *Zapp! The Lightning of Empowerment.* New York City: Fawcett Columbine, 1992, chapter 27.

2. Thomas, R. R., Jr. *Beyond Race and Gender.* New York City: AMACOM, 1991, p. 164.

3. Smith, F. W. Empowering employees. *Small Business Reports,* Jan. 1991. (First published in *Journal for Quality and Participation,* June 1990.)

4. Adizes, I. *Corporate Lifecycles.* Englewood Cliffs, NJ: Prentice Hall, 1990, p. 40.

5. Senge, P. M. *The Fifth Discipline.* New York City: Doubleday Currency, 1990, pp. 24–25.

6. Thomas, pp. 46–47.

7. Senge, pp. 226–27.

8. Adizes, pp. 87–88.

9. Thomas, pp. 56–57.

10. Loden, M., and Rosener, J. *Workforce America.* Homewood, IL: Business One-Irwin, 1991, p. 186.

11. Waterman, R. H., Jr. *Adhocracy: The Power to Change.* Knoxville, TN: Whittle Direct Books, 1990, p. 18.

12. Crosby, P. B. *Quality Is Free: The Art of Making Quality Certain.* New York City: McGraw-Hill, 1979, p. 9.

13. Adams, J. D. Networking: a catalyst for change. *J. C. Penny Forum,* Mar. 1983.

14. Orsburn, J. D., Moran, L., Musselwhite, E., and Zenger, J. H. *Self-Directed Work Teams: The New American Challenge.* Homewood, IL: Business One-Irwin, 1990. (For more information on work teams, see Byham and Cox and Waterman, previously cited.)

15. Owens, T. The self-managing work team. *Small Business Reports,* Feb. 1991.

16. Orsburn and others, pp. 30–34.

Appendix A

Diversity Management Resources

Diversity Videos

Bill Cosby on Prejudice. Budget Films. Phone: (213) 660-0187.

Bridges: Skills to Manage in a Diverse Workplace. Eight videos. BNA Communications, Inc., 9439 Key West Avenue, Rockville, MD 20850. Phone: (301) 948-0540.

Bridging Cultural Barriers. American Media, Inc. Phone: (800) 262-2557.

Choices: A Management Training Program in Equal Employment Opportunity. 12 videos. BNA Communications, Inc., 9439 Key West Avenue, Rockville, MD 20850. Phone: (301) 948-0540.

Flashpoint: When Values Collide. Dr. Morris Massey. Phone: (800) 824-8889.

Given the Opportunity. Meridian Education Corporation, 236 E. Front Street, Bloomington, IL 61701.

Harness the Rainbow. Dr. Samuel Betances. Phone: (312) 463-6374.

Living and Working in America. Via Press, Inc. Phone: (800) 944-8421.

Managing Diversity. CRM Films, 2233 Faraday Avenue, Carlsbad, CA 92008.

Managing a Multi-Cultural Workforce: The Mosaic Workplace. Ten videos. Films for the Humanities & Sciences, P.O. Box 2053, Princeton, NJ 08543.

Racial and Cultural Bias in Medicine. McCormick Learning Resource Center, Rush University. Phone: (312) 942-6799.

Serving the Diverse Customer. Salinger Films. Phone: (310) 450-1300.

A Tale of "O." Goodmeasure, Inc. One Memorial Drive, Cambridge, MA 02142.

Valuing Diversity. Seven videos. Copeland-Griggs Productions, San Francisco, CA 94121.

Winning Balances. BNA Publications, Inc., 9439 Key West Avenue, Rockville, MD 20850. Phone: (301) 948-0540.

Working Together: Managing Cultural Diversity. Crisp Publications, Inc., 95 First Street, Los Altos, CA 94022.

Diversity Tools

Bafa Bafa: Cross-Cultural Orientation is an experiential activity that simulates the contact between two very different cultures, Alpha and Beta. Gary R. Shirts. Phone: (619) 755-0272.

Barnga: A Simulation Game on Cultural Clashes is a card game for small groups in which participants experience the effect of cultural differences on human interaction. Thiagarajan, Sivasailam, Intercultural Press, Inc., P.O. Box 700, Yarmouth, ME 04096.

Diagnosing Organizational Culture is an instrument designed to help consultants and organizational members identify the shared values and beliefs that constitute an organization's culture. Pfeiffer & Company. Phone: (800) 274-4434.

Diversity Awareness Profile (DAP) is an instrument designed to help training participants become aware of their actions—both obvious and subtle—and how they affect people of different cultural, gender, or ethnic backgrounds. Available in both manager and employee versions. Pfeiffer & Company. Phone: (800) 274-4434.

Diversity Bingo, based on the traditional game of bingo, is an interactive group learning experience that is designed to explore the perceptions and assumptions that exist in regard to different dimensions of diversity. Pfeiffer & Company. Phone: (800) 274-4434.

Intercultural Communication Inventory is a learning instrument designed to improve the quality of communication and relationships among employees of different cultural backgrounds. Training Ideas. Phone: (904) 241-4388.

The Questions of Diversity: Assessment Tools for Organizations and Individuals is a series of surveys that assess personal and organizational issues of diversity in the workplace. ODT Incorporated. Phone: (413) 549-1293.

A Workshop for Managing Diversity in the Workplace is a trainer's guide offering workshop design including activities and lecturettes for building awareness, knowledge, and understanding of diversity. Pfeiffer & Company. Phone: (619) 578-5900.

Diversity Newsletters

Communique. Society for Intercultural Education Training and Research (SIETAR). Phone: (202) 737-5000.

Cultural Diversity at Work. The GilDeane Group. Phone: (206) 362-0336.

Extend: Multicultural Magazine. Vista-Multi-Cultural Group, Inc., 3302 N. 7th Street, Building C, Suite 12, Phoenix, AZ 85012.

Intercultural News Network. Pacific Area Communicator of Intercultural Affairs (PACIA). Phone: (213) 433-7231.

Managing Diversity. Jamestown Areas Labor Management Committee. Phone: (800) 542-7869.

Annotated Bibliography

Cox, T., Jr. *Cultural Diversity in Organizations.* San Francisco: BerrettKoehler, 1993.

> This book captures the enormous complexity of the topic of cultural diversity by employing three levels of analysis—individual, group, and organizational—as well as addressing the topic from multiple perspectives, including theory, research, and practice.

Fernandez, J. P. *Managing a Diverse Work Force.* Lexington, MA: Lexington Books, 1991.

> This book is based on a survey of managers and employees throughout the country and documents the racism, sexism, and the ethnocentrism present in today's organizations.

Gardenswartz, L., and Rowe, A. *Managing Diversity.* Homewood, IL: Business One-Irwin, 1993.

> This book serves as a complete desk reference and planning guide for managing diversity.

Gordon, E. E., Ponticell, J. A., and Morgan, R. R. *Closing the Literacy Gap in American Business.* New York City: Quorum Books, 1991.

> This book provides readers with a complete review of past, present, and future adult literacy programs and gives practical, real-life case study examples from successful on-site company programs. A blueprint on how to offer workforce education for any business, large or small, is provided.

Jamieson, D., and O'Mara, J. *Managing Workforce 2000.* San Francisco: Jossey-Bass, 1991.

> This book offers practical strategies to help organizations attract, make the best use of, and retain employees from different backgrounds in order to maintain a competitive advantage.

Johnson, W. B., and Packer, A. H. *Workforce 2000: Work and Workers for the 21st Century.* Indianapolis: Hudson Institute, 1987.

This book examines the census figures and demographic data that capture the attention of corporate America and inspire workforce diversity programs.

Knowles, L., and Prewitt, K. *Institutional Racism in America.* New York City: Prentice Hall, 1969.

This book gives a comprehensive account of the pervasiveness of racism in the institutions of American society.

Loden, M., and Rosener, J. B. *Workforce America.* Homewood, IL: Business One-Irwin, 1991.

This book is a practical guide that depicts managing diversity as a vital resource that can lead to increased creativity, innovation, and productivity, which are beneficial to both organizations and their employees.

Morrison, A. M. *The New Leaders.* San Francisco: Jossey-Bass, 1992.

This book reveals the country's best practices for promoting white women and people of color and offers a step-by-step plan for creating diversity strategies that achieve measurable results.

Schwartz, F. N. *Breaking with Traditions.* New York City: Warner, 1992.

This book reveals what life is like for women in corporations, professional firms, and academic and public institutions and how the bottom line of corporate America suffers when women's real needs are ignored or sabotaged by outdated traditions and views.

Tannen, D. *You Just Don't Understand.* New York City: Ballantine, 1990.

This book explores the problems of communication with the opposite sex in an accessible manner.

Thierderman, S. *Bridging Cultural Barriers for Corporate Success: How to Manage the Multicultural Work Force.* Lexington, MA: Lexington Books, 1990.

This book is a cross-cultural handbook filled with practical information about motivating, attracting, interviewing, retaining, and training the multicultural workforce.

Thierderman, S. *Profiting in America's Multicultural Marketplace.* Lexington, MA: Lexington Books, 1991.

This book explores how culture affects person-to-person behavior and how to communicate effectively with people of different backgrounds.

Thomas, R. R., Jr. *Beyond Race and Gender.* New York City: AMACOM, 1991.

> This book provides practical examples of how different organizations have set forth on their journey of diversity management. It includes a strategy for a cultural audit as well an action plan for change.

Thomas, R. R., Jr. *Differences Do Make a Difference.* Atlanta: The American Institute for Managing Diversity, 1992.

> This book is a series of individual accounts of corporate managers who are pioneers in being the first female, person of color, differently abled person, and so on to succeed in their organizations. It explores the barriers and obstacles faced as told by the participants.

Tichey, N., and Devanna, M. A. *The Transformational Leader.* New York City: John Wiley & Sons, 1986.

> This book is about leadership, corporate America's scarcest natural resource, and the need for American companies to make fundamental, revolutionary changes in order to stay competitive in an increasingly international business environment.

Books on Specific Cultural Groups

Andres, T. *Understanding Filipino Values: A Management Approach.* Quezon City, Philippines: New Day, 1981.

Condon, J. C. *Good Neighbors: Communication with the Mexicans.* Yarmouth, ME: Intercultural Press, 1985.

Condon, J. C. *With Respect to the Japanese: A Guide for Americans.* Yarmouth, ME: Intercultural Press, 1984.

David, G., and Watson, G. *Black Life in Corporate America.* New York City: Anchor, 1982.

Fieg, J. P., and Mortlock, E. *A Common Core: Thais and Americans.* Yarmouth, ME: Intercultural Press, 1989.

Gochenour, T. *Considering Filipinos.* Yarmouth, ME: Intercultural Press, 1990.

Kitano, H. L., and Daniels, R. *Asian Americans: Emerging Minorities.* New York City: Prentice Hall, 1988.

Knouse, S. B., Rosenfeld, P., and Culbertson, A. *Hispanics in the Workplace.* Newbury Park, CA: Sage, 1992.

Kochman, T. *Black and White Styles in Conflict.* Chicago: University of Chicago Press, 1981.

Mydell, M. K. *Understanding Arabs: A Guide for Westerners*. Yarmouth, ME: Intercultural Press, 1987.

Richmond, Y. *From Nyet to Da: Understanding the Russians*. Yarmouth, ME: Intercultural Press, 1992.

Wenzhong, H., and Grove, C. L. *Encountering the Chinese: A Guide for Americans*. Yarmouth, ME: Intercultural Press, 1991.

Articles

Adler, N. J., Doktor, R., and Redding, S. G. From the Atlantic to the Pacific century: cross-cultural management reviewed. *Journal of Management*, Summer 1986.

Baytos, L. M. Launching successful diversity initiatives. *HRMagazine*, Mar. 1992, pp. 91–97.

Braham, J. No, you don't manage everyone the same: companies are finding daring, different ways to manage an increasingly diverse workforce. *Industry Week*, Feb. 6, 1989, pp. 28–35.

Caudron, S. Monsanto responds to diversity. *Personnel Journal*, Nov. 1990.

The Conference Board. *Work Force Diversity: Corporate Challenges, Corporate Responses*. Report Number 1013, 1992.

Copeland, L. Learning to manage a multicultural workforce. *Training*, May 1988.

Copeland, L. Valuing diversity, part 1: making the most of cultural differences in the workplace. *Personnel*, June 1988.

Copeland, L. Valuing diversity, part 2: pioneers and champions of change. *Personnel*, July 1988, pp. 44–49.

Deutschman, A. What 25 year-olds want. *Fortune*, Aug. 27, 1990, pp. 42–50.

Dovidio, J. The subtlety of racism. *Training & Development*, Apr. 1993, pp. 51–57.

Edwards, A. The enlightened manager: how to treat all your employees fairly. *Working Woman*, Jan. 1991, pp. 45–51.

Eubanks, P. Workforce diversity in health care: managing the melting pot. *Hospitals* 64(12):48–52, June 20, 1990.

Geber, B. Managing diversity—changing corporate culture and managers' attitudes through diversity awareness training. *Training*, July 1990, pp. 23–30.

Goldstein, J., and Leopold, M. Corporate culture vs. ethnic culture. *Personnel Journal*, Nov. 1990.

Gunsch, D. Games augment diversity training. *Personnel Journal*, June 1993, pp. 78–83.

Kennedy, J., and Everest, A. Put diversity in context. *Personnel Journal*, Sept. 1991, pp. 50–54.

Kronenberger, G. Out of the closet. *Personnel Journal*, June 1991.

Laabs, J. Affirmative outreach. *Personnel Journal*, May 1991.

Lewan, L. Diversity in the workplace. *HRMagazine*, June 1990, pp. 42–45.

Overman, S. Different world brings challenge. *HRMagazine*, June 1990, pp. 52–55.

Peel, K. C. Learning to value differences. *Health Progress*, Sept. 1992, pp. 44–48.

Petrini, C. M. The language of diversity. *Training & Development*, Apr. 1993, pp. 35–37.

Sabatino, F. Culture shock: are U.S. hospitals ready? *Hospitals* 67(10):22–28, May 20, 1993.

Solomon, C. M. Are white males being left out? *Personnel Journal*, Nov. 1991, pp. 88–94.

Solomon, C. M. The corporate response to work force diversity. *Personnel Journal*, Aug. 1989.

Solomon, C. M. Managing today's immigrants. *Personnel Journal*, Feb. 1993, pp. 56–65.

Thompson, R. Equal access. *Successful Meetings*, May 1991, pp. 42–52.

Thomas, R. R., Jr. From affirmative action to affirming diversity. *Harvard Business Review*, Mar.–Apr. 1990, pp. 107–17.

Torry, K. 1990s workforce: ill-equipped for business. *Crain's Chicago Business*, Apr. 17, 1989, pp. 27–28.

Diversity Resources

Advanced Change Management, Inc.
361 W. Circle Drive
New Lenox, IL 60451
(815) 485-1026
Contact: Glen Crosier

The American Institute for Managing Diversity, Inc.
P.O. Box 38
830 Westview Drive, SW
Atlanta, GA 30314
(404) 524-7316
Contact: Terri Kruzan

American Society for Training and Development (ASTD)
P.O. Box 1443
1630 Duke Street
Alexandria, VA 22313
(703) 683-8123

BNA Communications, Inc.
9439 Key West Avenue
Rockville, MD 20850
(301) 948-0540

Catalyst
250 Park Avenue South, 5th Floor
New York, NY 10003-1459
(212) 777-8900

The Conference Board
845 Third Avenue
New York, NY 10022
(212) 339-0234

Copeland Griggs Productions
302 23rd Avenue
San Francisco, CA 94121
(415) 668-4200
Contact: Lewis Griggs

Gordon Martin Associates
5319 N. Wayne
Chicago, IL 60640
(312) 334-6383
Contact: Dr. Vicky Gordon Martin

Hudson Institute
P.O. Box 26919
5395 Emerson Way
Indianapolis, IN 46226
(317) 545-1000

Institute for International Research
437 Madison Avenue
New York, NY 10022-7001
(212) 826-3340

Jean Mavrelis Associates, Inc.
1018 N. Humphrey Avenue
Oak Park, IL 60302
(708) 383-3285
Contact: Jean Mavrelis

Karolus Incorporated
65 E. Wacker Drive, Suite 401
Chicago, IL 60601
(312) 346-8149
Contact: Karolus Smejda

Kochman Communication Consultants, Ltd.
2100 N. Racine
Chicago, IL 60614
(312) 477-3204
Contact: Thomas Kochman

Martin, Boone Associates
6166 N. Sheridan Road
Suite 14H
Chicago, IL 60660
(312) 761-0080
Contact: William A. Boone

Dr. Edwin J. Nichols
1523 Underwood Street, N.W.
Washington, D.C. 20012
(202) 723-2117

Project Reach
2 Pine Grove Road
Georgetown, SC 29440
(803) 520-4158
Contact: Wally F. Johnson III

Sanders and Associates
11300 52nd Avenue North
Plymouth, MN 55442
(612) 553-0492
Contact: Vapordeal Sanders

Svehla Consultants, Inc.
4808 Oakwood Drive
Downers Grove, IL 60515
(708) 968-6169
Contact: Trisha Svehla

Towers Perrin
245 Park Avenue
New York, NY 10167
(212) 309-3593

Appendix B

Model Internal Culture and Value Analysis Survey Form

Introduction

The purpose of this questionnaire is to assist us in a self-study of our organization so that we can improve patient services and make [health care organization's name] an even better place to work.

Please answer the following questions to the best of your ability. If you do not understand a specific question, you may ask the facilitator for assistance, or you may leave the answer blank. If English is not your first language, you may ask the translator [if available] for assistance.

The information that you provide will be kept strictly confidential. Your signature is optional, and your responses will not have any effect—positive or negative—on your job.

Thank you!

Section I. Your Background

1. Which of the following best describes your job? (check more than one if applicable)
   ____ Physician
   ____ Nurse (R.N.)
   ____ Nurse (other than R.N.)
   ____ Technician
   ____ Nonmedical professional
   ____ Management/supervisory
   ____ Nonmanagement/supervisory
   ____ Other

2. What is your educational level? (check one)
   ____ High school, but no diploma
   ____ High school diploma or general equivalency diploma (G.E.D.)
   ____ High school diploma plus some college course work
   ____ Two-year college degree: A.A., A.S., or technical school degree
   ____ Two-year college degree: A.A., A.S., or technical school degree plus some additional college course work

____ Four-year college degree: B.A. or B.S. degree
____ Four-year college degree: B.A. or B.S. degree plus some postgradu-
ate course work
____ Postgraduate degree: M.B.A., M.S., J.D., Ph.D.
____ Postgraduate degree: M.D., O.D., D.D.S. M.D., O.D., D.D.S., and
an additional postgraduate degree

3. What is your age?
   ____ 18 to 24
   ____ 25 to 34
   ____ 35 to 49
   ____ 50 to 64
   ____ 65 and older

4. How long have you worked here?
   ____ Less than 1 year
   ____ 1 to 3 years
   ____ 3 to 5 years
   ____ 5 to 10 years
   ____ 10 to 15 years
   ____ More than 15 years

5. What is your racial or ethnic background?
   ____ White
   ____ African-American
   ____ Native American
   ____ Hispanic
   ____ Asian or Pacific Islander
   ____ Other (please specify:)

6. Are you male or female?
   ____ Male
   ____ Female

7. What are the five best things about working at [health care organization's name]?
   (1)
   (2)
   (3)
   (4)
   (5)

8. What are five things about working at [health care organization's
   name] that you do not like or would like to change?
   (1)
   (2)
   (3)
   (4)
   (5)

9. Do you feel that your services and contributions are well appreciated here?
   _____ Yes
   _____ No

10. Do you feel that most employees' services and contributions are well appreciated here?
    _____ Yes
    _____ No

11. Would you like to have a greater role in planning the future of [health care organization's name] by participating on committees with fellow employees?
    _____ Yes
    _____ No

12. Do you prefer working with people who are similar to you in race, ethnicity, and sex?
    _____ Yes
    _____ No

13. Do you find it difficult to work with any of the following groups?
    _____ Males
    _____ Females
    _____ Whites
    _____ African-Americans
    _____ Native Americans
    _____ Hispanics
    _____ Asians or Pacific Islanders
    _____ Homosexuals (gays and/or lesbians)
    _____ Religious groups (please specify:)
    _____ People who are HIV positive
    _____ Others (please specify:)

14. Are there any segments of [health care organization's name]'s surrounding community for whom you find it difficult to provide services?
    _____ Males
    _____ Females
    _____ Whites
    _____ African-Americans
    _____ Native Americans
    _____ Hispanics
    _____ Asians or Pacific Islanders
    _____ Homosexuals (gays and/or lesbians)
    _____ Religious groups (please specify:)
    _____ People who are HIV positive
    _____ Others (please specify:)

15. What are five of the most important services [health care organization's name] provides for its patients and clients?
    (1)
    (2)
    (3)
    (4)
    (5)

16. Which of the services you listed in question 15 does [health care organization's name] perform best?

17. Which of the services you listed in question 15 does [health care organization's name] perform least well?

18. How would you describe the community or communities that [health care organization's name] serves?

19. How well does [health care organization's name] serve the community or communities you identified in question 18?

20. How can [health care organization's name] better serve the community or communities you identified in question 18?

21. Has your race, ethnicity, sex, religion, or any other factor affected your career at [health care organization's name]?
    ____ No
    ____ Affected positively (please specify:)
    ____ Affected negatively (please specify:)

22. Do you feel that race, ethnicity, sex, religion, or any other factor has affected other employees' careers here?
    ____ Yes (please specify:)
    ____ No

23. Are you interested in on-the-job classes and training to learn more about different ethnic groups, races, cultures, and religions?
    ____ Yes (please specify why:)
    ____ No (please specify why:)

24. Do you socialize at work with individuals whose ethnic groups, races, cultures, and religions are different from your own?
    ____ Yes
    ____ No

25. What are the five personal values (for example, family, religion, success) that are most important to you?
    (1)
    (2)
    (3)
    (4)
    (5)

26. Is the work atmosphere at [health care organization's name] supportive of the personal values you listed in question 25?
    ____ Yes
    ____ No (please specify why:)

27. Use the space below to write any other comments you might have regarding [health care organization's name] and any additional suggestions you might have.

Thank you very much for participating in this survey project! Remember, your responses will be kept strictly confidential.

Appendix C

Model Internal Culture and Value Analysis Focus Group Format and Questions

Setting for the Focus Group Session(s)

Focus group sessions may take place in meeting rooms on the health care organization's premises or at conference centers or consultants' offices off the health care organization's premises. Focus group sessions should usually have 10 to 12 participants and a moderator. There should also be a nonparticipant present to take notes. The optimum length for focus group sessions is one to two hours.

Focus group meetings should be arranged to minimize or eliminate the possibility of participants being interrupted by job-related activities. Consequently, it is probably most desirable to schedule focus group sessions during hours when the participants are not on duty. (Ideally, employees would volunteer their free time, but some organizations might be forced to pay overtime.)

Participants should be made to feel relaxed and comfortable. Light refreshments such as soft drinks and snack foods should be served and there should be periodic breaks. All participants should wear name tags.

Moderator's Introduction

The following is a sample speech that the focus group moderator can use to introduce the session:

> Thank you for joining us today. As you know, [health care organization's name] has begun a self-study of our organization so that we can improve patient services and make this an even better place for you to work. A key part of this self-study process is looking at the diversity of our staff and the diversity of the people they serve. By diversity I mean differences in race, sex, age, ethnicity, religion, culture, language, sexual orientation, income level, physical skill, ability, and so on—really, anything that makes each of us special.
>
> You have been asked to participate as representatives of the staff members that make up [health care organization's name]. I want to emphasize

that all of your opinions are equally important, regardless of your job title, department, or any other factor relating to your employment here. Although someone will be taking notes during this discussion, [he or she] will not keep track of who said what. This discussion will be kept totally confidential and will have no impact on your job status. We hope that what you have to say will help [health care organization's name] to make your job here even better.

Sample Suggested Moderator Questions

At the beginning of the focus group session, the moderator should ask each participant to briefly introduce himself or herself and identify his or her job title and function. The moderator should be alert to the fact that some participants will be more vocal than others and may try to dominate the discussion. In these cases, the moderator should encourage the contributions of less vocal participants and discourage obnoxious behavior. Additionally, to prevent the meeting from turning into a gripe session, it is important to begin the meeting with questions focusing on positive aspects of the health care organization. These questions might include the following:

- What are some of the best things about your job and the way you are treated at [health care organization's name]?
- What are some of the best things about the way [health care organization's name] treats its patients and the public?
- What special skills do you bring to [health care organization's name] as a result of your culture, background, age, gender, or abilities?
  - Do you think [health care organization's name] is making the best use of your skills?
  - What are some of the things [health care organization's name] could do to make better use of your skills?
- Do you feel that you fit in with your department or unit, as well as with the total organization?
  - Do you feel that your culture, background, age, gender, or abilities have any positive or negative impact on the way you do your job?
  - Do you feel that your culture, background, age, gender, or abilities have affected your ability to be promoted, receive pay increases, or otherwise move ahead at [health care organization's name]?
  - Do you feel that workers at [health care organization's name] who are similar to you in respect to culture, background, age, gender, or abilities would share your views concerning the previous question?
- What activities, if any, do you participate in that help create better working and social relationships with other staff members?

—Do you socialize in or outside of the office with [health care organization's name] employees whose culture, background, age, gender, or abilities are different from yours? If so, why? If not, why not?

- What are some of the biggest areas where [health care organization's name] should improve the working atmosphere for its employees from diverse backgrounds?

- What role do you think you could play or would like to play in helping [health care organization's name] to maximize the roles and contributions of employees from diverse backgrounds?

- What role do you feel the top-level management of [health care organization's name] should be playing to maximize the roles and contributions of employees from diverse backgrounds?

- How do you feel that patients and community members from various cultures and backgrounds and of various ages and abilities view [health care organization's name]?

- What types of ongoing activities should [health care organization's name] engage in to improve its image among and its services to all of its different types of patients and community members?

- As we bring our meeting to a close, let's go around the table and share any other thoughts or opinions you would like to express that we have not discussed already.

After this final discussion, some participants will probably ask what will be done with the focus group information and/or what will be the organization's next steps or overall plan. The moderator should state that the information will be studied, and as a result of that study, the organization will work on implementing organizationwide diversity programs. The moderator should add that as programs develop there will be official communications to all staff members. Finally, the moderator should close by thanking everyone for attending and contributing.

Model External Culture and Value Analysis Survey Form

Introduction

As part of its ongoing efforts to improve the quality of its services, [health care organization's name] is conducting a survey of individuals in the surrounding community. We would greatly appreciate your candid answers to the following questions. Community feedback provides important input that enables [health care organization's name] to continue providing the best health care services and programs possible. All of the information you provide will be kept strictly confidential.

1. Are you familiar with [health care organization's name]?
   ____ Yes
   ____ No

2. What are some of the services that you are aware that [health care organization's name] provides?

3. How would you define your geographic community in terms of ethnicity, culture, and/or economics?

4. On a scale of 1 to 10, with 10 being the best, how well do you think [health care organization's name] serves your geographic community?

   1   2   3   4   5   6   7   8   9   10

This survey can be adapted for a telephone interviewer or for a mailed response form.

5. Do you identify yourself with a particular racial, ethnic, religious, social, or other type of group?
   ____ Yes (please specify:)
   ____ No

6. If you answered "yes" to question 5, how well do you think [health care organization's name] serves that community on a scale of 1 to 10, with 10 being the best.

   1   2   3   4   5   6   7   8   9   10

7. Are you aware of any particular services or programs that [health care organization's name] performs particularly well?

8. Are you aware of any particular services or programs that [health care organization's name] does not perform particularly well?

9. Have you ever utilized [health care organization's name] for services?
   ____ Yes (please specify when you utilized the organization and for what reason:)
   ____ No (please specify why not:)

10. Do you have any personal preferences regarding the race, ethnicity, sex, religion, or any other factors (aside from professional competence) of the individuals providing health care services to you?
    ____ Yes (please specify:)
    ____ No

11. What factors do you consider when deciding whether to use a health care facility such as [health care organization's name]?

12. Would you like to receive information in the mail about [health care organization's name]?
    ____ Yes
    ____ No

13. Do you have any additional thoughts about [health care organization's name]?

Thank you very much for participating in this survey!

Model External Culture and Value Analysis Focus Group Format and Questions

Setting for the Focus Group Session(s)

The setting for the focus group should be similar to the setting described in appendix C for the internal culture and value analysis focus group session(s).

Moderator's Introduction

The following is a sample speech that the focus group moderator can use to introduce the session:

> Thank you for joining us today. [Health care organization's name] has begun a self-study of our organization as part of our ongoing efforts to continuously improve services to our patients and the community. A key part of this self-study process is looking at the diversity of our staff, our patients, and the community we serve. By diversity, we mean differences in race, sex, age, ethnicity, religion, culture, language, sexual orientation, income level, physical skill, and so on — really, anything that makes each of us special.
>
> You have been asked to participate because you are individuals who reflect the diversity of our patients and our community. I want to emphasize that each of your opinions is equally important, and I hope that everyone here will provide comments and suggestions. Although your comments are being recorded, they will be used by an outside consultant only and will remain totally confidential. We hope that what you have to say will help [health care organization's name] to improve its service to you — its patients and its community.

Sample Suggested Moderator Questions

At the beginning of the focus group session, the moderator should ask each participant to briefly introduce himself or herself and say a little bit about his or her background. The moderator should be alert to the fact that some participants will be more vocal than others and may try to dominate the discussion.

In these cases, the moderator should encourage the contributions of less vocal participants and discourage obnoxious behavior. Additionally, it is important to begin the meeting positively in order to elicit constructive comments and suggestions from focus group participants. The moderator might ask the following questions:

- Based on your perceptions, what are some of [health care organization's name]'s best qualities and how well does it serve its diverse patients and community?
- Based on what you have heard from others, what are some of [health care organization's name]'s best qualities and how well does it serve its diverse patients and community?
- How do you feel that [health care organization's name] benefits from the skills of its diverse employees?
  - Have you ever benefitted directly from the skills of [health care organization's name]'s employees?
- Do you feel that employee diversity has been a factor in the type of service you or someone you know has received at [health care organization's name]?
  - If so, has it been a positive or negative factor?
  - In what way was employee diversity a positive or negative factor?
  - Are you aware of others who have shared your experiences concerning employee diversity at [health care organization's name]?
- Based on your perceptions, do our diverse staff members work together in serving patients and the public?
- Do you feel that diverse patients and diverse members of the community perceive [health care organization's name] favorably?
- What are some of the biggest areas where [health care organization's name] should improve its service to its diverse patients and community?
- What types of ongoing activities should [health care organization's name] engage in to improve its image among and its services to all of its different types of patients and community members?
- What role do you think you could or would like to play in helping [health care organization's name] achieve the improvement goals that have been suggested here today?
- As we bring our meeting to a close, let's go around the table and share any other thoughts or opinions you would like to express that we have not discussed already.

After this final discussion, some participants will probably ask what will be done with the focus group information and/or what will be the organization's next steps or overall plan. The moderator should state that the information will be studied, and as a result of the study, the organization will work on implementing organizationwide diversity programs. The moderator should add that as programs develop there will be official communications to patients and the public through the organization's community services or public relations department. Finally, the moderator should close by thanking everyone for attending and contributing.

Model Five-Day Training Program Outline for Champions of Diversity

Day One

7:30 a.m.–8:00 a.m.	Continental breakfast
8:00 a.m.–9:00 a.m.	Program introduction

- Provide an overview of the entire five-day program.
- Detail the day's schedule.
- Emphasize the support and priority top-level management has given to the program and its goals.
- Emphasize the importance of the individuals who have been chosen and why they were chosen to be champions of diversity.
- Outline the training program's specific goals.

9:00 a.m.–10:00 a.m.	Presentation on the definition of diversity management

Learning objective: Understand the meaning of diversity management and how it applies to the organization.

10:00 a.m.–10:15 a.m.	Break
10:15 a.m.–11:15 a.m.	Presentation on workforce trends—nationally, in the health care field, and in the organization

Learning objective: Understand the impact of national and health care trends on the organization.

11:15 a.m.–12:00 p.m.	Open question-and-answer period

Learning objective: All participants should reinforce and support their understanding of diversity management principles and issues as they move forward to perform their mission as champions of diversity.

12:00 p.m.–1:00 p.m.	Lunch [including a motivational presentation on organizations exemplifying increased success resulting from effective diversity management—see appendix A for presentation resources]
1:00 p.m.–2:30 p.m.	Presentation on the summary of the organization's various self-assessments

Learning objective: Understand the current organizational culture, the organization's strengths and weaknesses, and how these strengths and weaknesses relate to the organization's goals.

2:30 p.m.–2:45 p.m.	Break
2:45 p.m.–4:00 p.m.	Individual group role playing—diversity bingo exercise

Learning objective: Identify prejudicial attitudes among the participants' groups and the organization.

4:00 p.m.–4:30 p.m.	Open question-and-answer period

Learning objective: Review the content of the day's training activities and identify issues and unresolved problems that need to be dealt with in upcoming days of the training program.

4:30 p.m.–5:00 p.m.	Participant feedback and planning for day two activities • Include a written evaluation questionnaire of day one activities. • Prepare and provide momentum to participants for day two activities.

Day Two

7:30 a.m.–8:00 a.m.	Continental breakfast
8:00 a.m.–8:30 a.m.	Program introduction • Summarize accomplishments and feedback from day one activities. • Detail the schedule of events for day two.
8:30 a.m.–10:00 a.m.	Presentation on the organization's diverse customer and community base

Learning objective: Provide an overview and perspective on the external diversity issues that affect the organization.

10:00 a.m.–10:15 a.m.	Break
10:15 a.m.–12:00 p.m.	Individual group role playing about the organization's contact with diverse customers and the community

Learning objective: Provide additional sensitivity to external diversity issues affecting the organization and also demonstrate how the organization's internal diversity can maximize the organization's delivery of services.

12:00 p.m.–1:00 p.m.	Lunch
1:00 p.m.–2:00 p.m.	Presentation on organizational barriers to managing and valuing diversity

Learning objective: Provide training on how to identify problems within the organization.

2:00 p.m.–2:15 p.m.	Break
2:15 p.m.–3:30 p.m.	Individual group role playing about barriers facing both newly entering and incumbent employees from diverse groups

Learning Objective: Promote increased sensitivity to and understanding of barriers faced by individuals from diverse groups currently employed and/or newly entering the organization.

3:30 p.m.–4:00 p.m.	Presentation on methods for breaking down subtle barriers to diversity management within the organization
4:00 p.m.–4:30 p.m.	Open question-and-answer period

Learning Objective: Review the content of day two training activities and identify issues and unresolved problems that need to be dealt with in upcoming days of the training program.

4:30 p.m.–5:00 p.m.	Participant feedback and planning for day three activities • Include a written evaluation questionnaire of day two activities. • Prepare and provide momentum to participants for day three activities.

Day Three

7:30 a.m.–8:00 a.m.	Continental breakfast
8:00 a.m.–8:30 a.m.	Program introduction

  • Summarize accomplishments and feedback
    from day two activities.
  • Detail the schedule of events for day three.

8:30 a.m.–9:30 a.m.   Presentation on the role of management in
                         managing diversity and the impact of differing
                         management styles

Learning Objective: Understand both generally
and specifically the different types of managers
with whom they will be interacting as champions
of diversity.

9:30 a.m.–10:30 a.m.   Individual group role playing—managers and
                          diverse employees

Learning Objective: Provide exposure to what current and newly entering diverse employees might
experience in the organization.

10:30 a.m.–10:45 a.m.   Break

10:45 a.m.–12:00 p.m.   Presentation on techniques for champions of
                           diversity to utilize with different types of
                           managers

Learning Objective: Provide champions of diversity
with support and reinforcement in their efforts to
work with managers for effective diversity
management within the organization.

12:00 p.m.–1:00 p.m.   Lunch

1:00 p.m.–2:15 p.m.   Individual group role playing on the interaction
                         between champions of diversity and different
                         types of managers

Learning Objective: Provide champions of diversity
with experiences they may confront during
implementation of the organization's diversity
management program.

2:15 p.m.–2:30 p.m.   Break

2:30 p.m.–3:15 p.m.	Presentation on techniques for champions of diversity to utilize with different types of nonmanagers
	Learning Objective: Provide champions of diversity with support and reinforcement in their efforts to work with nonmanagers for effective diversity management within the organization.
3:15 p.m.–4:00 p.m.	Individual group role playing on the interaction between champions of diversity and different types of nonmanagers
	Learning Objective: Provide champions of diversity with experiences they may confront during implementation of their role in the organization's diversity management program.
4:00 p.m.–4:30 p.m.	Open question-and-answer period
	Learning objective: Review the content of day three training activities and identify issues and unresolved problems that need to be dealt with in upcoming days of the training program.
4:30 p.m.–5:00 p.m.	Participant feedback and planning for day three activities • Include a written evaluation questionnaire of day three activities. • Prepare and provide momentum to participants for day four activities.

Day Four

7:30 a.m.–8:00 a.m.	Continental breakfast
8:00 a.m.–8:30 a.m.	Program introduction • Summarize accomplishments and feedback from day three activities. • Detail the schedule of events for day four.
8:30 a.m.–10:00 a.m.	Presentation on total quality management/customer service/change management concepts and applications
	Learning objective: Understand what these concepts mean and how they are synthesized with diversity management to benefit the organization.

10:00 a.m.–10:15 a.m.	Break
10:15 a.m.–12:00 p.m.	Presentation on identifying supporters, resisters, and fence-sitters/bandwagon supporters of diversity management change

Learning objective: Understand the different types of players within the organization with whom the champions of diversity will have to work with in their efforts to implement diversity management change.

12:00 p.m.–1:00 p.m.	Lunch
1:00 p.m.–2:30 p.m.	Individual group role playing on the interaction between champions of diversity and different types of players in the diversity management change process

Learning objective: Provide champions of diversity with experiences they may confront during implementation of the organization's diversity management program.

2:30 p.m.–2:45 p.m.	Break
2:45 p.m.–4:00 p.m.	Presentation on team work techniques for groups of champions of diversity

Learning objective: Provide support and reinforcement to champions of diversity that they are not working alone as individuals, but instead as part of a team, and provide them with team work techniques.

4:00 p.m.–4:30 p.m.	Open question-and-answer period

Learning objective: Review the content of day four training activities and identify issues and unresolved problems that need to be dealt with during the next and final day of the training program.

4:30 p.m.–5:00 p.m.	Participant feedback and planning for day five activities

- Include a written evaluation questionnaire of day four activities.
- Prepare and provide momentum to participants for day five activities.

Day Five

7:30 a.m.–8:00 a.m.	Continental breakfast
8:00 a.m.–8:30 a.m.	Program introduction • Summarize accomplishments and feedback from day four activities. • Detail the schedule of events for day five.
8:30 a.m.–10:00 a.m.	Presentation on organization's timetable for effectuating its change program for diversity management

Learning objective: Provide champions of diversity with detailed orientation on the organization's strategies, long-term plans, and measurable goals.

10:00 a.m.–10:15 a.m.	Break
10:15 a.m.–12:00 p.m.	Presentation on organization's planned activities and specific assignments to champions of diversity for their role in effectuating the change program for diversity management

Learning objective: Provide champions of diversity with detailed orientation on their specific role within the organization's overall plan.

12:00 p.m.–1:00 p.m.	Lunch (should include a motivational speech by the organization's CEO to support and reinforce the importance of the program and the role of the champions of diversity)
1:00 p.m.–2:15 p.m.	Open question-and-answer period

Learning objective: Provide a forum for the participants to offer input on what they think will work, will not work, what should be added, and/or what should be modified regarding the overall organizational plan for diversity management and the role of the champions of diversity in assisting with its implementation.

2:15 p.m.–2:30 p.m.	Break

2:30 p.m.–3:30 p.m.   Training program feedback and evaluation process
                            • Include written evaluation questionnaire for
                              day five activities as well as the total training
                              program.
                            • Obtain objective feedback on suggestions for
                              modifying the training programs for future
                              champions of diversity.

3:30 p.m.–4:00 p.m.   Graduation ceremony
                            • Participants should receive some type of
                              individualized certificate or other memento
                              acknowledging their completion of the training
                              program and their appointment as a champion
                              of diversity.

4:00 p.m.–5:00 p.m.   Graduation party